Teaching about Doublespeak

Edited by Daniel Dieterich

Members of the Second NCTE Committee on Public Doublespeak

Clare Barkley, Urbana High School, Illinois
Mildred Berkowitz, Dartmouth Middle School, Massachusetts
John A. Black, Darien High School, Connecticut
Haig Bosmajian, University of Washington, Seattle
George R. Bramer, Lansing Community College, Michigan
Walter A. Buchmann, Union for Experimenting Colleges and
    Universities, Yellow Springs, Ohio
David Burmester, Davis High School, California
Robert Cirino, University of Hawaii
Edward P. J. Corbett, Ohio State University
Brenda Danet, Boston University
Daniel Dieterich, National Council of Teachers of English, chair
Stephen Dunning, University of Michigan, *ex officio*
Paul Eschholz, University of Vermont
F. Richard Friedman, Central Oregon Community College
Richard Gambino, Queens College, CUNY
H. Lee Gershuny, Manhattan Community College, CUNY
Walker Gibson, University of Massachusetts
Gloria Glissmeyer, California State University
Daniel Hahn, Queens College, CUNY
Francine Hardaway, Scottsdale Community College, Arizona
Peter Hasselriis, University of Missouri, Columbia
Sidney J. Hormell, Hawaii English Project
Herb Karl, University of South Florida
D. G. Kehl, Arizona State University
Gerald Kincaid, Minnesota State Department of Education
William Lambdin, University of Northern Colorado
Donald Lazere, San Jose State University
Howard Livingston, Pace University, New York
William Lutz, Rutgers University
H. Thomas McCracken, Youngstown State University
Nancy McCracken, Youngstown State University
William Miller, Diablo Valley College, California
Terence Moran, New York University
Don L. F. Nilsen, Arizona State University
Christine Nystrom, New York University
Richard Ohmann, Wesleyan University, Connecticut
Wayne O'Neil, Massachusetts Institute of Technology
Ernest Page, San Diego State University
Neil Postman, New York University
Ivan L. Preston, University of Wisconsin
Hugh Rank, Governors State University
Bruce Reeves, Acalanes High School, California
Alfred Rosa, University of Vermont
Vernon Smith, Indiana University, *ex officio*
Julia P. Stanley, University of South Dakota
Daniel Tutolo, Bowling Green State University
Charles Weingartner, University of South Florida
Howard Ziff, University of Massachusetts

Teaching about Doublespeak

Edited by Daniel Dieterich

National Council of Teachers of English
1111 Kenyon Road, Urbana, Illinois 61801

Acknowledgments   Frances B. Cacha, "Propaganda Techniques via Children's Literature," from *Elementary English* (April 1975), pp.527–528. Copyright © April 1975 by the National Council of Teachers of English. Reprinted with permission / Robert Cirino, "Surveying Your Information Environment," from *Power to Persuade: Mass Media and the News* by Robert Cirino. Copyright © 1974 by Bantam Books, Inc. by permission of the publisher / Christopher Lehmann-Haupt, "A Fish Story . . . or Two," review of *Jaws* by Peter Benchley in the *New York Times,* January 17, 1975. © 1975 by The New York Times Company. Reprinted by permission / Howard Livingston, "Approaches to the Study of Public Lying," (originally titled "Some Antidotes for Public Lying"), from *Maryland Journal of English,* vol. 13, no. 1 (Fall 1974), pp.38–40. © 1974 by Maryland Council of Teachers of English. Reprinted with permission / Jeffrey Schrank, "The Language of Advertising Claims," from *Media & Methods,* March 1974, pp.44–48, 51. Reprinted by permission of the author / Sandra Schurr, "Consumerism," excerpted from the February issue of *Teacher* magazine with permission of the publisher. This article is copyrighted. © 1974 by Macmillan Professional Magazines, Inc. All rights reserved / Charlene W. Smith, "Evaluating Advertising." Adapted from material originally published in *Instructor,* vol. 84, no. 2 (October 1974), pp.64–65, "Huh, Wadja Say? Index to Better Listening," by Charlene W. Smith. This material was later published by Fearon Publishers, Inc. in *The Listening Activity Book: Teaching Literal, Evaluative and Critical Listening in the Elementary School* by Charlene W. Smith. © 1975 by Fearon Publishers, Inc., Belmont, California. Quoted by permission of publisher and author.

Contents

Theory

Practice
Multi-level

*which might be read to heighten students' perception
of public language.*

The Language of Advertising Claims
Jeffrey Schrank
*Describes and gives examples of ten types of adver-
tising claims which students should be able to recognize. Provides suggestions for a unit on advertising
interpretation.*

Speaking of People: Teaching about Sexism in Language
Sidney J. Hormell
*Provides a variety of techniques for exploring sex
stereotyping and sexist language (especially as they
are found in the mass media) with junior high school
students.*

College

The Stylistics of Belief
Julia P. Stanley
*Provides a method of linguistic analysis of language as
social contract, encompassing both sentence structure
and word choice.*

Practical Applications of Public Doublespeak Teaching: A Crap Detector for the Junior College Student
Francine Hardaway
*Describes a junior college course in doublespeak for
consumers, a course which analyzes the misuse of
language in ads, in instruction manuals, in directions
on medicine bottles, in real estate terminology, and
in college catalogues.*

Training College Students as Critical Receivers of Public Persuasion
Daniel Dieterich
*Describes a survey of teachers of persuasion in
Illinois institutions of higher education, suggests
directions which the training of college students as
critical receivers of persuasion might take, and
encourages the preparation of college teachers so
that they might teach about public persuasion.*

Resources

Resolutions

National Council of Teachers of English, 1975

BACKGROUND: Both the NCTE Committee on Public Doublespeak and the CEE Committee on Teacher Training in the Nonprint Media advocate the preparation of students in a new literacy. This new literacy requires that individuals exercise critical abilities in reading, listening, viewing, and thinking in order to cope with the persuasive techniques found in political statements, advertising, entertainment, and news. Be it therefore

RESOLVED, That NCTE, through its publications and its affiliates, continue to support curriculum changes designed to promote sophisticated media awareness at the elementary, secondary, and college levels. And be it further

RESOLVED, That NCTE continue to encourage teacher education programs which will enable teachers to promote media literacy in students. And be it finally

RESOLVED, That NCTE cooperate with organizations and individuals representing teachers of journalism, the social sciences, and speech communication to promote the understanding and develop the insights students need to evaluate critically the messages broadcast by the mass media.

Speech Communication Association, 1972

WE ACCEPT the responsibility of cultivating by precept and example, in our classrooms and in our communities, enlightened uses of communication; of developing in our students a respect for precision and accuracy in communication, and for reasoning based upon evidence and a judicious discrimination among values.

WE ENCOURAGE our students to accept the role of well-informed and articulate citizens, to defend the communication rights of those with whom they may disagree, and to expose abuses of the communication process.

WE DEDICATE ourselves fully to these principles, confident in the belief that reason will ultimately prevail in a free marketplace of ideas.

National Council of Teachers of English, 1971

On Dishonest and Inhumane Uses of Language
RESOLVED, That the National Council of Teachers of English find means to study dishonest and inhumane uses of language and literature by advertisers, to bring offenses to public attention, and to propose classroom techniques for preparing children to cope with commercial propaganda.

On the Relation of Language to Public Policy
RESOLVED, That the National Council of Teachers of English find means to study the relation of language to public policy, to keep track of, publicize, and combat semantic distortion by public officials, candidates for office, political commentators, and all those who transmit through the mass media.

Introduction

Daniel Dieterich

This is the National Council of Teachers of English Committee on Public Doublespeak's second book. The first, *Language and Public Policy*, edited by Hugh Rank, is designed "both to inform our colleagues and to persuade them" by providing perspectives on doublespeak in advertising, politics, the military, and the news media. These perspectives, offered, in many cases, by prominent authors, educators, and politicians, provide a sound justification for the study of public doublespeak, a justification encompassing several political and educational philosophies. However, it should be noted here that although *Language and Public Policy* emphasizes theory, it also contains two excellent articles on practical classroom techniques for teaching about doublespeak: Bruce Reeves' "Ad-Man, Business-Man, Teacher-Man," a discussion of Reeves' methods for involving high school students in the verifying of advertising claims, and Robert Cirino's "Bias in the Mass Media: A Student-Consumer Approach to Analyzing News Products."

Whereas *Language and Public Policy* was written in response to the charge given to the committee to "alert the profession generally to the forces that in the committee's judgment are misusing the language," *Teaching about Doublespeak* was written in response to the other charge to the committee: "to create a series of concrete classroom exercises (lesson plans, discussion outlines) which would focus students' attention on irresponsible uses of language."

Thus, *Teaching about Doublespeak* was not written in order to encourage teachers to study doublespeak. *Language and Public Policy* and the committee's columns in *College English* and *English Journal* have already undertaken that task.* Instead, it was written to provide those teachers who are already interested in teaching about doublespeak with practical information on how to go about doing so.

The essays which follow have been written by women and men teaching at all educational levels and living in communities all across the United States. Some of the authors answer to the name of English teacher, others to language arts teacher, and still others to speech or education teacher. Most are not nationally recognized authorities on education. All have a solid contribution to make to the study of doublespeak.

The majority of the articles in this book describe successful units, classes, or courses on the misuse of public language. Others suggest specific techniques for the study of doublespeak or discuss theoretical frameworks within which to approach the study of doublespeak. As was the case with the committee's first book, no orthodoxy is being preached here. Instead, I have attempted to provide materials for teachers with a variety of philosophies regarding doublespeak.

The first section of this book deals with the theory behind the study of doublespeak. In this section I am proud to include Hugh Rank's recently completed schema for use in training students to deal with public persuasion. The first new schema for analyzing public persuasion since the one developed by the Institute for Propaganda Analysis in the 1930s, the Rank schema should be of great benefit to teachers at all levels. Dennis Gouran's "Guidelines for the Analysis of Responsibility in Governmental Communication" is an excellent companion to the Rank schema. Where Rank contends that the various aspects of communication are in themselves neutral, and may in certain contexts be used for good or ill, Gouran describes some of the contexts in which governmental communication is inappropriate and irresponsible. In "Communication Contexts and Pseudocommunication," Richard Beach once more emphasizes the importance of contexts, describing how the contexts of television programs and advertising can lead to "pseudocommunication."

The second section, "Practice—Multi-Level," contains materials suitable for use at more than one educational level (e.g.,

---

* For the editor's justification of the study of public doublespeak, see "Public Doublespeak: Teaching about Language in the Marketplace," *College English,* 36 (1974), 477–481.

for use at the elementary, secondary and college levels). Beginning this section is the teaching kit "Doublespeak and Ideology in Ads," which was produced during the committee's summer 1974 Conference on Doublespeak under the direction of Richard Ohmann. This discussion of ways to approach the study of ideology in advertising is an excellent introduction to a very important, though frequently overlooked, aspect of advertising: the economic or political philosophies taught by means of ads. Daniel Tutolo's "Classroom Techniques to Evaluate Advertising in Magazines" is an introduction to a new educational approach. It describes how "counterattitudinal advocacy" may be used to inoculate students against advertising propaganda. In "Politics and Practical Semantic Analysis," Sanford Radner describes how general semantics may be used to study deceptive political language. Pat M. Taylor's "Doublespeak and Spoken Communication" presents techniques for analyzing political speeches which are broadcast nationwide or presented near to home. In "Books, Bookmakers, and Blurbs," John H. Hershey suggests a fertile source of doublespeak for classroom analysis, blurbs on book jackets and in advertising for new publications. This section closes with "Approaches to the Study of Public Lying," a few suggestions by Howard Livingston on how to study the misuse of language in advertising, political speeches, and the news media.

The third section, material for the study of doublespeak at the elementary level, is perhaps the most important section in the book. Students are bombarded by propaganda long before they enter the classroom. Unless they receive early instruction about the purpose and tools of propaganda, they soon become the gullible marks of public persuaders. Children have little exposure to political propagada, and thus the emphasis of the six articles in this section is on preparing children as critical evaluators of advertising propaganda. Frances B. Cacha describes how the study of doublespeak may be joined to the study of children's literature. Daniel Tutolo suggests an approach for improving students' critical listening skills in regard to radio commercials. Sandra Schurr suggests several techniques which can help children acquire a better overall picture of the nature and function of the American marketplace. Mildred Berkowitz describes a successful month-long unit on consumer education. Charlene W. Smith shows how critical listening and reading skills can be developed by studying public service advertising, and local and national commercial advertising. Finally, Jane M. Hornburger mentions a variety of classroom activities which would be useful in teaching elementary school students how to cope with doublespeak.

The fourth section contains six articles on how to develop the critical skills of secondary students with regard to their language environment. Robert Cirino provides a method by which students may assess the political opinions expressed in the mass media. Clare Barkley describes a course in which her students attend the public meetings of their city legislative and administrative bodies (committees, boards, etc.) and observe the ways in which language is used and misused there. Nancy McCracken describes her course, which uses both literature and the language of everyday life to heighten students' critical skills. Christine Fontenot presents a number of different techniques for approaching the study of both the language of advertising and the language of politics. Jeffrey Schrank discusses and gives examples of ten types of advertising claims which are often used to sell products. Sidney J. Hormell suggests ways to study sex stereotyping and sexist language in the mass media.

The fifth section, on teaching doublespeak at the college level, contains three essays, which supplement those appearing in earlier sections, especially sections one and two, which are of interest to the college teacher. Julia Stanley suggests how the study of linguistics can help students become critical listeners and readers. Francine Hardaway describes a junior college course about doublespeak addressed to consumers, a course analyzing the ways that public language is used and misused in a variety of different areas. The final article reports on my survey of college teachers of public persuasion and recommends ways of teaching college students and teachers to deal with public persuasion.

The twenty-four essays included in this book exemplify the many pieces that have been written and are being written about the study of doublespeak. Some other sources of information about doublespeak are "Resources," the concluding section of this book; "Public Doublespeak: A Personal Reading List," the concluding section of Language and Public Policy; and the quarterly Public Doublespeak Newsletter, available through the Committee on Public Doublespeak, 1111 Kenyon Road, Urbana, Illinois 61801 ($2.50/year).

Theory

Teaching about Public Persuasion: Rationale and a Schema*

Hugh Rank
Governors State University

Rationale

In the mid-1930s, Adolph Hitler began exploiting the fears and hopes of the people by means of a propaganda blitz, an unprecedented organized campaign of persuasion, using new media—radio and motion pictures—and traditional persuasion devices to such a degree that it transformed modern propaganda. In America, some scholars and teachers recognized early that Hitler's propaganda blitz had serious consequences for the world and that "something ought to be done." Thus, a small group of concerned people joined together, formed a group which called itself the Institute for Propaganda Analysis, and managed to publish a few pieces, including what became a well-publicized and widely used list of what they considered to be the seven most common propaganda devices: glittering generalities, name-calling, transfer, testimonial, plain folks, card-stacking, and bandwagon.

Since the 1930s, the world has changed. On the international scene, population has almost doubled; whole new cities of people are being born each day. Two, then three, massive superpowers have emerged in world politics. A dozen nations have gained the power to destroy, with one weapon, more than all previous wars in human history.

But, in a world of change, some things haven't changed. Despite the growth of commercial advertising from a cottage industry in 1945 to a $31 billion a year industry in 1976; despite the

---

* Revised and adapted from the script of a slide show first presented at the 1974 NCTE convention in New Orleans. The original version, "Teaching Counter-Propaganda Techniques" is available on audio cassette, NCTE #74035.

increase in the sophistication of modern persuasion and the development of technological aids to persuasion (from color TV to computers); despite the growth of the Pentagon into the world's largest, richest, most sophisticated propaganda machine; despite the fantastic changes in American political campaigning since the first awkward use of television by Eisenhower; despite all these changes, some things haven't changed. For example, after 40 years of the most significant changes in communications, in persuasion techniques, and in propaganda, the most commonly used item to analyze such propaganda is still the old list of the Institute for Propaganda Analysis.

Very few textbooks discuss propaganda analysis, and more than half of those textbooks which even deal with it still rely upon the IPA list as their basic teaching device. Though the IPA list has been of value in the past, it is too limited for the complexities of modern propaganda. It also has intrinsic errors of classification. For example, "transfer" or the association technique is a way, a method, whereas "plain folks" (the common people), "bandwagon" (the most people), and "testimonials" (the best people, the admired people) are all subject matters with which one seeks to associate. But that technicality of cross-classification is not the main problem with using the old IPA list; the list simply doesn't have the scope or flexibility to deal with contemporary propaganda.

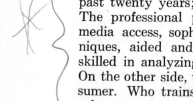

We've experienced a significant change in persuasion during the past twenty years; we are now in a state of gross inequality. The professional persuaders have the upper hand: money, media access, sophisticated personnel utilizing scientific techniques, aided and abetted by psychologists and sociologists skilled in analyzing human behavior. All of that on one side. On the other side, the persuadees: the average citizen and consumer. Who trains the citizen? Not the schools. There is no coherent, systematic effort in the schools today to prepare our future citizens for a sophisticated literacy. In many schools there is more attention given to a minor nineteenth-century writer than to the major language developments of the twentieth century. In American colleges and universities, English departments are essentially *literature* departments. Speech, journalism, and communication departments in most colleges are designed to train the persuaders of the future, not to enlighten the persuadees. In the schools, the most sophisticated techniques of persuasion are being taught (usually in business colleges- under the labels of "salesmanship," "public relations," "consumer behavior," "marketing research," and so on. Perhaps schools should shift their emphasis in order to train the larger segment of our population in a new kind of literacy so that more citizens can recognize the more sophisticated techniques and patterns of persuasion.

We have sixty million children in our schools, millions more on their way during the next decade, and we do very little about the real facts of life and language today. These kids are growing up in a propaganda blitz unparalleled in human history. By the time they enter school at the age of five or six, they've watched thousands of skillfully devised commercials. John Wilpers estimates that by the time children are 16, they have seen over 640,000 commercials. Thus, while the schools do little to instruct and to inform the persuadees, the persuaders continue; the propaganda blitz intensifies. Will the advertisers and political persuaders of 1980, or 1984, be less sophisticated, less informed, less funded than they are today? If we close our eyes, will they go away?

If one accepts the premises of an accelerating propaganda blitz and of an increasing imbalance between the professional persuaders and the average untrained persuadee, then it would seem reasonable in a democratic society to seek as a goal a systematic method within the schools to inoculate future citizens, to immunize them from the potential dangers of organized public persuasion.

But such a goal is not easily achieved; not because of external restraints, but primarily because of internal problems within the academic world. Entrenched special interests account for some of the problems; departments and professors who have established empires or staked out turfs in traditional literary studies are not likely to abandon their claims to their own primacy and importance in education. Yet, even the most altruistic teacher, willing to change or to learn new ideas, would be bewildered as to what direction to take. During the past generation, there have been more new developments and new breakthroughs in the study of human communication than in centuries of previous scholarship. Since 1957, for example, the whole study of linguistics has changed direction, and there have been significant insights introduced through the study of cybernetics and semiotics. Such major shifts in thinking contribute to our present dilemma; despite the genuine promise for the future, problems exist in the present. Right now, within the schools, the study of and the teaching about human communication is in a state of chaos, incoherence. In a great sense, it parallels the study of

biology before Linneaus, before biology began to be systema-
tized, coherent, coordinated.

A few years ago, in 1971, the National Council of Teachers of
English passed two resolutions expressing their concern, that
"something ought to be done" about the growing influence of
the organized professional persuaders. One resolution, "On the
Dishonest and Inhumane Use of Language," called for NCTE
members to organize, "to propose classroom techniques for preparing children to cope with commercial propaganda." The
other resolution, "On the Relation of Language to Public Policy," was politically oriented; it resolved "to keep track of,
publicize, and combat semantic distortion by public officials,
candidates for office, political commentators, and all those who
transmit through the mass media." During the next year, the
NCTE formed the Committee on Public Doublespeak, designed
to work with those two resolutions to "do something." With a
title suggesting Orwellian overtones of a 1984 society, the committee began to organize and to concern itself with propaganda
analysis, semantics, persuasion, language manipulation, lying,
deceit, and omission—all of which conceivably fell under the
metaphoric label of "doublespeak."

Shortly afterwards, political scandals erupted in Washington,
and for the next two years public attention was focused daily
on the corruption exposed by the Watergate affair and the
crafty manipulation of language by politicians. During these
years, the NCTE Committee on Public Doublespeak increased
in membership, activities, publications, publicity, and in the
number of speeches delivered at major academic meetings. Such
activities were designed to persuade those within the teaching
profession to re-examine priorities.

As the original chairman of this committee, I took part in this
development. I considered these in-house activities (the convention speeches and seminars) to be immediately important
and necessary, but ultimately subordinate to a program which
would have broader effects in the classroom. My own personal
priority was to create some kind of simple teaching device which
would replace the old IPA list. Because I did not anticipate any
speedy consensus, agreement, or coherent effort from the diverse
groups within the profession, I sought to provide some kind of
interim "first aid," something we could use now in the classrooms to teach kids about propaganda. To replace the IPA list
(and subsume 25 other random lists I've come across) and to
expand the scope so that it includes a wider range of human

communication—including nonverbal and verbal languages both spoken and written, and other symbolic communication (such as mathematics) I devised a chart, or schema, working from the following criteria:

1   It should be a *simple* explanation of a complex reality; simple enough to be understood by very young children, and by adults not keenly interested in reading scholarly papers about language.

2   It should be *flexible* enough to be a common denominator and thus useful within the diverse disciplines which actually exist in the schools today, in departments of English, speech, language arts, communications, media, journalism, psychology, and so on. And it should be flexible enough to be used at all educational levels, from kindergarten to graduate school.

3   It should be *accurate*. To avoid promulgating error, it must have an inner consistency, and must avoid contradiction of known truths.

4   It should be *useful*, practical, teachable, reproducible in many forms.

Schema: Intensify/Downplay

Intensify/Downplay focuses attention on a simple pattern useful to analyze communication, persuasion, and propaganda techniques. Binary computers, working on a very simple two-part positive/negative (+/−) basis, can generate very complex combinations. So also, one way of looking at human communication is to see that we can produce an almost infinite number of variations and combinations by intensifying or downplaying the various parts, or bits of information, communicated.

Sometimes this pattern is very easy to recognize: people *intensify* by raising their voice, shouting, making certain gestures, using certain words or patterns of words. People *downplay* by silence, and by other kinds of words (e.g. euphemisms) and gestures. Downplaying is often harder to recognize. Some very sophisticated techniques (e.g., satire, irony, concessive arguments) are often very difficult to analyze. But, people do not need to be "experts" to recognize the *most common ways* in which we all intensify or downplay.

The three most common ways to intensify are *repetition, association*, and *composition*. Their counterparts, the three most common ways to downplay are *omission, diversion*, and *confusion*.

Each of these subdivisions can be further broken down into

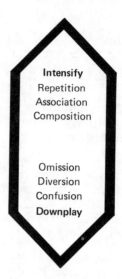

Figure 1.

parts. Before such analysis, a warning is useful: avoid rigidity
or confining things into one category. Recognize that these
categories and terms may be useful, but are arbitrary (created
by observers); recognize that many parts often function simultaneously.

Repetition
Intensifying by repetition is a simple, but very effective, way to
persuade. Some scholars believe that certain redundancy is
essential in all communication simply because there are so many
distractions that messages would get missed unless our languages
had a built-in repetition factor. Other experts emphasize the
psychological comfort we get from repetition. We love the familiar, the known. As children, we want to hear the same stories
over and over. Later, we listen to our "favorite" songs, watch
"favorite" programs, read "favorite" kinds of books, play "favorite" sports and games, and so on.

Commercial advertising recognizes the effectiveness of repetition. Every American knows that Budweiser is the King of
Beers, Miller is the Champagne of Bottled Beers, Coke is the
Real Thing, and that you can double your pleasure, double your
fun with Doublemint, Doublemint, Doublemint gum. The *last*
singing commercial for cigarettes was aired on TV in 1970; none
since; yet most people today can still sing or whistle the Salem
commercials: "You can take. . . ."

Thus, slogans, signs, symbols, logos, brand names are repeated often to intensify. All education, training, indoctrination, conditioning, propaganda is largely based on repetition, and is concerned with the receiver's memory; the ability of the receiver to identify or recognize and *respond* appropriately.

Politicians know the importance of repetition. In the early 1976 primaries, for example, a critical problem in the Democratic party was the lack of recognition of the names of the many candidates. Simple repetition of names (posters, bumper stickers) to identify the candidates became important. Naturally, incumbent politicians who have a high visibility have an advantage over the unknowns. Repetition of politicians' names and slogans is not a new technique; Kenneth Clark, in *Civilization*, describes the ancient Egyptian hieroglyphics as the first recorded "propaganda" based on repetition. But, even before that, most primitive cultures had established religious and social customs involving verbal repetition (chants, prayers, litanies) and nonverbal repetition (dances, rituals). The repeated pleas of cheerleaders today (Hold that Line! Hold that Line!) have their ancestral roots far back in human history.

Technology—ranging from the invention of the printing press to the most modern Xerox machine or videocassette recorder—makes repetition a lot easier to disseminate to mass audiences. But the basic patterns of verbal repetition (assonance, alliteration, anaphora, etc.) were cataloged by the Greek rhetoricians. Although random repetition is possible, it's much more likely that repetition will have some kind of *patterning*—in time or space.

Association
Intensifying by association is a technique of persuasion which links (1) the idea, person, or product with (2) something already loved or desired—or hated or feared—by (3) the intended audience. Thus, it is very important to know the audience. Aristotle, 2500 years ago, devoted a major portion of his *Rhetoric* to audience analysis; today, millions of dollars are spent by advertisers in such "market research": ranging from simple polls, surveys, questionnaires, and contests to sophisticated psychological and sociological research. Politicians have advisors, and governments have agencies, whose function it is to provide such "target audience" information so that political persuasion campaigns can be based on an assessment of the audience.

Verbal association can be done by direct statements, allusions, or a wide variety of metaphoric language: direct comparisons (metaphors), indirect comparisons (similes), etc. Many English teachers have great ability in analyzing metaphoric language in "poetry" as commonly taught in literature courses. Perhaps these insights can be expanded or applied by analyzing the mundane metaphoric language of everyday life: viewing commercial advertising as the "poetry of the corporation" and clichés as the "poetry of the people."

Nonverbal association techniques follow the basic pattern of putting the item into a *context* which already has emotional significance for the intended audience. Consider, for example, the *visual* background settings and *musical* accompaniment in television commercials.

Although there are an almost infinite number of possible combinations of subject matters and intended audiences, some patterns of human behavior are predictable (for example, attitudes toward God, country, nature, etc.) and are commonly exploited by the persuaders. Variations occur in different cultures, different eras, but essentially the subject matter of the association technique extends to all of the pleasures and ideals for which people live and die. In contemporary American culture, for example, any listing of the most common favorable associations as seen in commercial advertising and political persuasion would include: God (God-on-our-side); Flag (Flag-waving); Tribal Pride (ethnic groups, alumni, sports fans, etc.); Ideals (virtues or movements); Heroes and Experts (testimonials); Folk Sayings; the Most People ("bandwagon"); the Best People ("status"); the Average Person ("plain folks"); Heritage ("good old days"); Progress ("exciting, new"); Science; the Arts; Domestic Pleasures (Ma, apple pie, dogs, babies); Sensual Pleasures (especially sex). Some of these appeals contradict each other; what would delight one person would offend another. Compare the ads in *Playboy* with those in *Good Housekeeping:* different strokes for different folks.

Composition
Intensifying by patterns and arrangements uses design and order, variations in sequence and in proportion to add to the effectiveness of words, images, movements, etc. Choice of words, their level of abstraction, and their patterning within sentences are important; in longer messages, overall strategy is involved in planning patterns (grouping, structure, divisions, sequence, climax, etc.). Logic, both inductive and deductive, deals with the systematic patterns of linking ideas together. Nonverbal patterning includes visual aspects (color, size, shape), aural

(music), mathematics (quantities, relationships, etc.), and time and space patterns in relation to whole context.

In verbal communication, diction (word choice) and syntax (arrangement within the sentence) are both basic in patterning. The words we choose will either intensify or downplay the information transferred and the emotional associations of our communication. In old fashioned terms, all adjectives and adverbs are intensifiers, adding some information to the nouns and verbs which they modify. All nouns and verbs have a level of abstraction or specificity. We have options, as we speak and write, of choosing not only the linear sequence of words following after each other, but also selecting the "vertical" level of specificity of the nouns and verbs, and whether or not we'll add more information.

While there is no such thing as a neutral transfer of information from one person to another, we commonly use the terms "denotation" and "connotation" to indicate the relative degree of emotional associations involved in the diction. What a word connotes or suggests is not intrinsic to the word, but relative to the situation and the experience of both the speaker and audience.

In written languages, we often use certain customs or conventional patterns to signify when we want something intensified: we use CAPITALS, underlining, some punctuation marks! Sometimes we can intensify, attract attention, by violating standard conventions: Cummings' poetry is a good example of the conscious artist doing this; but consider also the protestors' banners which deliberately misspelled Nixxon (or used a swastika for the x) and U$A.

In spoken language, we can intensify by raising our voice, by changing the patterns of the tone, pitch, stress, or by pausing; by differing these things from what is "normal" for the situation, we can change the meaning conveyed. Using the same words, we can be sweet or sarcastic. The subtle nuances of languaging here are very intricate; certainly, foreigners wouldn't catch all the subtle implications which native speakers pick up. And, even within a homogenous "native" group, some people simply "can't take a hint." That is, some people are not aware or do not understand the nonverbal communication which contradicts and overrides the verbal message.

Within the schools today, a good portion of the instruction in "English" is concerned with sentence patterning and the overall structure of larger compositions. The earliest Greek rhetoricians gave us long lists of rhetorical schemes and tropes, and worked out some of the basic structural patterns for the oration. Many "rhetoric and composition" teachers today carry on in this same tradition. Literary criticism today also gives much attention to the structural composition of poems, plays, essays, short stories, and novels. Thus, we do have a large number of teachers who are well able to analyze certain aspects of communication, but who have not been trained in other aspects: e.g. nonverbal communication and symbol systems, such as mathematics.

In contrast to the rather overt techniques of *intensifying* elements of communication (by repetition, association, composition) we have extremely limited awareness of the techniques of *downplaying*, of the tactics of omission, the strategy of silence. We don't even have an adequate vocabulary to label or to identify the variations of downplaying which are more obscure, more subtle, more difficult to analyze. It's much easier to spot examples of intensification: there's something out there to analyze. But, it's extremely difficult to know when things are being withheld, hidden, or omitted. Much more attention must be paid by scholars and analysts, by teachers and students, to the whole problem of downplaying as a form of communication, because it has such importance to us in terms of political life (secrecy and censorship, classified documents, and cover-ups) and corporate advertising (half-truths, confusing claims, etc.), as well as in our daily affairs with others.

Omission, diversion, and *confusion* are suggested here as three major categories of downplaying. If one intensifies by repeating things frequently, then one can downplay by omitting them. If one intensifies by association, which brings things together, then one can downplay by diversion, which splits things apart. If one intensifies by composition, which lends order and coherence, then one can downplay by confusion, which creates disorder and incoherence.

Omission
The basic selection/omission process *necessarily omits* more than can be presented. Thus, all communication is edited, is limited, is biased or slanted to include and exclude items. But, omission can be used deliberately, as a calculated and systematic strategy of silence. As such, it is the most difficult aspect of communication to analyze, since we must attempt to detect that which is withheld, concealed, hidden, or omitted. Political examples would include many forms of governmental *censorship,*

book-burning, cover-ups, managed news, and activities involving *secret police* and *secret diplomacy.*

Euphemisms—words which downplay the unpleasant or unpopular—are a form of omission, a substituting of a more socially acceptable word for one which is "offensive." Forbidden words (especially concerning death and deities, sex and bodily functions) are common in many cultures. Euphemisms downplay; in contrast, one can intensify, can shock an audience, by using the "forbidden" words: profanity, vulgarity, cursing, etc. Euphemisms are frequently condemned as being "bad" *per se*; but, here too, one must make value judgments in relation to the situation. To comfort a grieving friend, it may well be humane to use "passed on" rather than "died." But, the euphemism "nuclear device" may be inhumane if it disguises reality.

Diversion
Downplaying by diverting attention, distracting focus away from key issues or important things; usually by intensifying, emphasizing, the side-issues, the unimportant, the trivial, the nonrelated. Common variations have been called *"red herring," "straw man," "hairsplitting," "nit-picking,";* also, emotional attacks and appeals *(ad hominum, ad populum),* plus activities which drain the energy of others *("busy work,"* legal harassment). Humor and entertainments *("bread and circuses")* are often used as pleasant tactics to draw attention away from significant issues.

Confusion
Downplaying key issues by making a situation so complex, so chaotic, so unintelligible that people often weary, get "overloaded," "drop out," "give up." This can lead to dangerous situations if people are unable to understand, comprehend, take necessary actions; or if people follow leaders offering a panacea, a simple solution. Chaos can be the accidental result of a disorganized, confused mind, or it can be the deliberate flim-flam of the con man or the demagogue. Confusion can result from *faulty logic, shifting definitions, equivocation, circumlocution, multiple diversions, contradictions, inconsistencies, jargon,* or anything which obscures clarity or understanding.

To avoid confusion, or cut through the maze, one should seek careful definitions, precise diction, clear syntax, strong structure, exact logic: in brief, all of those ideals of the counterpart, composition. Yet, such clarity is difficult in real situations when everything seems to demand our attention at once and leads us to the feeling of weariness, chaos, overload. Confusion is a

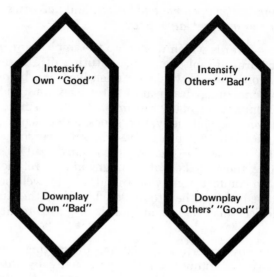

Figure 2.

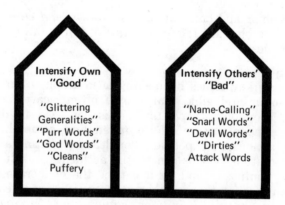

Figure 3.

strategy of some persuaders who think, "If you can't convince 'em, confuse 'em." Anything we can do to slow down the speed and sort out the junk, any kind of outlining, listing, or chart-making may be helpful to avoid that very common feeling of being overwhelmed by the "information explosion."

Thus far, this Intensify/Downplay schema is *static*, an analysis breaking some concepts into parts for clarity. In reality, communication is a *dynamic*, fluid, ever-changing process with many things going on at once, always in a wider context.

Based on observation, it would seem that people manipulate communication: (1) to *intensify* their own "good"; (2) to *intensify* others' "bad"; (3) to *downplay* their own "bad"; and (4) to *downplay* others' "good." "Good" and "bad" are in quotation marks here deliberately to suggest the qualifications and reservations needed in order to avoid setting up rigid dichotomies. An assumption: All people, in all eras, in all countries, intensify or downplay elements of communication as a natural human activity.

The moral and ethical judgments which have to be made about any human activity, including language manipulation, must be made in the context of specific situations: *who is saying what to whom, with what intent, with what result.* Such moral issues are complex, and important, but they are *distinct* from an analysis of how the elements of communication can be intensified and downplayed. As Cardinal Newman said: "Knowledge is one thing, virtue is another; good sense is not conscience. . . ." For further discussion of the moral issues involved, see my concluding essay in *Language and Public Policy* (Urbana, Ill.: NCTE, 1974, pp. 216–223). In this schema, the focus is on *how* communication can be manipulated.

These ideas are not new. This is simply a resorting, a translation into a simple language and a simple pattern. It's quite probable that you already accept these basic ideas, and that you are already familiar with many of the metaphoric words and labels currently in use to describe the parts of this schema. For example, focus on the top section of Figure 2. Depending on the textbooks you've already used, you've read other authors who discuss the intensification process, labeling concepts usually in paired terms: "glittering generalities" and "name-calling," "purr words" and "snarl words," "god words" and "devil words," "cleans" and "dirties," and so on.

When communication is intensified to focus on the others' "bad," we already have a vocabulary to describe such attacks: catty, snide remarks, mud-slinging, smear campaigns, and confrontation tactics. Such attack language would include not only verbal insults—shouted obscenities and scrawled graffiti—but also a whole cornucopia of intensified nonverbal communication: fist-shaking, teeth-clenching, sneering and smirking, ranging from the silent malice of the "hate stare" to the actual use of physical violence.

In our era, in our country, Watergate may well be the classic example of downplaying: omission, secrecy, deletions, half-truths, concealment, and cover-up. If we were to analyze Watergate language manipulation using the four-part pattern, certainly it would be reasonable to emphasize one area: downplay own "bad."

Yet the Watergate affair provides a good illustration of how all aspects of language manipulation can work together simultaneously. By recognizing such multiplicity and simultaneity, we may be able to avoid the trivial, hair-splitting arguments of previous techniques of propaganda analysis which sought to pigeonhole things into single categories, attempting to force a complex reality into simplistic packages. While Watergate was primarily a "downplaying own 'bad' " by the Nixon conspirators, at the same time some things were being intensified—such as the emphasis on Nixon's successful foreign relations with China and Russia, and the intensified attacks on the press, and on other politicians for being "biased" and "partisan."

Many Americans have been frightened by the abuses of power as evidenced in the Watergate affair, in the CIA involvement in foreign assassination plots, and in the FBI record of illegal domestic spying. Many investigators (e.g., David Wise in *The Politics of Lying*) have documented the systematic deceptions, the overclassification of government documents, the growing web of secrecy, censorship, concealment in recent years in the United States. Such fears of a totalitarian police state are reasonable fears. We have seen other nations in this century so abuse power. For example, the brutal history of the Soviet Union has been so revised by Kremlin historians as to downplay their own bad: to omit, to delete references, to ignore those whole ethnic groups and millions of political enemies who were purged, murdered, or enslaved by the USSR during the past half century. Today, it is not fashionable in an era of detente, or in an academic atmosphere of polite liberalism, to allude to the Gulag Archipelago. But I'm simply pointing out that the Soviet leaders are downplaying their own bad, concealing that which is not favorable, while they intensify the glories of their space programs, industrial and technological progress.

If you accept this four-part pattern as being a reasonable way of describing human behavior; if you accept the premise that all people in all eras for all kinds of motives, good and bad, intensify and downplay certain elements of communication; and if you recognize the recent growth in organized corporate persuasion, the concentration of power, money, and media access, then you may see some of the possible political and social implications resulting from a widespread use of this pattern as a teaching device, and from some of the axioms which can be inferred from it for use in analyzing public persuasion.

Intensify Own "Good"	Intensify Others' "Bad"
Stress foreign affairs, detente, peace, end of war, return of POWs.	Attack on press, on "leaks" as being treasonous, dangerous to national security.
Image building: protestations of innocence ("I am not a crook"); Operation Candor.	Attack on any factual press errors, misquotations.
Appearance of disinterest in matter—too busy with important affairs of state.	Attack on Democrats as being partisan, biased.
	Attack on credibility of witnesses (untrustworthy, disloyal "squealers").
Downplay Own "Bad"	**Downplay Others' "Good"**
In general, the whole cover-up conspiracy; some specifics: 1700 "inaudibles" and "unintelligibles" on the tapes; 150+ "expletives deleted" and "characterizations deleted"; 18-minute gap in tape; key tapes missing; documents withheld, shredded; silence of witnesses; evasive answers; perjury, etc.	Denying, ignoring, not responding to opponents' true claims.
	Denying valid motives, good intent of others.
	Denying competency of others (e.g., of the judge, the jury, the evidence, the tape experts, etc.).

Figure 4.

For example, assuming that any concentrated propaganda blitz in the future will come from governments or corporations, one might recommend to the citizen: *"When they intensify, downplay."* That is, when we recognize the propaganda blitz, we should be cool, detached, skeptically alert, not only to the inflated puffery of advertising with its dreams and promises, but also to intensified attack propaganda, the threats and the exploitation of fears by a demagogue or a government.

Conversely, we could recommend to our fellow citizens and to our students, our future citizens, that when a government or corporation hides or suppresses something, citizens should intensify and seek out: *"When they downplay, intensify."* Obviously, not everyone can be an expert investigative reporter, nor do we all have access to materials closely guarded, covered up, or concealed. But a whole citizenry can be taught in the schools about the need for openness in government, the need for a free press if we are to retain our democratic freedom.

People trained in recognizing the intensify/downplay patterning might even start seeing this pattern in the apparently random efforts of those various consumerists and reformers who urge a variety of *disclosure* laws (truth-in-lending, truth-in-packaging, truth-in-advertising, etc.), political campaign reforms, and corporate reporting practices designed to make public that which has been hidden in the past. Today, after a decade of consumerism and highly visible reformers, relatively little progress has been made because of the general randomness of the reformers and the confusion of the public. Such confusion works in favor of those who wish to conceal. With training, future citizens might be better able to recognize patterns and to see the implications of various "Shield Laws," full disclosure laws, standardized systems, clear record keeping, and reporting of data.

Thus far, I've emphasized verbal communication, but have made some allusions to the importance of nonverbal communication. The intensify/downplay pattern is also a useful way to analyze many elements of spacing and distancing, gestures, clothing, and ornamentation. It's also very probable that those who are concerned with visual literacy, especially with the analysis of photography and the cinema, will recognize the intensify/downplay elements involved in lighting, in audio techniques, in background setting, in camera angles, in pacing and timing, and so on.

For the average person, perhaps the most complicated kind of intensifying and downplaying occurs in our system of symbolic communication, mathematics. For most people, the manipulation of numbers, figures, and statistics is very confusing, as it takes special training and aptitude to understand how to intensify and downplay the various elements involved.   ·

The language of business is the language of money. Most people are not able, or do not wish, to be expert in this form of human languaging. But it would be valuable to have a larger population of citizens and consumers who have a basic "liberal education" in the intricacies of this language. We need more "common people" or "non-experts" who are able to recognize the basic ways of manipulating figures and statistics; how governments or corporations can intensify—inflate—certain figures to give favorable illusions (seeking votes, selling stock), and can downplay other items to conceal losses and income. "Juggling the books" is not a new human activity, but, with the advent of the computer, it's going to be an increasingly complex one— with the odds favoring the rich, the powerful, the huge corporations and governments.

If we are to seek equity and balance, the citizenry should recognize some of the basic problems, and some of the possible solutions: laws and lawmakers intent on counterbalancing power; and an educational system "of the people, by the people, and for the people," which seeks to train future citizens in a more sophisticated literacy in order to cope with the propaganda blitz of today, and of tomorrow.

Guidelines for the Analysis of Responsibility in Governmental Communication

Dennis S. Gouran
Indiana University

When I first agreed to write a paper developing guidelines for the analysis of responsibility in governmental communication, I believed the task would be a relatively simple one. During the period I have been studying the matter, however, I have altered my perspective considerably and, I hope, constructively. Initially, I had assumed that one need only identify the more glaring examples of irresponsible behavior in governmental communication and from those instances extrapolate a set of general principles to serve as criteria for judging future cases. Finding appropriate illustrations was no problem, for the number of governmental actions susceptible to the charge of irresponsibility is indeed substantial, and one would experience great difficulty listing them, let alone analyzing and discussing each. What perplexed me most was the inadequacy of my own conception of responsibility. What does it mean to communicate responsibly, and what are the indices by which one can make such determinations? In grappling with these questions, my impulse to be objective came into sharp conflict with the recognition that any assessment of responsibility, of necessity, entails a value judgment, regardless of the care exercised in the identification of standards. Consequently, anyone in my position would run the risk of making what Bergmann refers to as ideological statements: that is, observations confusing one's value judgments with propositions of fact.[1] To avoid this complication, I have tried to acknowledge that much of what I have to say is cast in the form of value judgments even though factual considerations are involved in their formation.

Adding to the problem has been my realization that judgments of responsibility, in part, depend on the context in which the behavior at issue is manifest. The same behavior exhibited

under different circumstances might warrant discrepant judgments. To some, this type of seeming inconsistency would be
tantamount to hypocrisy. A realistic and fair appraisal of official
conduct, however, dictates consideration of such circumstantial
factors before any final judgment concerning the responsibility
of one's communication behavior in a given situation can be
reached.

I have not intended to imply by the preceding remarks that
members of our association should refrain from judging the
extent to which people in government conform to the standards
of responsibility on which we might agree. On the contrary, my
study of governmental behavior has convinced me of the need
for scrutiny, evaluation, and response. What concerns me in
raising these types of issues is that we avoid becoming the very
thing we are trying to combat, namely, irresponsible communicators. With this in mind, I have tried as carefully as I can to
outline a set of conditions that frequently stimulate social interest in responsibility and to develop a corresponding set of guidelines for use in the evaluation of given instances of questionable
conduct. The specific examples chosen to illustrate problem
types are in many cases controversial. Accordingly, I have attempted to identify the assumptions one must make before
reaching the conclusion that a particular standard of responsible
communication behavior has been violated. Whether the standards themselves appear reasonable I assume I shall discover
from the responses to what I say. In short, the approach to this
paper is to raise issues, not to resolve them.

On the basis of the many and varied materials I have consulted
in preparing for this program, it seems clear that there are at
least seven areas of activity in which, historically, the behavior
of governmental officials has been subject to possible indictment
as irresponsible. Included are the falsification of information
released to the public, classification of documents, news management, intimidation of the news media, interference with the
exercise of free speech, political espionage, and disguised communication. Let me discuss these subjects in greater detail and
present the standard of evaluation I believe appropriate to each.

In the recent past, perhaps the two most discussed cases of
falsifying information released to the public are President Johnson's assertions underlying the need for the Gulf of Tonkin
Resolution and President Nixon's repeated denials of any knowledge of or involvement in the Watergate Coverup. At 1:30 p.m.
on August 4, 1964, Commodore John J. Herrick reached the
Pentagon with the following cable:

> Review of action makes many recorded contacts and
> torpedoes fired appear doubtful. Freak weather ef-
> fects and overeager sonar man may have accounted
> for many reports. No actual visual citings by Mad-
> dox. Suggest complete evaluation before any further
> action.[2]

In spite of the uncertainty involved, President Johnson that
very night addressed the American people and reported that
vessels of the U.S. Navy on patrol in the Gulf of Tonkin had
been attacked by the North Vietnamese. Three days later, a
Joint Session of Congress sanctioned the President's response
to that alleged attack and thereby assured continued involvement in our nation's longest war.

On March 30, 1973, President Richard M. Nixon announced
that he had for the first time on March 21 become aware of
attempts by members of the White House staff and other officials
in his administration to prevent public disclosure of administrative involvement in the break-in of National Democratic Headquarters.[3] Despite this and other frequent denials of knowledge
of the coverup, the June 23, 1972 transcript of a Nixon–Haldeman conversation clearly reveals that not only did the President
know about the coverup but that he may well have ordered it.[4]

If one assumes that the statements of these two men are sub-
stantially at odds with the facts and that, at the time of utterance, they were fully aware of the discrepancies, then the indictment of irresponsibility is clearly warranted. The consequences
of President Johnson's actions and the destructive potential of
Richard Nixon's were far too serious to dismiss with the cliché
that "all politicians lie." So, probably, do most other human
beings, but that neither justifies the behavior nor the activities
to which it leads. The general guideline suggested by the preceding and similar instances is that *the deliberate falsification
of information released to the public, especially under circumstances involving the general welfare, is inappropriate and irresponsible.*

I suppose one could advance the argument that, in both of the
cases cited, the parties involved honestly believed that their
actions were serving the public interest; hence, the charge of
irresponsibility is undeserved. Such a position might have credibility if one were able to convince oneself that plunging the
nation into an undeclared war at uncalculated human and material costs and sanctioning illicit activities while at the very same
time publically decrying the country's burgeoning crime rate

serve the public interest. Personally, I find myself unable to reason to such a conclusion.

The unwarranted classification of government documents is an issue brought into focus by the Pentagon Papers.[5] The facts in that particular case are by now so familiar that a summary statement seems unnecessary. Of greater importance is the general concern triggered by the release and publication of those documents; that is, the question of national security versus the public's right to know. Although a system of classification for documents whose public availability might jeopardize the nation's capacity for protecting itself, to conduct foreign policy, or to prevent our enemies from achieving their objectives (when those objectives are patently destructive) seems desirable, one must also question the wisdom of a practice that can maintain ignorance, lead to the continued misuse of public funds, and involve the country in commitments its citizens and duly elected representatives might not willingly make.

Some obvious problems exist with respect to determining whether information has been justifiably classified. First, we do not know frequently what has been selected for classification. Second, when a document has been declassified, in retrospect, the security rating may seem to have been unwarranted even though at the time of original classification the designation appeared necessary. Finally, there are literally millions of documents which have various levels of security ratings. Trying to determine if the assigned rating of each is appropriate would be almost impossible. Still, the question of the public's right to know keeps the matter alive.

When asked what he thought of the principle of the people's right to know, General and former Ambassador Maxwell Taylor responded, "I don't believe in that as a general principle."[6] It is, of course, this type of attitude that leads many to the belief that government officials are desirous of only two things from the public: the people's economic support and the granting of the freedom to do whatever they please. Moreover, the public is to expect nothing in return.

In some cases, the information held inaccessible is probably not worth knowing. For example, the Pentagon has classified a 1912 document outlining one of the Defense Department's then current contingency plans.[7] On the other hand, the release of the Pentagon Papers made it apparent that United States citizens had been continuously deceived on the matter of our involvement in Vietnam. The government argues that classification was necessitated by national security interests, yet as Richard Harwood has pointed out, "The substance and in some cases the precise details of virtually everything the *Washington Post* and the *New York Times* have printed from the Pentagon Papers is ancient history."[8]

If it is true that the Pentagon Papers contained no information injurious to national security and that the motives of those insisting upon continued classification were to mislead Americans about their role in the Southeast Asian adventure, the charge of irresponsibility again seems called for. Although it is likely that few documents wrongly classified will come to our general attention, it nevertheless seems desirable to propose an evaluative criterion for the cases that do arise. Such a standard might be that the *classification of government documents for the purpose of deceiving or otherwise keeping the public uninformed on matters affecting private citizens' well-being is inappropriate and irresponsible.* This criterion will be difficult to apply because of the varied interpretations of what in any given instance constitutes deception. Nonetheless, it should aid in focusing on the behavior one is trying to characterize.

News management is a third area of concern in assessing the communication behavior of governmental figures. The Presidential news conference and press briefing are possibly the two most conspicuous forums in which such behavior arises. Certain questions are precluded while others are answered with "No comment!" On occasion, outright lies are told. As *News Republic* journalist John Osborne observed after five years of watching the Nixon White House, "The consensus of reporters who regularly cover the White House is that Ron Ziegler is a proven deceiver and liar and that Mr. Nixon will have no credibility so long as Ziegler continues to be his chief spokesman."[9]

A fascinating example of news management in process is revealed in the eighteen-minute conversation held by Richard Nixon, John Ehrlichman, and Ron Ziegler on March 30, 1973.[10] At issue was the preparation of Ziegler for his afternoon press briefing in which he was to create the appearance that the White House was doing everything possible to get to the bottom of the Watergate case. The fact that it had done nothing to that point was apparently a matter of no concern. Only the illusion of activity was.

The generation and dissemination of news, of necessity, is a selective process. As a result, all news that reaches the consumer has been to some extent managed. The crucial questions underlying the management of news by governmental officials are "How?" and "Why?" When news has been deliberately manipulated to mislead, conceal embarrassing facts, or cover up wrongdoing, the grounds for assessing responsibility are clear. The activities of the White House staff on March 30, 1973, to which I referred earlier, point to news management in its worst sense. Unfortunately, this type of behavior has not been characteristic of only the Nixon administration.

The handling of the Bay of Pigs Invasion by the Kennedy administration[11] and Eisenhower's response to the U-2 Incident[12] are replete with examples of conscious deception of the public through news management. In each of these cases, the truth surfaced in time; however, the possible consequences the country faced while its leadership was "managing" the situation represents, in my judgment, the very height of irresponsibility.

In cases such as the Bay of Pigs and the U-2 Incident, there has been a general lack of concern about censure. Perhaps the embarrassment to the individuals in question seemed a sufficient punishment. In fact, when Kennedy finally shouldered responsibility for his fiasco, his popularity rating shot up to 82 percent.[13] A possible reason for such a charitable response might be that people felt that these men were doing what they believed to be best for the country at the time. I have a hunch that such was not the case and that political survival rather than public interest was the stronger motivating force. The paradox of resentment toward news management and tolerance of it under circumstances of disclosure notwithstanding, I would argue that news management of this type is reprehensible and that we should judge individual cases of suspected management against the following standard: *The deliberate use of official news sources for the purpose of obscuring embarrassing and deceitful governmental acts is inappropriate and irresponsible.*

Consistent with the desire of some governmental figures to put the best possible face on their acts through news management has been an underlying tendency to intimidate the press. The most celebrated instance of such intimidation in recent years was Vice President Agnew's speech in Des Moines on November 13, 1969.[14] Were the speech but an isolated event, one might argue that Mr. Agnew was simply exercising his right to criticize, an act certainly no worse than those of the commentators about whom he was speaking. There is, however, a whole catalog of activities that suggest the speech was part of a concerted effort to assure that the Nixon administration would be portrayed only in the most favorable terms by the news media. Included in the list were threats of antitrust action, attempts to force reporters to reveal confidential sources, court action to prevent the publication of the Pentagon Papers, and an unannounced search of the Pentagon press room by agents of that organization's Counterintelligence Force.[15]

John Mitchell's response that "Katie Graham's gonna get her tit caught in a big fat wringer if that's published" to reporter Carl Bernstein's announcement that the *Washington Post* was about to publish a story identifying Mr. Mitchell as the controller of CRP's secret fund[16] is one of the more blatant examples of attempted intimidation. One also finds it difficult to believe that the Nixon people's posture toward the press was anything other than threatening when one examines the President's own statements. Shortly before his reelection in 1972, Nixon issued the following directive to aides Haldeman and Dean:

> I want the most comprehensive notes on all those who tried to do us in. They didn't have to do it. If we had a very close election and they were playing the other side I would understand this. No—they were doing that quite deliberately and they are asking for it and they are going to get it. We have not used the power in this first four years as you know. We have never used it. We have not used the Bureau and we have not used the Justice Department but things are going to change now. And they are either going to do it right or go.[17]

Considering the number of journalists on the "Enemies List," one is drawn to the undeniable conclusion that the statement calls for nothing short of intimidation. How ironic that this voice, a decade earlier, could have indicted President Kennedy for not understanding the role of a free press.[18]

The right of officials in government to be critical of news media is not in question here. At issue is the ability of a free press to function when threatened or subjected to other forms of intimidation. To me, the standard of judgment is clear. *Criticism of the press for the purpose of assuring that governmental acts are viewed only in favorable terms is inappropriate and irresponsible.*

Closely related to intimidation of the press are attempts to control the exercise of free speech. In his testimony before the Senate Select Committee on Presidential Campaign Activities, John Dean related the following example of directed interference with a citizen's right to free expression:

> I was made aware of the President's strong feelings
> about even the smallest of demonstrations during the
> late winter of 1971 when the President happened to
> look out the windows of the residence of the White
> House and saw a lone man with a large ten foot sign
> stretched out in front of Lafayette Park. Mr. Higby
> called me to his office to tell me of the President's
> displeasure with the sign and told me that Mr.
> Haldeman said the sign had to come down. When I
> came out of Mr. Higby's office, I ran into Mr. Dwight
> Chapin who said he was going to get some 'thugs' to
> remove that man from Lafayette Park. He said it
> would take him a few hours, but they could do the
> job.[19]

Although the demonstrator was not physically removed from
the scene, he was shuttled around the corner out of the President's sight.

Perhaps a more impressive example from the point of view of
the numbers involved was the mass arrest of 12,000 antiwar
protesters in Washington, D.C. between May 3 and 5 of 1971.[20]
The official justification was that the demonstrators were disrupting traffic and otherwise creating problems for the safety
of the city. Some probably were. If all those arrested had been
breaking the law, they should have been charged accordingly.
As it turned out, the majority were simply detained. Since
formal charges were not brought in most cases, it seems likely
that the real concern was in minimizing the protesters' impact.
If so, then undue interference with the right of free expression
was exercised in this situation.

Freedom of speech is one of our most important Constitutional
guarantees, and we should be ever mindful of threats to its
continuance. Although it is the responsibility of the courts to
define the limits of free expression, we cannot assume that attention will always be paid to their definitions. As the Mosher
Committee pointed out in reaction to the troop of witnesses
appearing before the Senate Watergate Committee, "Very few
of the top witnesses indicated any sense of understanding or
appreciation of democratic ideals or principles."[21]

Cases involving the possible abridgement of free speech can be
judged against the following criterion: *Deliberate attempts by
governmental agents to suppress or otherwise interfere with an
individual's legitimate exercise of free expression within the
limits defined by our courts are inappropriate and irresponsible.*

The McCarthy and Nixon eras and all that they augured for the maintenance of civil liberties are too recent memories for any of us to be unconcerned about the implications of permitting the abridgement of this most fundamental right.

Some individuals believe that we have never been closer to one man rule in our history than we were during the five and one-half years of Richard Nixon's administration. The truth of this proposition is probably best left to future scholars to decide; however, it is now already apparent that the power of the Presidency has grown enormously in the twentieth century, a fact which Arthur Schlesinger, Jr. has carefully traced in his recent book *The Imperial Presidency*.[22] Strong presidents have brought increasing power to their office, but the means by which the Nixon administration attempted to strengthen the hand of the Presidency appear unique. The perception may be only the result of our having a more thorough record of its activities. Whatever the case, the acts of political espionage that have surfaced in the investigations of the past two years constitute a cause for alarm.

In 1971, Donald Segretti was hired by the Committee to Re-elect the President.[23] Sometimes portrayed by his apologists as just another Dick Tuck type of fun-loving political prankster, within the space of eighteen months, Mr. Segretti and his staff had arranged for hecklers to be present at Democratic candidates' rallies, falsified campaign literature, attributed the slogan "If you liked Hitler, you'll just love Wallace" to the Muskie organization, forged a letter on Muskie stationery accusing Senators Jackson and Humphrey with sexual impropriety, advertised free lunches and liquor at Muskie headquarters, announced the cancellation of a speech by former Secretary of the Interior Udall, ordered an airplane carrying the sign "Peace, Pot, and Promiscuity. Vote McGovern" to fly over the Democratic Convention Center, and engaged in a host of other abusive, malicious, and frequently illegal activities.[24]

In addition to the types of campaign practices carried out by Segretti and associates, let us not forget some of the other kinds of activities in which members of the Nixon political family were either directly or indirectly involved, including the Huston Plan, the "Plumbers" operations, and the Watergate break-in.[25] Frequently excused as security measures, actions such as these point to a pattern of behavior directed toward a concentration of power heretofore unknown in the national experience.

In spite of Congressional efforts to enact legislation minimizing the occurrence of political espionage, I rather suspect that, at the very least, "dirty tricks" will continue to be a part of the American political scene. Moreover, while it is possible to separate legal from illegal activities, some of those that are not illegal may still be irresponsible. Hence, it seems to me that we need to be prepared to examine given cases of political activity and render ethical judgments regardless of legality. A standard for making such judgments might be: *Overt and covert governmental acts designed to misrepresent a political candidate's, or any other citizen's character or position or to violate said individual's rights are inappropriate and irresponsible.*

Finally, I turn to the issue of disguised communication. Because the National Council of Teachers of English Committee on Public Doublespeak has done an admirable job of exposing and commenting on this phenomenon, I shall not dwell on the subject. I would like to suggest, however, that, from the point of view of responsibility, it is not ambiguity or euphemistic language per se that are at issue. The focus of our interest should be on governmental communication in which ambiguity, euphemism, and other forms of disguise are employed to mislead or deceive. The expression "protective reaction strike," for example, to me represents more than just another illustration of the type of jargon commonly used by military personnel. Rather, it has a strategic purpose; that is, leading the public to believe that we are not engaged in a type of activity which, in fact, we are. During the Vietnam war, an attack on the North might not be tolerated whereas a protective reaction strike would.

Another invidious, if not insidious, expression popularized during the period when John Mitchell was Attorney General is "Preventive detention." Ostensibly, the term is a label for the act of incarcerating individuals with potentially dangerous criminal tendencies. In practice, however, it could easily refer to the imprisonment of anyone whom a government in power happens to believe is its enemy.

Remembering that we are concerned with language chosen to conceal intentions rather than with all forms of ambiguity, I propose the following criterion: *Language employed by governmental figures for the purpose of deliberately obscuring the activity or idea it represents is inappropriate and irresponsible.* Because of the availability of public statements, one could harbor the illusion that this evaluative standard is easy to implement. Actual application, however, may be complicated by the difficulty of identifying intentions. As a result, I trust that we would utilize this criterion with as much care and caution as any of the others.

Hans Morgenthau has recently suggested that:

> If democratic government is defined as the choice by the people at large, according to preestablished rational procedures, of the personnel and, through it, of the policies of the government, then the decline of democratic government throughout the world is an observable fact.[26]

By being sensitive to the actions and public statements of government officials, and by willingly pointing to instances of irresponsibility, we can, I think, develop a constructive, even if small, role in the maintenance and evolution of our social institutions. But even if the prospect of achievement is minimal, I would urge us to take such action, not because it is fashionable nor because we are morally superior. We should undertake such activity because it is right.

Notes

1 Gustav Bergmann, "The Concept of Ideology," *Ethics*, 61 (April, 1951), 205–218.

2 Cited by David Wise, *The Politics of Lying* (New York: Vintage Books, 1973), pp. 62–63.

3 *The End of a Presidency*, compiled by the staff of the *New York Times* (New York: Bantam Books, 1974), p. 186.

4 *The End of a Presidency*, pp. 323–353.

5 Wise, pp. 213–218.

6 Maxwell D. Taylor, Interview on CBS News, June 17, 1971.

7 Wise, p. 100.

8 Richard Harwood, *Washington Post*, June 29, 1971.

9 John Osborne, *The Fifth Year of the Nixon Watch* (New York: Liveright, 1974), p. 106.

10 *The Presidential Transcripts* (New York: Dell Books, 1974), pp. 220–226.

11 See James David Barber, *The Presidential Character* (Englewood Cliffs, New Jersey: Prentice-Hall, 1972), pp. 319–330.

12 Wise, pp. 47–51.

13 Barber, p. 324.

14 Wise, p. 336.

15 Wise, pp. 336–356.

16 Carl Bernstein and Bob Woodward, *All the President's Men* (New York: Simon and Schuster, 1974), p. 105.

17 *The Presidential Transcripts*, p. 38.

18 Cited by Arthur Schlesinger, Jr., *The Imperial Presidency* (New York: Popular Library, 1973), p. 328.

19 John W. Dean, *Hearings Before the Select Committee on Presidential Campaign Activities of the United States Senate*, vol. 3 (Washington, D.C.: U.S. Government Printing Office, 1973), p. 917.

20 *The Fall of a President*, compiled by the staff of the *Washington Post* (New York: Dell Books, 1974), pp. 177–178.

21 Frederick C. Mosher, *Watergate: Implications for Responsible Government* (New York: Basic Books, 1974), pp. 12–13.

22 *The Senate Watergate Report*, vol. 1 (New York: Dell Books, 1974), p. 249.

23 *The Senate Watergate Report*, pp. 255–271.

24 All of these operations are described and discussed in *The Senate Watergate Report*, pp. 51–316.

25 Schlesinger, *op. cit.*

26 Hans J. Morgenthau, "Decline of Democratic Government," *The New Republic*, 9 November 1974, p. 13.

Communication Contexts and Pseudocommunication

Richard Beach
University of Minnesota

Talking about pseudocommunication or doublespeak in the classroom is generating interest in language among students because they are now discussing the actual uses of language in social, economic, and political contexts. By discussing actual contexts, students intuitively sense that they are dealing with language as they use it in their own lives. They know that differences in contexts affect changes in their language. They know that they alter their speech as they move from classroom to classroom, audience to audience, street corner to street corner. They also know that they often misjudge the unspoken rules operating in certain contexts—rules contingent upon the expectations and needs of audiences, the status relationships between speaker and audience, the social setting, the roles assumed, the kinds of speech-acts performed, etc. And some sense that this rhetorical guessing/switching process stems from the larger forces of social and economic values. Some become devilishly proficient at this process, while others never transcend the narrow boundaries of their own egocentric, provincial contexts. Others become cynical, viewing it all as a phoney game.

The fact that students do sense that unspoken rules or conventions differ with different contexts and that these unspoken rules derive from values speaks directly to the problem of dealing with doublespeak in the classroom.

One problem with simply listing examples of doublespeak isolated from the context in which these examples occurred is that students may not be learning the influence of unspoken rules in those contexts. Students may simply learn that "peace with honor" is a deceptive slogan, an example of doublespeak, instead of understanding the political values underlying its use, and therefore its meaning, in the 1972 Presidential campaign.

32

Students may also recognize that the words "peace with honor" in other contexts might be used in an ethical manner without the intention to deceive. By carefully studying the contexts in which technical jargon, slogans, neologisms, euphemisms, or bombast is used, students could learn to generalize about the effects of these contexts on speakers' verbal behavior.

Moreover, simply citing examples and saying that these examples represent bad or unethical uses of language without considering the particulars of the context—who said what to whom in what situation for what purpose—may perpetuate the same prescriptive attitude towards certain types or modes of language use that characterizes traditional English instruction. Blanket generalizations about the "rightness" or "wrongness" of language use without consideration of the particulars of contexts exhibit the same insensitivity that some English teachers have shown towards variation in dialect, speech community, or social values. Labeling the Pentagon spokesman or the huckster as a no-good liar does not appreciate the fact that speakers are often the unwitting pawns of the rules and conventions operating in certain contexts. It is these rules and conventions which underly and dictate the use of pseudocommunication that students could examine in a descriptive rather than prescriptive manner. To draw on Kenneth Burke's pentad, if attention is focused on the speaker (agent) who uses doublespeak (agency) to produce pseudocommunication (act) in order to confuse or deceive (purpose), then the explanation is incomplete because context (scene) has been ignored.

Studying the complicated relationships between context and pseudocommunication requires some understanding of how speakers conceive of contexts or situations. By now we have some understanding of how Richard Nixon, during the final years of his administration, conceived of himself and the world: he saw himself as a man against enemies who were out to get him and who misunderstood him. That conception influenced his use of language: simplistic labels of his enemies, scapegoating, slogans playing upon connotations, deceptive summaries of optional approaches to a problem.

The speaker's conception is also influenced by social, economic, and political values. Group consensus develops out of agreement on values as to certain rules or conventions governing appropriate or inappropriate discourse. In the drawing-room conversations of Victorian England, for example, conventions reflecting the wealthy class's values produced an elaborate system of conventions.

Speakers accept the group consensus, conceiving of contexts according to the rules or conventions of the group, institution, corporation, school, etc. They thereby conform to institutional or others' conceptions of appropriate verbal behavior. Supermarket checkout clerks are told that as employees they are to be polite and friendly to customers by telling customers "Thank you for shopping at Grandway." The clerks then chant this refrain to each customer even though they don't mean it and the customer also knows that the whole ritual is simply pseudocommunication. My point is that the clerk conceives of the situation according to the rules and conventions of the store, reflecting the larger values of an impersonal consuming society. Speakers therefore assume that certain rules or conventions dictating verbal behavior are appropriate in certain contexts. In television commercials, speakers who are interviewed about a product say what they have learned as appropriate language in the context of television commercials: "It has made me a new man" or "I don't know how I got along without it."

These speakers are therefore not deliberately lying, deceiving, evading, concealing, or distorting because they are the unwitting pawns of the rules and conventions of contexts. The boss who talks to employees about "maximizing the potential for output" instead of simply telling them to work harder may not be deliberately trying to deceive or evade. Moreover, the workers have heard these words enough times to know what the boss means; what they resent is the boss's impersonal conception of the situation—instead of simply telling them to work harder, they seen him or her adopting the role of bureaucrat. The boss is conceiving of the context in a highly stereotyped manner, a conception which assumes that bureaucratic or technocratic conventions are valid.

My examples pose a further question about the relationship between contexts and pseudocommunication: Where do people learn some of the unspoken rules that legitimize pseudocommunication? Students could examine several influences on language behavior—peers, family, school, social milieu, etc.—beginning with a study of how conventions or rules generally govern behavior, and then applying the results of this study to specific examples of pseudocommunication.

One starting point for working with students would be a general look at the effect of conventions and rules on verbal behavior. Students could talk about the conventions governing talk in their classroom or the rules involved in telling a joke, giving a speech, writing a formal business letter, bartering, proposing marriage, "putting someone down." One approach for discussing conventions is to use the conventions governing the performance of speech-acts, conventions originally proposed by J. L. Austin in *How to Do Things with Words*, and outlined in Martin, Ohmann, and Wheatley's *The Logic and Rhetoric of Exposition*. To cite their list of conventions: In order to successfully perform certain speech-acts (1) a conventional procedure must exist for performing the act; (2) the participants must be the right ones for the act in question; (3) the circumstances must be appropriate; (4) the procedures must be executed correctly and completely; (5) the speaker must have the appropriate feelings and beliefs; and (6) the speaker must behave appropriately afterward (Martin, Ohmann, and Wheatley, pp. 56–59).

Students could role-play situations in which these conventions are violated. They could then explore examples in which speakers conceive of the same speech situation in different terms— the procedures, the status of the participants, the circumstances, the appropriate feelings or behavior afterwards. One student may conceive of proposing marriage as a very serious, solemn occasion in which the male dominates, while another student may conceive of it as open, honest discussion between equals.

Students might examine cases in which certain kinds of language are considered as appropriate or inappropriate. A Biblical style is often considered appropriate for praying in churches; the language of the "here-and-now" for encounter groups; oratory for commencement addresses; a terse, code-like style for military and police operations, etc. These conceptions often dictate the use of jargon and cliché. Students might discuss examples of speakers who followed these dictates, regardless of differences among audiences.

Once students are accustomed to recognizing the components of communication contexts, they could focus on a thorough analysis of the effect of certain contexts on the misuse of language. For example, they could define and discuss the various conventions that dictate the use of language on television. While television portrays many different kinds of discourse, it imposes its own set of well-defined conventions onto these different kinds of discourse. These conventions evolve out of television producers' conceptions of appropriate and inappropriate behavior on television, generally on the basis of what will satisfy or not offend a mass audience, an audience conceived of in highly stereotyped terms. The conventions are slavishly followed regardless of differences in programs; students should be able to recognize certain conventions simply by watching and discussing several programs and commercials.

Let me mention some of the conventions dictating language use on television and the manner in which these conventions generate certain kinds of pseudocommunication.

Television gives its viewers hours and hours of talk—news, quiz shows, talk shows, sports play-by-play, panel discussions. Viewers assume that all of this talk is more immediate, direct, and, to use the jargon of television public relations, more "in touch with what's going on in the world while it's happening, where it's happening" than is the print media. One of the dangers of this assumption is that viewers also begin to assume that the immediacy of TV talk is to be valued as more authentic, sincere, genuine, or natural than the print media. This assumption legitimizes any kind of talk as somehow authentic, or of worth. Because TV needs to fill up hours of time with talk and tends to homogenize differences and extremes between speakers, regardless of their verbal abilities, a perceptive discussion will be followed by the illogical claims of an ad and then by the prepackaged banter of a talk show without any critical distinction between the quality of talk. When a speaker on a talk show says, "I'm really into trying to put it all together—that's my thing," that speaker is really communicating little, but within the context of the talk show, speakers are immune from criticism because it is assumed that their talk is of worth.

Commercial television also attempts to perpetuate the myth that its viewers are in constant need of novelty in the products advertised. When a new or improved product is advertised, the primary appeal is that because it is new it must be better than other products. Nonsensical neologisms are used in commercials to give an impression of novelty; the product is portrayed as "better" because it has a new name or new description. A new deodorant is described as "macroencapsulated" or an airline talks about its "all-new Comfort Class." Because producers and viewers both conceive of commercials in terms of the assumption that new is better, they are not critical of this verbal nonsense.

Another characteristic of television language is that speakers appear as representatives for organizations, corporations, institutions, movements.

A certain standard verbal style, slogan, or technical jargon portrays a certain public relations image. All those speaking for a particular organization, regardless of individual differences among them, use the same prepackaged language. Viewers do not question speakers' use of language because they learn to associate the language with the organization represented rather than with the speaker. When all of the scientists and engineers who appear for an oil company say, "We're doing our part to clean up the environment," the viewer does not hold the speaker accountable for those words.

Let me outline a few conventions I have observed which seem to dictate the use of language on television. For one, language is used on television primarily for definite pragmatic ends: to impress, entertain, inform, request, cajole—all of which are based on underlying commercial motives. This is a limited focus because it is concerned with the consequences or effects of language use: will it sell or entertain? Speakers who would use language to reminisce, philosophize, be poetic—that is, to use language without any predefined effect, any definite payoff—are discouraged.

The formats are highly ritualistic, fulfilling a pragmatic appeal to the viewer's sense of security and stability. For example, news programs always include reports on the weather, the stock market, and sports, as well as casual chatter among speakers, visual backgrounds, and an emphasis on the personality image of the principal newscaster. As Kingsley Widner has noted:

> Not the world reported on but the *process* itself becomes the crucial experience. The processing-programming style consumes all, merging every reality into the arbitrarily delimited package, equalizing the sporting game and the genocide war, a commercial quip and a social philosophy, the trivial and the magic. . . . Some recent studies suggest that many people follow the sports "scores" who do not otherwise relate to the athletic activity and who understand few of its nuances.*

These well-defined formats limit what speakers can say. For example, in interviews, questions are designed simply to test the interviewee's allegiance to a group, cause, or product. "A lot of people have said that your team hasn't got a chance. What do you think?" or "You have tried all of the products on the market. How does our product stand up?" Viewers know

* Kingsley Widner, "Sensibility Under Technocracy: Reflections on the Culture of Processed Communication," *Human Connections and the New Media*, ed. Barry Schwartz (Englewood Cliffs, N.J.: Prentice-Hall, Inc., 1973), p. 30.

what to expect in the answers because they recognize the staged questioning/affirming sequence.

Another characteristic of TV language use is that the roles of speakers, formats, sequences of units, and verbal style are well defined so as to deliberately limit the possibility of varying interpretations and connotations. The producer wants to communicate one definite meaning with a definite effect on the viewer. By carefully defining the context, the range of potential interpretations may be limited to the intended message. If speakers on commercials communicate a slight hint that they really do not care about the product they are praising, then the audience might pick this up. Thus the need for careful control.

One method for controlling potential interpretation is that the units or segments of television are distinctly separate; commercials are obviously separate from the programs and programs have no overlapping relationship. Viewers learn to distinguish between units because the same predictable formats are equated with the same predictable speech-acts. For example, one way to distinguish commercials from conversation on a talk show is by having the speaker suddenly address the camera, shifting attention away from the guests and studio audience to the viewer, with questions such as, "Do you feel tired and run down?" If the speaker had posed the same question in the talk show role, the viewer would have been confused.

Another technique for reducing the range of potential interpretations is the use of visual illustrations, particularly on news and commercials. When a concept is used, the producer can use an illustration which emphasizes interpretations of the concepts, "fast relief," "the good life," "youthful," "first class," "escape," by showing people consuming products. The viewers' attention is focused on the illustration, so they do not question the equation between the concept and the illustration. Likewise, news broadcasts flash stereotyped pictures or symbols when changing topics to illustrate concepts such as women's liberation, protest march, the ghetto, war, the Congress.

By trying to describe some of the conventions dictating language use on television and in other arenas of social discourse, students may be able to define some of the institutionalized conventions responsible for pseudocommunication. It is to be hoped that by increasing students' awareness of the function of contexts, we can encourage them to favor openness and honesty in communication.

Practice
Multi-level

Doublespeak and Ideology in Ads: A Kit for Teachers

compiled by Richard Ohmann and the Amherst Conference on Public Doublespeak, Summer 1974*

> How can business defend itself? The answer is not distant. . . . Pick up the weapon lying idle at your side, your advertising budgets.
>
> Patrick Buchanan

Mr. Buchanan, a speechwriter for former President Nixon, was talking about difficulties the oil companies had in 1974 in telling the public their views on energy and the environment. He went on to say, "Oil companies spend billions each year in advertising. Mobil's creation of 'idea advertising,' in lieu of the happy-motoring nonsense, is a first step." Whenever Mobil follows Buchanan's advice—as it has often done and will doubtless continue to do—it uses money spent by consumers for gas in order to educate those same customers in Mobil's *ideas*. Not having either the billions or the organization of oil companies, there's little that consumers can do to control such education except be alert to and critical of such ideas.

* Those who helped put together these materials at the Amherst conference were: Susan Allen, Meramec Community College, Missouri; John Bacich, Diablo Valley College, California; John Black, Darien High School, Connecticut; Jack Boozer, Warren Wilson College, North Carolina; Stella Bruton, West Chester State College, Pennsylvania; Walker Gibson, University of Massachusetts, Amherst; Francine Hardaway, Scottsdale Community College, Arizona; Andrea Johnson, Trinity College, Vermont; Howard Livingston, Pace University, New York; Dwight Marsh, Hastings College, Nebraska; David Milan, Tacoma Community College, Washington; Lee Morgan, Centenary College, Louisiana; Karl Oelke, Union College, New Jersey; Richard Ohmann, Wesleyan University, Connecticut; Jeffrey Roberts, Worcester State College, Massachusetts; Arthur Young, Michigan Technical University, Michigan.

The following material, an abbreviated version of a teaching kit prepared at a workshop in Amherst in the summer of 1974, is about the kind of advertising that Patrick Buchanan had in mind, and about any ads that sell ideas, with or without products. It offers ways to help alert students to business' ideas, and to ways of expressing them that are misleading, confusing, deceptive, manipulative. In other words, to what members of this NCTE committee have come to call "doublespeak."

You could think of the kit as an aid to self-defense, since without critical instruments a student has a handicap in sorting out the hundreds of messages she or he gets daily from advertisers. But we hope that the kit will be more than that, too. We'd like it to help you help students understand how ideology works, *whoever* the seller or giver. We'd like it to help you and your students define and understand the widespread thing we call doublespeak. And we think it will be useful in teaching some general points of rhetoric and semantics.

One obvious deficiency of the kit needs mentioning. We haven't been able to reproduce the photographs or layout of print ads, or the music or voice of radio ads, or the visual sequences of TV ads. These modes of presentation may contain nonverbal doublespeak, if you will, and we hope you will supplement the kit with whatever criticism you can bring to bear on the sounds and sights of advertising.

The explanations, checklists, and analyses here are addressed to you. They are no more than a sketch of the one- to three-week unit we imagine you may teach on doublespeak. And most of this material will need expansion or simplification, depending on the level of your college or high school students. Further—and perhaps this goes without saying—an effective unit on this subject cannot be "canned" for students. Everything depends on their becoming actively critical, finding their own instances, doing their own analyses.

Basic Principles
Ideology is the ideas of a group of people with common interests—a nation, a party, a government, a social or economic class, an occupational group, an industry, etc. The most common tactic of ideology is to show how the interests of the group are "really" the same as the interests of the whole society or of humanity in general. The famous remark of Charles Wilson some years back, "What's good for General Motors is good for the country," encapsulates the root principle of ideology. General Motors, the American Medical Association, the AFL-CIO,

the National Rifle Association, garmet workers, English teachers, college professors, businessmen—whatever group is organized and conscious of a common interest turns out ideology.

Ideological talk does not always amount to doublespeak, but it easily can. And for a simple reason: the interests of various groups in a society are *not* all compatible—not all the time in all respects. Poll taxes were good for white politicians but not for black tenant farmers. Higher faculty salaries at a private university with finite resources may mean *lower* salaries for secretaries or less scholarship money for students. And so on. Usually the conflict of interest is not so dramatic. Then ideology has its best opportunity—and runs its greatest risk of doublespeak. For then it can be rather abstract, hitching on to generally accepted ideas like (in this society) freedom, technological problem-solving, individualism, the family, "ecology." And if conflicts are obscure or buried, the grand concepts smooth a surface over them. Oil companies and consumers are both for a clean environment, and also for free choices in the marketplace; so (say the oil companies) let us work together to solve our problem. To paraphrase an anecdote of Lincoln's, the wolf and the sheep are both for liberty. So long as the discussion remains on this level, bystanders might be content to let the wolf and the sheep resolve their own differences, not noticing that the wolf's desired liberty is to eat the sheep, the sheep's not to be eaten. One person's solution may be the other person's problem. Not *always*, but often. And in such a situation ideology is often doublespeak.

It's an important kind of doublespeak for people to study, for these reasons: (1) If they can't decode it, they are likely to make major social choices for bad reasons, and against their interest. (2) Powerful groups in a society have ideological advantage over the poor, weak, or unorganized. Welfare mothers doubtless have an ideology, too, but lacking the resources to buy prime TV time they are less able to confuse us with doublespeak than groups that *can* buy prime time. (Remember Buchanan's advice to business.) Ideological doublespeak always tends to keep power where it is in a society. So in the Soviet Union it would be well if young people could detect Communist Party doublespeak. Here, the doublespeak of the U.S. Communist Party is less a force to contend with than that of the Pentagon. Ideology-detection is a weapon mainly of those without much wealth or power—e.g., most of us and most of our students. (3) For all that, much ideology does not *intend* to deceive. People often deeply believe their own doublespeak. And sincerity and good will make ideological doublespeak especially hard to detect.

This "kit" concentrates on advertisements. But early in a unit on this subject it is useful to have students look at some examples of more direct ideological argument, to see how it works, and how deception (conscious or unconscious) is likely to creep in. Choose one example of ideology that is unfamiliar to your students and one that is familiar. Needless to say, the choice will differ from one group of students to another, depending on their experience and stations in American society. It may be well to start with an argument quite foreign (literally) to them— say some Soviet or Chinese ideology.

How to Look for Ideology and Doublespeak in Ads: Questions to Ask

1 Who is the advertiser?
2 What is the explicit purpose of the ad?
3 Does the advertiser have any purpose other than the explicit one?
4 What kind of person or company does the advertiser claim to represent?
5 What audience does the advertiser assume?
6 To what qualities of that audience does the advertiser appeal?
7 What self-interests does the advertiser assume the audience to have? To *think* it has?
8 How does the advertiser relate the product, company, industry, or ideas to the audience's self-interest?
9 What common interests does the advertiser claim or imply between the company or person and the audience?
10 Are there possible *conflicts* of interest between advertisers and audience?
11 Does the ad refer, directly or obliquely, to such conflicts?
12 Does the advertiser call any widely accepted values or beliefs into play in pointing to the audience's and the company or person's common interest?
13 What words does the advertiser use for such values and beliefs? How abstract are these words? How easy are they to tie down to concrete situations and events?
14 What language does the advertiser use to suggest harmony between the company or person and the audience? Is it warranted?

Thirteen Items of Ideological Stock in Trade

Here's a highly selective list of ideological themes to look for in what American industry says:

1   Anything wrong in our society is a problem, amenable to a solution in the interest of all.
2   Corollary: all conflicts of interest are only apparent.
3   We'll all be best off if business manages the development of resources in the future.
4   It can do this only if (a) profits are high, and (b) there is a minimum of government interference.
5   Solutions to problems are generally technical; we need new technology, but not any change in the system.
6   Hence, what the experts decide is best for all. The people are often deficient in understanding.
7   On the other hand, neither business nor technocrats have much power: in the present system, *the people* are the ones who decide.
8   They decide best through individual purchases in a free market; voting is secondary, other kinds of politics a potential threat to free choice.
9   The United States can solve its problems apart from those of the rest of the world, and do so without creating problems elsewhere.
10 Freedom is good for both individuals and corporations, and pretty much the same thing for both.
11 Growth and productivity are good for all.
12 Our needs—for pleasure, love, approval, security, etc.—can best be met by consuming products.
13 Consumption should generally be done by units no larger than the nuclear family. And the nuclear family is the social ideal.

(Remember: Taken as ideas, these are of varying merit. They can be openly debated. Certainly they are not in themselves doublespeak. What earns them their places on this list is their very wide acceptance, coupled with their loose formulation: they can easily be appropriated for almost any purpose, including honest and dishonest ones. It is their abuse we should attend to.)

Short Guide to Ideological Doublespeak
Look for doublespeak in these areas of semantics and rhetoric:

1   *What you mean "we," paleface?* The homogenizing "we," and "us," and "our." Particularly, watch for shifts in the reference of "we," and for instances where "we" purports to refer to everyone in the society, but where what is said is in fact only true of some. (Recall the Lone Ranger's saying "There are Indians closing in from all sides, Tonto: we're in trouble." Tonto: "What you mean 'we,' paleface?")

2 *"America."* And "the people," "our society," etc. When you read "America needs. . . ." stop and ask if all Americans need it, or only some, or some more than others. The use of "America" is often coercive, not referential.

3 *Abstraction away from people.* When someone proposes to fight "poverty," does that mean getting more money to poor people, and perhaps less to the wealthy? If not, what? Again, can we be for "ecology" without being against those who upset the ecological balance?

4 *Liberty. Or, the sheep and the wolf.* Both are for liberty, but one's liberty is the other's death. Watch for plus-words like "liberty," used as if they had the same meaning for all. In many situations they conceal conflict of interest.

5 *It's a problem.* An American habit of mind conceives any difficulty, crisis, disaster, social conflict—ANYthing BAD—as a problem. This move always implies that we're in it together, faced with the same problem, and all with the same interest in a solution. Remember that your solution *may* be my problem, or that your problem may even be *me.* Be watchful, especially, for distinterested formulation of "problems" by those who have helped create them, and whose livelihoods are at stake. Another thing: labeling something a problem obviously implies that there *is* a solution—but in some situations there may be no approved solution, or even no solution at all.

6 *The technological fix.* Fusion will solve our problem, or a new emission control device, or a new ingredient, or a new kind of glass, or just "research." The technological fix is usually aimed at symptoms, not causes. Now sometimes technical solutions are what we (all of us) need. But often they're *more* needed by those who supply the technology. And very often the technological fix is offered as remedy for social or political problems. When some technological term is the subject of an active verb, try to put people back in the picture: Technology does nothing by itself. *Who* will set the machine going? With what interest?

7 *Experts know best.* A corollary of the above, this idea always merits some skepticism. But it leads to doublespeak especially when the ideologue says (a) the people must decide, (b) the people don't/can't understand what the experts understand, (c) let the experts decide.

8 *Hard facts or iron laws.* "The hard fact is that America progresses only if business prospers." Query: What makes a fact hard? Query: What issues are excluded from debate by this

hard fact? Well, the equation of progress with economic growth, for one. And the question of alternatives to free enterprise for another. The hard fact move leads to doublespeak when it treats a present social arrangement as iron law, and so rules out choices that might not be good for the advertiser. Watch for law-like statements in present tense (like the invented one above), which foreclose discussion of the system itself, and its assumptions. And watch for coercive uses of words and phrases like "necessary," "only possible," "required," "essential to economic health," and "inevitable unless."

9 *There's nobody here but us chickens.* Watch for formulations like "the people will decide," or "we will all be ruled by free choices in a free market." They imply that no one has more power than anyone else in determining the future—or even that big corporations have *less* power than ordinary people. Check these formulas against the facts of how decisions will be made on a particular issue. And remember to ask who paid for the ad, and whether ordinary people have any matching power.

10 *What can one man do?* To stop pollution, buy brand X gasoline. To handle the trash menace, dispose of your bottle properly. To deal with the energy shortage, turn your lights off when not using them. Some of this may be good advice (but not *all* of it), but none of the individual actions proposed will make a dent in the "problem." Watch for ads that urge independent acts of consumers, and stay silent about broader "solutions," like new laws, regulations of industry, etc.

11 *Corporations equal people.* A blend of 9 and 10. "We're all in this together—*you* conserve heat in your house, and *we'll* build more nuclear plants." Beware of hearty invitations to collaborate in making America better; ask whether the proposed "partnership" is one of equals, or one of chickens and foxes.

12 *Blurred ownership.* "The people's coal." "Your power company." "America's resources." "Our industrial system." And so on. Ask who, in cold financial and legal fact, owns the thing in question, who has power to determine its future, and why the possessive noun or pronoun is so generalized.

Kinds of Ads, and How They Sell Ideas (Not Just Products)
Probably all advertisements contain or imply some ideology. They are trying to get the audience to do something or believe something that's in the advertiser's interest. One natural meeting ground of audience and advertiser is broad ideas or images of the good life, the good society. As lots of people have said,

advertising taken as a whole conveys some important ideological messages:* commodities can solve just about all human problems; business is meeting "our" deepest needs; the American way of life is OK basically as it is; there are always problems, but they will be solved by business and consumers in league with each other—and solving problems is progress.

But these and other points of ideology appear very differently in different kinds of ads, and only some involve doublespeak. It helps, then, to have a classification of ads for this particular purpose. Here's a handy one, moving from specific to general rhetorical aims.

1 Ads that make a factual claim about a product to persuade you to buy it. (Our razor blade lasts longer; our car gets the best mileage.) Subject to empirical test; no ideology in the foreground; doublespeak at a minimum.

2 Ads that sell a product by vague and untestable claims about it ("gets teeth whiter"), or by associating it with some reliable image—the happy family, youth, sexual success, etc. There's a good deal of deception in such ads through implied associations (cigarettes don't make you young, fresh, and healthy, in spite of what the picture suggests). Doublespeak here resides mainly in vagueness, evasion, empty language, rather than in ideology.

3 Ads that invoke current social concerns and the anxieties they stir, in order to increase the motivation for buying the product. (Your house will be cold this winter; buy sweaters.) Ideology in the background, except for the usual implication that social problems can be solved by individuals, for themselves.

4 Ads that refer to the same current problems, but say that the consumer can help solve them—not just for the individual, but for all of us—by making the right purchase. (You can help the energy crisis by buying our gas.) Much ideology here, and often much doublespeak.

5 Ads that sell a company or an industry, not a product, by showing how its activities benefit all. These ads are a goldmine of ideological doublespeak.

6 "Responsible" ads that state the manufacturer's concern over the social consequences of the use of a product. The prod-

* See, for instance, Marcuse's *One Dimensional Man,* or Ronald Gross's short essay, "The Language of Advertising," in *Language in America,* ed. Neil Postman, Charles Weingartner, and Terence P. Moran.

uct, say the ads, is beneficial to all, *if* used properly. Where does responsibility lie for abuse, bad side effects, and the like? In the area of this question there is much room for doublespeak.

7   Explicitly ideological ads that defend high profits, argue against government regulation, etc.

8   And most general, what we might call "philosophy of life ads." They seem not to be about a product, a company, an industry, *or* the American way of life, but to offer disinterested wisdom. Great ideas (of Plato, Shakespeare, etc.) presented as a public service by the X Company. Ideology is deeply buried here.

A unit on ideological doublespeak in ads should concentrate on types 4–6. But we'll at least glance at the doublespeak potential in each category.

1   Watch for the general motto that sometimes accompanies class 1 ads. An insurance company ad describes the economic difficulties a small business can get in when its owner is disabled; then it offers a policy to prevent such difficulties. All factual. The motto at the end is "We add assurance to life in an unsure world." Here is ideological doublespeak of the "hard fact" type. *Is* the world simply "unsure"? Well, yes, continued life and good health are always unsure. But no, the world is not inherently unsure in the other sense required—economic consequences of accidents could be absorbed by the entire society, not left to individuals. The ad makes a social choice seem an inevitability. Why? Insurance companies, of course, have an interest in keeping the world economically unsure, and in convincing us that it *is* intrinsically unsure. Therefore, the role of insurance companies is in the interest of all of us.

2   A Colgate ad explains that Billie Jean King wins friends as easily as tennis tournaments. "Liking people comes naturally to Billie Jean. Which is one reason she's a long-time user of Colgate." The ideology is in the casual connective, which not only sells Colgate as a friend-maker (garden-variety doublespeak), but also reinforces the idea that social anxieties, personal failures, loneliness, can all be resolved by buying something. Ideology in class 2 ads is mainly on this level of abstraction. Get students to ask what assumptions these ads make about the kind of society we have, and how to face problems within it.

3   Closer to ideology here. Libbey-Owens-Ford titles an ad "INSULATION YOU CAN SEE THROUGH, FROM LOF," and goes on to cite rising energy costs as a reason for buying

two special kinds of glass, to keep your view and still "save . . .
energy dollars." Here the garden-variety doublespeak is in the
implication that glass insulates better than other materials.
"Save energy dollars" compared to what? Not to insulated
walls, but only to ordinary, cheaper glass. Glass is not "insulation." But the ideological doublespeak lies in the casual
implication: energy crisis—buy glass. No real sacrifice is necessary, no change in our pattern of life or the economic system,
not even the loss of your picture window. The crisis is presented as a problem of individuals, not a social problem. LOF
asks us to rely on patchwork technological remedies, and on
the market. This approach rules out, of course, the possibility
of legally limiting the amount of glass in the new buildings,
and so forecloses the possibility of a conflict between LOF's interests and ours. In class 3 ads, get students to look at the
casual connections between the social crisis and the individual
act recommended: what possibilities for action are omitted?
Why?

4   What class 3 ads imply, class 4 ads more directly state.

> What can one man do, my friend,
> What can one man do,
> To fight pollution in the air,
> That's closin' in from everywhere?
>
> There's a lead-free gasoline, my friend,
> And it's name is Amoco,®
> Two lead free brands, one for every car,
> The one sure way to go.

Lots of doublespeak here.

a   Abstracting. Not "fight polluters," but "fight pollution."
Not "that's coming from combustion of gas," but "that's closin'
in from everywhere."

b   Presenting individual purchases as a general problem-solver.
The pertinent chemistry is such that if *you* switch to an un-
leaded or low lead gas, then either you increase hydrocarbon
pollution by your own car or you leave *me* to purchase gasoline
with *more* lead in it. Always ask of class 4 ads: What would
be the result if everyone did what the ad recommends? And:
Could everyone do what it recommends? Generally, class 4 ads
imply the impossible.

c   The "one person" ploy is common in free enterprise ideology.
The point is to defer collective action in favor of individual action. Needless to say, one person can't do anything to fight

pollution so long as he or she is restricted to choosing among brands, disposing of containers "properly," and the like. But encouraging this approach leads a consumer to (1) feel personally responsible, (2) overlook the advertiser's responsibility, and (3) accept the present means of making social decisions. "One person" is led to believe he or she has power that in fact could only be possessed in league with many men and women.

5   Here's an example of a sort common today:

What's My Electric Company Doing about the Energy Problem?

America's fuel shortage problem is so big that it seems difficult for one individual or even one industry to influence it very much. And there are no quick and easy solutions to the fuel shortage facing the nation.

But almost every individual and every company uses energy so we all should try to help by using fuels wisely.

The electric light and power industry is helping because we have some degree of flexibility in the way we can design our plants to use various fuels now and in the future.

Using Fuels Wisely

At the present time, about half of America's electric power is generated with coal. Natural gas and oil account for a little more than a third.

As we all know, supplies of oil are limited.

So, where changes are feasible, electric companies are burning coal in some of their power plants that once depended on oil. And the expanded utilization of coal, America's most plentiful fuel, is an important goal in our immediate and long term generating plans. Along with the increased use of nuclear energy.

Searching for New Ways

The electric companies, in partnership with the federal government and others, are involved in research and development in a wide variety of new methods of power generation: developing nuclear "Breeder" reactors that would create more useable nuclear fuel than they consume; experimenting with fusion which would create energy by combining the atoms available in ordinary water; producing electricity directly from the sun's energy; using the earth's heat, deep underground, as a generating source.

Research has been going on in these areas for a number of

years, and it will continue long into the future, for there are no instant answers.

But the important thing is, we in the electric companies are doing everything we can today to find ways to ease the energy problem. We are also doing everything we can for tomorrow.

Outlook for the Future

The time is past when any of us can use energy carelessly. But if everyone uses energy wisely in his home, or at his place of business, or when he travels, he will be helping with the nation's fuel shortage problem.

And if we in the electric industry can use those fuels to generate power that best conserve the nation's reserves, America will have gone a long way toward assuring an ample supply of energy for generations to come.

The people at your Investor-Owned Electric Light and Power Companies.

Places to look for doublespeak:

a   The generalization of a problem: "America's fuel shortage problem." The power companies' problem is, in part, to stay in command of this economic area, to keep Nader-like consumers from interfering with free choice and profits. The consumer's problem is, in part, to get the power companies to be more farsighted and public spirited in the future than in the past. (The wolf and the sheep again.)

b   Equating corporations and individuals through the familiar doublespeak "we": "we all should try to help by using fuels wisely." But "we" consumers can only choose among fuels and technologies made available to us by the power companies and others. The we're-all-in-this-together approach is particularly misleading here.

c   Excluding the layman: See the paragraph about new ways to generate power. Only big industry in "partnership" (suppression of conflict, again) with government could do research on this scale. No effort made here to explain to consumers what the experts are doing, or what consequences to expect from one or another of these technologies. In what sense is it, then, "my" electric company?

d   The technological fix. This is so universal in American society that it passes almost unnoticed. We read that the power companies are "doing everything we can today to find ways to ease the energy problem." What is that "everything"? Trying out technical solutions. Other possibilities occur: helping to reduce our dependence on power (who encourages us to buy all those appliances in the first place?); submitting energy decisions to voters; changing the companies from "investor-owned" to public. Ads like this treat technology as the only way out, and do not explain why the technological fixes of the future will be better than those of the past, which created the "problem" in the first place. And they assume that technology is, simply, good. Look in such ads for the presentation of social and political problems as purely technological. This tactic makes it seem that our interest is in leaving the problem to the companies, since they are the ones with the technical expertise.

e   America as abstraction. "America's electric power," "America's most plentiful fuel," "America will have gone a long way toward assuring an ample supply of energy for years to come." Who, specifically, uses the power? produces it? owns the fuel? will make the crucial decisions about energy in the future? Confront these aggregates with questions that make the concrete situation visible and like as not you'll uncover doublespeak.

6   An ad of the Distilled Spirits Council of the United States:

What's the best way to enjoy a drink? Slowly.

A social drink with good food and good friends. That's a traditional custom observed by most people in this country.
Like any other custom, of course, it can be abused.
Hastily downing glass after glass, for example. Or drinking with no food and no company. That's hardly the way to enjoy the products we make so carefully.
Most Americans, fortunately, make responsible decisions in this respect—drinking and dining leisurely in a relaxed setting.
And with ordinary common sense, that's what liquor is—a pleasure, not a problem.
If you choose to drink, drink responsibly.

This ad trades mainly on "There's nobody here but us chickens" and "What can one man do?" Liquor is traditional, a "custom," etc. But "it can be abused." So you individual drinkers should moderate your drinking, and that will make liquor "a pleasure, not a problem," i.e., no social control is needed; the problem is some people who abuse alcohol, and it can be solved by continuing the free economic relationship between drinkers and distillers—if the drinkers will just be reasonable. (As usual in this type of ideology, the people are held responsible for all problems.)

"If you choose to drink, drink responsibly." Is the word "choose" appropriate, for many drinkers? Is this really an area where the concept of free individual choice applies? The *New York Times* on July 11, 1974 carried a front page story headlined "Alcoholism Cost to Nation Put at $25-Billion a Year." Among other things, the study suggested that "alcohol control laws and regulations are grossly ineffective in dealing with alcohol problems." But it's in the interest of the distillers to conceive of these as basically individual problems, hence matters of free choice, hence not amenable to social control.

7   In these ads, the argument is openly ideological. A United States Steel ad (written by the Chairman of the General Electric Company) explains that "we" need to have higher profits between now and 1985 so that "we" can meet the "capital needs of this country," so that "we" won't have to live with worsening shortages. Note shifts in reference. The homogenized "we" are also asked "to improve our personal productivity on the job. . . . This will not only help industry earn more and invest more in America's future, it will also help each of us earn more as we produce more." The "personal productivity" of assembly line workers may be in the interest of the Board, but is the Board's productivity so certainly in the interest of workers? It's a debatable question, side-stepped by "we" and "our." The same ad also relies heavily on the hard facts approach: In the next twelve years our capital *needs* will come to $3 trillion. Most of it "will *have to* be raised and invested by the business community." And the iron law approach: "The capital available to business comes *only* from profits. . . . The *higher the profits, the higher the levels of investment* that are *possible*." (Italics added.) Ask students to imagine alternatives to these hard facts and iron laws, and consider why the language might be excluding them. And in such ads, watch also for leave-it-to-the-experts, for the portrayal of conflicts as "problems," and for blurred ownership. (On this last: an ad of the American Electric Power system asks for the Government to "release" the resources of coal it "owns" in the West. "This coal is the people's coal and the people need it." Query: Is the government the people? Are the power companies the people? Just who is to release whose coal and to whom?)

8   The Atlantic Richfield Company has a series of philosophy of life ads under way at this writing. One begins with, "the real": "People become obsolete before their time in our assembly line culture," talks about how "we" have made the aged into a problem, offers examples of achievements by old people

(Churchill, Sandburg, Grandma Moses, Frank Lloyd Wright, Schweitzer), and ends with "the ideal": "The maturity and social flexibility to recognize that for some, life reserves its greatest rewards until later." In such ads doublespeak is muted or absent. But they bear examination for the usual marks of ideology. How did "our assembly line culture" get that way? Whose interest is served by automatic retirement? By making it hard for older people to find work? What do "maturity and social flexibility" boil down to? What attitude do such ads encourage toward social "problems"? Toward the status quo? And, of course, why is Atlantic Richfield spending money in this way?

Study and Writing for Students
A *Alternate points of view.* Ideology tries to draw all points of view together into one—the common interest. So one antidote to ideological doublespeak is consciously to shift point of view. Students can do this in a variety of ways. For instance:

1 Keep the same speaker, but change the audience. Take a passage like the following from Richard Gerstenberg, former Chairman of General Motors:

> In addition to our efforts at General Motors to earn a profit, and largely because of our success in those efforts, we are helping to create a better balanced system of transportation in this country and throughout the world; to explore space; to cleanse our air and water; to develop new materials and means of manufacture; to recruit, hire, and advance minority employees and women; to foster minority enterprise; to support education and a wide range of other community and civic programs. In short, to help do what must be done if our country and the world are to become all that we want them to be.

Ask students to imagine Gerstenberg talking to some close associates in camera, and describing to them in backroom terms this same program of public service. A cynical version:

> OK, look: we're going to keep making a profit; that comes first. Right? And to persuade the public that we deserve it, what can we do? Well, we have to keep them dependent on their private cars, but we can build a few buses on the side (and make a profit on them, too.) Then we'll glamorize ourselves and the whole technological shtick by sending a few space cowboys out into the solar system. If Nader and that gang of hoodlums in Congress keep

after us, we'll cut down on. the gunk our cars spill
out the exhaust pipe, and claim credit as environ-
mentalists. We'll hire enough spics and spades and
broads to satisfy HEW, and we'll give blacks a few
franchises in places like Watts and Hough that aren't
safe for white salesmen anyhow. That way we'll
build a good image, racewise. And we'll keep up the
usual PR—you know, have our top men on school
boards and their wives ornamenting the heart fund.
With this combination, we ought to have no trouble
keeping the U.S. and the world the way we want
them—a happy home for GM.

This kind of exercise, of course, can't be accurate and certainly
shouldn't claim to be "fair." The point is to expose latent conflicts between points of view, and the language used to smooth
them over.

2 Change the speaker. For instance, ask students to write a
discussion of the energy shortage parallel to that of the Power
Companies, but from the point of view of a beleaguered consumer (or environmentalist, socialist, etc.):

What's my electric company doing about the energy
problem, having created it in the first place? The
fuel shortage may be a huge problem, but one certain
thing is that the power companies can do a lot about
it and individuals can't influence it at all. There are
no quick and easy solutions, but you can bet that
whatever solution we end up with will be a lot easier
on the power companies than on me.

It's irritating, at best, to be told that "we" should
save fuel, when for me that means shivering in
winter, while for the power company management
and stockholders that means hiking prices to keep
profits as high as ever.

And so on. Needless to say, this kind of exercise can attune
students to doublespeak in ideology of left, right, and center,
and to media other than advertisements.

B Parody. Students can often bring out the special interests
behind doublespeak by parody, by keeping the rhetoric and some
of the language of an ad, but changing the subject matter.
Here's a job on the Distiller Spirits Council's ad:

What's the best way to enjoy heroin? Slowly.

A social hit with some food and friends. That's a
traditional custom observed by many street gangs,
derelicts, and pimps in this country.

Like any other custom, of course, it can be abused.
Taking heroin daily, for instance, or nodding off by
yourself. That's hardly the way to enjoy the shit
we make so carefully.
Most users, fortunately, make responsible decisions
in this respect—mainlining at leisure in a relaxed
setting.
And with ordinary common sense, that's what heroin
is—a pleasure, not a problem.
If you choose to take heroin, do it moderately.

Ankara, Marseilles, and Harlem
Poppy Advancement League

C   Research. Projects for studying the relations of ideology
and doublespeak to different audiences.

1   Select a variety of magazines: *Newsweek, Good Housekeeping, Hot Rod, Time, True Confessions, Business Week, Cosmopolitan, Harper's, New Republic, Guns and Ammo, Forbes, Sports Illustrated, Ebony,* etc. Describe the assumed reader of
each, basing your characterization on analysis of both text and
ads. Then find examples of ideology and doublespeak: how do
these vary, if at all, in keeping with the assumed audience?

2   Select a group of magazines that appeal to women: *Woman's Day, Viva, True Romance, Redbook, Ladies Home Journal, Seventeen, Ms., Madamoiselle, Cosmopolitan.* What subgroup
among the female population does each try to reach? How
do you know? What background ideas are used to help sell
products? If you find ideological doublespeak, is it especially
likely to succeed with the intended audience of the particular
magazine?

3   Do the same for a group of men's magazines: *Playboy, Field and Stream, Penthouse, Esquire, Forbes, Money, Popular Mechanics, Motor Trend, Guns and Ammo, American Legion Magazine.*

4   In these same groups of magazines, consider ads of classes
5–8—ads not trying to sell a product. What assumptions about
the world, the nation, and the good life are common to ads in
a particular magazine? a group of magazines? all magazines
in all groups?

5   Become an expert on some consumer issue—cholesterol, the
fuel shortage, lead poisoning, pollution, etc. Examine ads by
companies whose products are involved. How do they select
from the whole range of facts and arguments available? How

do they differ from, and respond to, claims of consumer advocates? What ideological bridges do they build between themselves and audiences? If they fall into doublespeak, how would you explain that?

6   Study ideology in TV commercials. How much is communicated by the words, and how much by the images? Can there be visual doublespeak?

7   Study relations of TV shows to business and industry, *aside* from commercials. What products appear during the show, and in what setting? What airline is the only one seen on "Hawaii Five-O"? What kind of car does "Mannix" drive? What prizes are given away on "The Price Is Right"? What do TV's "hidden" commercials sell, besides products?

D   Imagining

1   Invent a magazine designed for you and your friends by big business interests. What kinds of ideological ads would appear? How would ideology figure in ads designed to sell products? Write copy for sample ads.

2   Invent a magazine designed for some rather different audience—old people, successful financiers, revolutionaries, freaks, whatever group you'd define as most antithetical to your own. Write ideological ads for this audience, designed to sell your own values and beliefs, in a way that would make them palatable to the audience.

3   Take some ads of classes 5–7 from one magazine, and rewrite them as if for the audience of another quite different magazine—e.g., translate from *U.S. News & World Report* to *Rolling Stone*, from *New Republic* to *Guns and Ammo*, etc.

4   You are the head of the President's Council of Economic Advisors. You have just gotten the latest figures on the economy, and they are bad: Prices are up 2% over last month; unemployment is up .4%; housing starts are off 20% from this same month last year; and retail sales are down. Can you write a statement to be given out to the newspapers, which will make the picture sound hopeful? Do not falsify the facts.

5   A bill is coming up in Congress to extend price supports to tobacco growers. You are a southern representative to Congress whose state grows a lot of tobacco, so you intend to vote for the bill. (You personally stopped smoking five years ago and you know two people who have died from lung cancer.) A high school senior writes to you and asks how you can spend public

money on something that is (according to the cigarette pack-
age) "injurious to your health." Write that student an answer
that makes it sound reasonable and good for the U.S. to support
tobacco growers.

6   You are a manufacturer of polyurethane. A TV network
has made a short film for its news program showing some tests
in which fire swept through structures coated with this substance. You have demanded time on the network to respond
to the TV newsman's remarks that your product is dangerous
and that a ban is being considered. Write the speech you would
use. Do not "lie," but try to make your product sound safe.

Classroom Techniques to Evaluate Advertising in Magazines

Daniel J. Tutolo
Bowling Green State University

It is no small task to ferret out dishonest and inhumane uses of language by advertisers. Rarely is an advertisement by a large company blatantly dishonest for all ads appearing in national media have been carefully scrutinized by appropriate members in the advertisinig agency that generated the ad and staff members of the company that will run the ad under its name. These highly trained individuals are schooled in the latest legislation covering permissible statements etc. which may appear legally in advertisinig matter.

Yet those of us as consumers who are exposed to these ads—some would say bombarded by these ads—frequently have occasion to question at least part of the message, feeling a degree of annoyance at the seeming gall of the advertiser because of some of the claims made. Although appropriate government agencies—the Federal Trade Commission and the Federal Communication Commission—would decree that no law has been violated, our sensibilities as buyers with unlimited wants and scarce means to satisfy these wants are often offended.

We must find appropriate classroom procedures to help children deal with this very powerful and persuasive institution we call advertising. To do this we must develop a good understanding of how the goliath functions, and how it manages to persuade us to commit, and sometimes overcommit, our scarce reseources.

The Persuasion Process

Our understanding of the function of advertising is enhanced if we recognize some basic contributions made by communication theorists and motivational research psychologists. Traditionally in persuasion research this formula was accepted: $M \times A = E$ where M is the message, A is the appeal and E is the effectiveness of the appeal. With the contributions of the motivation

60

researcher a new element was added to the formula. Now the formula reads $(M \times A) P = E$. The addition of the P for predisposition revolutionized the persuasion formula, for it suggested the persuadee contributes in large part to the success of any communication. Successful appeals must consider the needs and assumptions, in short, the psychological characteristics of the receiver of the persuasive message.

An advertiser or any other persuader must first isolate the needs and assumptions of the intended audience and prepare an appeal to meet those needs. Communication will take place if the receiver agrees with the message and perceives the message as compatible with personal needs.[1]

As psychologists focused on predisposition or the contribution of the receiver in the communication process, they discovered that receiver response or cognitive functioning took place at four levels, each with several dimensions.

The level of prime importance in the approach to be outlined here is the immediate cognitive response that a receiver has while exposed to an advertisement. It encompasses the receiver's feelings, emotions, personal experiences and attitudes. It has to do with how people perceive and affectively interpret a message.

The immediate cognitive response level is the focus of this teaching approach. Students can be asked to bring to class youth magazines they read regularly.[2] Perhaps some of the class will need to bring in several issues for those who cannot readily supply their own. After specific instructions, the students leaf through the magazine until they find an ad they wish to study. After they find an ad for which they have a certain fascination, they are encouraged to study the ad and to prepare to rate it.

The attitude rating scale which they will employ was developed after extensive research into attitude formation. Ads are rated on three factors: attractiveness, meaningfulness, and vitality. Attractiveness suggests whether the ad is liked. Meaningfulness measures whether the ad delivers a message that is understood and considered important and believable. Vitality reflects the liveliness of the ad. (Attractiveness and meaningfulness are well established by the research while vitality must be verified by additional research.[3])

This attitude scale for print ads has been constructed to reflect readers' attitudes toward the message. The student responds on a five-point scale. High scores represent strong positive attitudes toward the message. An extremely high score of forty-five or better would suggest a strong predisposition toward the product. The advertisement strongly encourages a want or need on the part of the reader. Since predisposition is considered by researchers as a precursor to behavior, it is entirely likely that the reader will buy the product in the near future. The respondent agrees with the ad if it is compatible with perceived needs.

	5	4	3	2	1	
Beautiful	—	—	—	—	—	Ugly
Attractive	—	—	—	—	—	Unattractive
Appealing	—	—	—	—	—	Unappealing
Interesting	—	—	—	—	—	Uninteresting
Meaningful	—	—	—	—	—	Meaningless
Convincing	—	—	—	—	—	Unconvincing
Honest	—	—	—	—	—	Dishonest
Fresh	—	—	—	—	—	Stale
Lively	—	—	—	—	—	Lifeless
New, different	—	—	—	—	—	Common, ordinary

We have now established that psychologists involved in motivational research have shown us that attitudes toward products can be determined by the use of attitude scales. We now know that a person's predisposition toward a product is a good prediction of whether the person will buy the product. What can we do with this knowledge in classroom settings to help children to be better buyers? We need to alert our students to the consumer movement which is currently growing in momentum to strengthen the relative position of buyers.

What is Consumerism?
Consumerism is a social movement seeking to augment the rights and power of buyers in relation to sellers. To understand this definition and its deep social meaning, we need to examine the traditional rights of sellers and buyers and to scrutinize the efforts being made by consumer advocates to modify the relative influence of the sellers.

Certain sellers' rights have been well established by law and custom in the United States[4]:

1 To introduce any product into the marketplace so long as it is not hazardous to personal health or safety. If it is judged hazardous, it may be introduced with certain safeguards.

2 To set the price on the product so long as there is no discrimination among similar classes of buyers.

3 To promote the product so long as it does not limit competition.

4 To formulate any message about the product that is not misleading or dishonest.

5 To introduce buying incentive schemes.

The courts have interpreted these rights over the years in such a way that businessmen have had a great deal of flexibility and freedom. To limit these rights materially would greatly change our marketing arrangements in this country.

Buyers, too, have rights protected by law:

1 To refuse to buy a product offered to them.

2 To expect the product to be safe.

3 To expect the product to be essentially as represented by the seller.

A review of the rights of both buyers and sellers suggests the balance of power lies with the seller. The seller has the services of motivational research personnel to help in determining buyer wants and plan messages to appeal strongly to these wants. Consumers are not collectively organized and represented by equally qualified researchers who can suggest ways to resist appeals which reach us through the media.

Only lately have consumer advocates begun to speak out for additional rights. These demands include:

1 To have adequate information about the product.

2 To obtain additional protections against questionable products and marketing practices.

3 To influence products and marketing practices in directions that will increase the "quality of life."

Until such time as favorable legislation is forthcoming to realize these demands, consumers are left largely to their own resources to carefully select the products purchased. Even so, consumer influence can be quite formidable when given some direction or guidance.

The model in Figure 1 can be used to make judgments about products. Salutary products are those which have low appeal but which are also highly beneficial to the consumer. Some examples of products often resisted by students are foods, such as liver, and warm durable clothing which may not be high

Daniel J. Tutolo

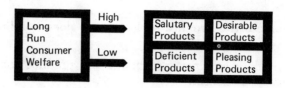

Figure 1. Immediate Satisfaction

fashion. Deficient products have neither immediate appeal nor salutary qualities. Poorly constructed toys and some sports equipment made of nondurable materials fall into this category. Desirable products are those which combine high immediate satisfaction and high long-run benefit. Tasty nutritious breakfast foods can be considered in this category. Pleasing products are those which give high immediate satisfaction but which may hurt the consumer interest in the long run. Alcohol and nonprescription drugs are examples of this category.

If students can be helped to identify deficient products and pleasing products for which they respond favorably on the attitude scale shown above, classroom instruction in counterattitudinal advocacy can encourage a move to salutary products and desirable products. A look at consumer behavior in the past suggests that immediate gratification through pleasing proucts has been more highly valued than delayed gratification through salutary products. There is some evidence that this may be changing. Certainly appropriate classroom instruction can hasten this process.

Counterattitudinal Advocacy
In counterattitudinal advocacy the student encodes (either speaking or writing) a message at odds with prior beliefs.[5] An argument against a product is created despite having previously expressed on an attitude scale strong positive feelings toward the product. This serves as a kind of self-persuasion. The individual will modify personal attitudes toward the product to conform with the argument presented against the product. Earlier it was suggested that attitudes precede behavior. This theory suggests that attitudes are modified as a result of behavior.

Perhaps this can be best explained by use of an example. The students selected several ads from youth magazines and employed the reaction profile. One high-scoring ad was selected for class discussion. After thorough review of the message, general agreement was forthcoming that the product being advertised was one appropriately categorized as a "pleasing product."

It provides high immediate satisfaction but may hurt consumer interest in the long run. One student who rated the ad very highly volunteers to role play a situation where he or she must find arguments against the product.[6] Let us say the product is a beauty aid and widely used by girls in the school. Several students testified that under certain circumstances, the user loses sight of the amount of cosmetic applied and produces a look that is anything but glamorous.

The role player is assigned the task of informing a friend that she is using too much of the product. Her responsibility is to prepare arguments against overuse of the product. The theory suggests that by creating an argument against overuse of the product, the role player's own attitude toward the product will change. Indeed, a sort of self-persuasion against the product or at least excessive use of the product will take place. Counterattitudinal advocacy can change attitudes toward a product which could result in not using the product or at least using the product more moderately.

Counterattitudinal advocacy is strong medicine. There are certain moral considerations in its use with students in a classroom situation. If, after careful consideration, the teacher feels that it should not be used, then so be it. But, when we consider the tremendous efforts being made by advertisers to encourage us to buy products, perhaps strong measures are needed. There are many deficient products and pleasing products which do not contribute to the long-range good of society.

As a member of the Committee on Public Doublespeak, I have assumed the responsibility, along with my fellow committee members, to identify ways we teach children about advertising. Heretofore our efforts have been sporadic and based on antiquated research concerning persuasion. In this new approach the student selects an ad that is of personal interest, rates the ad on an attitude scale, determines whether the product contributes to the long-range good of society, and presents arguments against products which do not. This seems a good way to help children to evaluate carefully their wants for commercial products. Now there is something to do about products that do not seem to contribute to society. Counterattitudinal advocacy deserves a try. Only time will tell whether it will have staying power.

Notes

1 Hans H. Foch, "Psychological Research and Effective Persuasion," *The Journal of Communication*, 8, No. 4 (Winter 1958), 196.

2 For a bibliography of youth periodicals see: Lavina Dobler and Muriel Fuller, *Dobler World Dictionary of Youth Periodicals* (New York: Citation Press, 1970), pp. 25–30.

3 William D. Wells, "EQ, Son of EQ, and the Reaction Profile," *Journal of Marketing*, 28 (October 1964), 51.

4 Philip Kotler, "What Consumerism Means for Marketers," *Harvard Business Review*, (May–June 1972), 49.

5 Gerald R. Miller and Michael Burgoon, *New Techniques of Persuasion* (New York: Harper & Row, Publishers, 1973), pp. 59–75.

6 Fannie Shaftel and George Shaftel, *Role Playing for Social Values* (Englewood Cliffs, N.J.: Prentice Hall, Inc., 1967).

Politics and Practical Semantic Analysis

Sanford Radner
Montclair State College

Politics may be briefly defined as conflict between those who have power and those who do not. We may speak of political conflict not only between nations, but between races, sexes, or socioeconomic classes. The assumptions and perspectives of powerful and powerless in these conflicts are consistent. Those in power try to communicate (1) we really don't have power, or, we do, but we don't profit from it or enjoy it; (2) our power is for the benefit of the powerless (the "White Man's Burden"); (3) any shift in power would be calamitous for the entire community.

On the other hand, the powerless, organized as a radical action group, declare that such a shift in power is both desirable and possible; they seek to frighten those in power, raise the morale of their own constituents, and appeal to the self-interest of neutral groups.

At least in recent human history, *language*, almost as much as brute force, has been the medium of this conflict, as each side seeks to persuade both its own members and those of the opposing group. In attempting to do so, *deception* of others (and self-deception), at least as much as truth, characterizes language use on both sides.

Semantics, the scientific study of meaning, offers five especially cogent perspectives from which to analyze the deceptiveness of political language. In our time of Doublespeak and Watergate, English teachers ought to make their students aware of these perspectives, and skillful in the practical applications which follow from them.

1   *The reciprocal relationship between language and reality.* Language not only reflects reality, as a map does its territory; it

also influences reality and, in the hands of unscrupulous politicians, language may become a precise substitute for reality:
John Kenneth Galbraith's wordfact. Instead of confronting
economic problems honestly, a leader may assert, "We are not
in a recession." This assertion makes it unnecessary to do anything about the harsh reality. Applications:

a   Analyze the following as wordfact: "Wear your WIN but-
    ton to beat inflation."
b   Take the role of a leader who has to defend or cover up
    some calamity (epidemic, unjust war). Compose a speech
    to your constituents reassuring them through wordfact.
c   Verbal maps of the future: Identify a political campaign
    promise or slogan from the mass media. What is the likli-
    hood of future reality conforming to this map?
d   Verbal maps of the past: Discuss an historical event, the
    meaning or significance of which has subsequently changed
    (e.g., causes of World War I). Explain the reason(s) for
    this map-territory readjustment.
e   Euphemism: Explain the difference between these pairs of
    different verbal maps for the same territory: 1. war—police
    action; 2. relief—unemployment insurance; 3. strolling—
    marauding.

2   *Language and the individual: self-reflexiveness.* The self-
reflexiveness of language means that while statements we make
may refer to things outside of us (the subject of our discourse),
our words simultaneously project our own hopes and fears. It is
this subjective dimension of language, the connotation of words,
which is the heavy carrier of political appeal: "Power to the
People." Students need to become more aware of how, in certain
uses, connotation swamps denotation. Applications:

a   Conjugations: Make up conjugations similar to the follow-
    ing, explaining the different perspective of each of the three
    persons in the conjugation: I am slim. You are skinny. He
    is a toothpick.
b   Explain the appeal of each of the following: 1. "Black
    Power!" 2. "The hand that rocked the cradle rules the
    world!" 3. "The Marine Corps wants real men."
c   Taboo: Find examples in your newspaper of statements em-
    bodying each of the following taboos; explain the power of
    the taboo. 1. death. 2. body odor. 3. failure.
d   Stereotypes: Explain, from the standpoint of personal fear,
    verbal stereotypes of each of the following groups: 1. Orien-
    tals. 2. Blacks. 3. Russians. 4. Italians. 5. Jews.

e   Analyze examples around you of hairstyling, including beards and mustaches. What is the individual trying to communicate about him/herself through this hair fashion?

3 *Language and the culture: contexts.* We are prisoners of our culture insofar as we remain unaware of the basic assumptions of our group, and how these assumptions, reflected in the structure of our native language, influence our behavior. Thus, members of a powerless group (blacks, women) growing up in a culture dominated by others, may see their disadvantaged position as "natural" rather than humanly created and therefore changeable. For example, our connotations of the words "right" and "left" make it difficult for a left-handed person not to see him/herself as at least mildly freakish. Applications:

a   Explain the cultural differences implied in these verbal expressions of the same visceral condition: I am hungry (English); I have hunger (French); The spirit of hunger is within me (Pueblo Indian).
b   Analyze the use of *natural* in the following: 1. It's natural for wives to do the housework. 2. Blacks have natural rhythm. 3. Indians are naturally lazy.
c   Discuss the following headline from a San Francisco paper: JAPANESE IN MOSCOW COMPLAIN. MISTAKEN FOR CHINESE, ABUSED.
d   Discuss the political implication of a specific color (red, yellow, white, black) for different cultures or national groups.
e   Identify and discuss instances where the same hand signal or facial gesture (e.g., lowering of the eyes) has different meanings in two different cultures.

4 *The sign-symbol distinction.* Signs *point* to something; symbols *stand for* something. What symbols stand for are often intensely important feelings and values, just those which are the targets of political manipulation. A basic problem is that the same linguistic expression often *simultaneously* functions as both sign and symbol. "Wall Street" as a sign is innocuous enough, pointing to a specific locale in downtown New York City; as a symbol of economic, therefore of political power, it is the carrier of strong emotional implications, both positive and negative, depending on the power-perspective of the user and the audience. Students need to be made more aware of this simultaneous functioning. Applications:

a   Explain how the entity, *the rich*, is being used as a symbol by one speaker, a sign by the other in the following exchange:

FitzGerald: The rich are not as we.
Hemingway: No, they have more money.

b Explain how the following may function as both sign and symbol: 1. The Kremlin. 2. Harlem. 3. Henry Aaron.
c Explain which is more meaningful, a *signifying* or a *symbolic* interpretation of the following statement: Watergate was undoubtedly a national disaster. (Focus on the word *Watergate*.)
d Discuss the differences between sign and symbol in the ways we use the following: 1. pig. 2. snake. 3. fox.
e Identify a partisan political statement from the mass media. Rewrite it with exactly the opposite connotation (symbolic meaning) while keeping the denotation (sign meaning) the same.

5 *The process of abstracting.* Language gives us an advantage in talking about increasingly complex phenomena by allowing us to "leave out" characteristics as our field of discourse enlarges. In abstracting, we arbitrarily choose to include certain items, leaving out others; we thus create "classes" which are more manageable than the raw reality out of which they are mined. Students need to be aware of the process of abstracting and classifying because what is "left out" may be of crucial emotional and political importance. In particular, labels such as *liberal, conservative, radical* need to be examined to prevent the danger of oversimplification. In the following example it is important to see that statement two, being less abstract than statement one, is really much more informative:

1 X is a liberal politician.
2 X voted for public health bill #462.

Applications:
a Arrange the following in order of increasing abstraction. As one ascends this "abstraction ladder," what qualities are left out from one step to the next? 1. school supplies. 2. pens. 3. material wealth.
b Explain the dangers of classification from the following statements: 1. Republican presidents are dishonest. 2. Southerners are more prejudiced than Northerners. 3. No basketball players under six feet in height can make it in the NBA.
c *Killing* and *bombing* are less abstract than *protective reaction* and *air support.* Why do politicians and generals prefer using the latter two expressions?
d Write a short essay analyzing a *classification conflict;* for example, under what conditions is a *riot* a *rebellion?* a *heroic* act an *immoral* act?

e   Students are to write a sentence using a high level abstraction like democracy; then, a paragraph defining this concept. Discuss differences in the paragraphs.

Two matters should be kept in mind in applying all of the five perspectives discussed in this article. Students should be encouraged, from the very beginning of their study, to keep a log of distorted and dishonest use of language gleaned from the mass media as raw material on which to operate. In the analysis itself, the watchwords for such concepts as *stereotype, euphemism,* and *abstraction* should be awareness and selective use rather than avoidance.

Doublespeak and Spoken Communication

Pat M. Taylor
University of Alabama in Birmingham

With the ever-burgeoning amount of information an individual is exposed to, the ability to spot doublespeak upon first encounter becomes more and more important. An examination of isolated rhetorical events, although of obvious benefit in that they clearly expose one to specific examples, fails to show the dynamic moving quality of rhetoric. A solution to this problem was submitted at the recent workshop on Doublespeak and General Semantics held in New Orleans: have students write a speech with a conscious effort to include doublespeak and have others in the class discover the techniques that were used.

Serious problems exist within the submitted plan, but emerging from it is a method that I have found most workable. The purpose of this paper, therefore, is twofold: to show why I disagree with the method suggested in New Orleans, and to discuss its workable offshoot.

To suggest that a student simply sit down and write a speech shows complete ignorance of the basic tenets of speech-making. First, such a suggestion implies that the construction of a speech is the same as the construction of an essay. That is simply not the case. If the reader does not comprehend the significance of an essay, he or she is able to read it a second and even third time. If the consumer of a speech does not understand its content, all opportunity to learn from the message has been lost. Thus, the organization is obviously different.

As organization differs, so do language and grammar. In a speech, incomplete sentences are permissable, where they would not be tolerated in a more formal written exercise. Also, in a speech a "simple" vocal inflection can be used to convey meaning that would take paragraphs to explain on the printed page.

More fundamental, however, is the questionable practice of having a student deliberately practice and attempt to deceive an audience. An examination of the Aristotelian persuasive mode of *ethos* shows the harm in such an activity. If instructors were to encourage students to actively practice communicating a message using doublespeak, they could do great damage to their students. Speakers must accept responsibility for their words. When students, in advocating a policy, approach it knowing they are misleading an audience, they cannot put forth their greatest thought and effort. Thus they fail to fulfill their obligations as communicators. Later, when students are communicating outside of the classroom situation, there is liable to be a carry-over of the negative effects created by the initial intentional use of doublespeak. The classroom practice in doublespeak may make future doublespeak easier.

The suggestion that one write a speech also implies that a speech will have universal application. Again, this is simply not the case. A speaker must consider the audience while preparing a message. What is appropriate for one group in one situation may not be for another—even if it is the same group of people meeting at a different time and place. Thus, having a message to communicate is not sufficient, unless one has a specific audience in mind. The speaker will be able to interact with the specific audience via feedback to further gain acceptance of the advocated policy. Thus, the audience involvement of the speaker is entirely different from that of a writer.

Finally, I believe such an exercise misses the whole point of discovering doublespeak in spoken communication. In an exercise such as this, the listeners will find doublespeak because they know—absolutely—that doublespeak is being used; this was the assignment. Armed with this knowledge, they are in a much better position to discover the techniques used. This, in turn, precludes any real discovery or learning on the part of the students.

The above discussion leads us to the conclusion that a speech is not an essay on its hind legs. To treat one as such disregards fundamental differences between the two.

On the other hand, the disavowing of any significant learning taking place from specially prepared student speeches does not preclude benefit accrued from the analysis of other spoken materials. The material is part of a dynamic continuum—not an isolated item. This places discovery in a real world situation—outside the classroom—and in turn makes such analysis applicable to realities the student will face in the future.

The sources available for such analysis are limitless. I have found it best to start with some sources where the student might expect to find doublespeak (expect, not be assured) and move on to other sources.

An excellent source included in the former are governmental short wave radio stations. Every night one can hear (sometimes even drowning out local AM stations!) news and views from Radio Moscow, Radio Havana, etc. It is a relatively simple matter to tape-record some of these programs one evening and bring them to class for analysis the next day. In this way the student is faced with a contemporary situation. Soft-sell stations should not be excluded. Interesting examples can be found interspersed with the charming chiming music box of Radio Switzerland and Radio Portugal's offer of free correspondence lessons in Portuguese.

While listening to foreign stations' English language broadcasts is beneficial, one should not forget the programs beamed by our own Radio Free Europe and Radio Liberty. Basic information on these stations can be obtained by writing Radio, 2 Park Avenue, New York, N.Y., 10016. Likewise, advertisements presented on those American stations having their transmitting antennae in Mexico can prove to be enlightening.

Included in the same category are some other favorites of mine. I have a personal recording of a speech presented by the late George Lincoln Rockwell. This speech has made students aware of the power of the spoken word—particularly when spoken by a person with apparent conviction.

Also, tapes of Axis Sally and Tokyo Rose are readily available from the Office of War Archives in Washington, D.C. Although the recording quality leaves a great deal to be desired, one can be exposed to a certain type of doublespeak by these materials.

Finally, after literally years of search, I obtained a copy of a recording of a radio message by Father Charles E. Coughlin of the Church of the Little Flower, Royal Oak, Michigan. This, too, is available from the Office of War Archives for a nominal charge. The recording is owned by the Rare Books Library of Columbia University. It is necessary to obtain written permission from them before the Washington office will release the materials. When I first contacted Washington they were hesitant to let me have the speech and told me they "washed their hands of the whole deal" once the tapes were in my possession.

Once such "expected" sources have been investigated and analyzed, it is time to move to other sources. Political speeches, lectures, NOW meetings, city council meetings, etc., offer excellent sources. It is impossible to take recording equipment to some of these, but this does not make the challenge insurmountable. Rather, since speeches encountered after the course is over will probably demand immediate evaluation, this is simply a further step in the desired direction—developing students' ability to analyze doublespeak as they encountered it.

By following such a plan, the study of public doublespeak directly links the student with the world outside the classroom. Also, it serves to integrate the various disciplines to which the student has been exposed. These elements, under the guise of "how to use," require further exploration.

It seems fashionable, particularly among certain advocates of interpersonal communication, to allocate considerable time to the playing of "communication games." This same practice, seemingly, has been adopted by many in their instruction concerning doublespeak. While games are always fun, it seems to me that such an approach is shallow. This shallowness, in turn, almost precludes any carry-over from the "fun" of the classroom to the seriousness with which doublespeak is really used. If the student is to become an adroit participant in the community, the importance of the subject needs heavier emphasis.

With any of the speeches, I have found it beneficial to begin with an examination of the *context* in which the message was presented. This allows the student to view a situation in the light of it's own time frame, and not from today's viewpoint. Each year I discover this factor is more vital. What I view as yesterday's headlines are seen by my students as ancient history. This approach also allows us to see the refinements taking place in the use of doublespeak.

Specifically, I pay attention to several items (individually and in combination), such as delivery, logical fallacies, loaded language, unsupported generalizations, half-truths, total deception, etc. Especially in the early part of instruction I feel it is best to analyze the items separately; to do otherwise seems to confront the beginning student with too many variables. The items I stress for the particular exercise change from class to class. I do this to adjust the material to the class and to keep it fresh for myself. As one progresses with this program, it is easy for the students themselves to see the interconnections between the various items. This is important in reaching the final goal—getting the student to react to the totality of the spoken communication.

As the students' ability to analyze increases, they are also attaining the second goal I established—integrating the various subjects. Outside the classroom situation experiences are not as neatly compartmentalized as they appear within the confines of a school environment. One can see the interaction of history with both oral and written communication, experience the psychological and sociological development of arguments, and discover why people act and react in the ways they do. Perhaps more importantly, it arms students with the knowledge necessary to combat the influence of doublespeak on themselves.

When students conduct the various analyses, they use a number of different methods—oral reports, written reports, group reports. Enterprising students use these in combination. Some have even compared contemporary events with those of the past. For example, after a discussion of myths as exploited (and sometimes created) by some users of doublespeak, one group compared the myth presented by the Revolutionary Student Brigade with that found in the pages of *Reader's Digest*. Granted the message and myths are completely different, but some similar techniques were found.

In conclusion, the analysis of doublespeak in spoken communication is certainly desirable, but it should be as closely related to the world in which the students will find themselves as possible. To do otherwise—especially to have students themselves practice the fine art of doublespeak—can have no advantages.

Books, Bookmakers, and Blurbs

John H. Hershey
Academic Interest Center, Lansing, Michigan

Some practices of the publishing industry are as questionable as those of another sort of bookmaker. Since books are an essential concern of language arts, teachers ought to expose their students to some of the marketing methods used by the industry.

Peter Benchley's best-selling novel, *Jaws*, offers a fine opportunity. The April 21, 1974, *New York Times Magazine* gives a detailed account of the selling of the book. Students who have teachers who insist on perfect manuscripts when themes are submitted would find it educational to read about the extensive editorial assistance given in the course of writing the book. Like so many sensational best-sellers, the book was originally sold as an idea, with all ingredients carefully calculated.

Certainly Benchley's name was no drawback. Nearly every review points out that his father, Nathaniel, and his grandfather, Robert, make him a third generation popular writer. *Jaws* was an assured success from the start. "Eight weeks before its official release," says *Publishers Weekly* (Feb. 11, 1974) "[it] had already earned over a million dollars in subsidiary sales." It was picked up by three book clubs, sold to seven foreign language publishers, and peddled to the movies for $100,000. Obviously the publishing house (Doubleday) had a big stake—and a big opportunity. In order not to miss a marketing trick, they turned to the blurbs.

On the back cover of the paperback edition are five quotes, the last of which reads:

> "Powerful climax . . . His story grabs you at once
> . . . Read *Jaws*—by all means read it."
>
> The *New York Times*

77

Any bookstore customer who has come to place some reliance on the book reviews in the *Times* might be surprised to discover that the blurb comes from the following review (quoted portions in italics):

> A Fish Story . . . or Two
> *Jaws*, by Peter Benchley. 311 pages. Doubleday $6.95.
>
> Most of the way through *Jaws*, it looks as though Peter Benchley is going to pull off the rare trick of writing a slickly plotted thriller with substance. After all, *his story grabs you at once:* On a dark spring night just off the shore of the town of Amity, Long Island, a "great fish moves silently through the night water, propelled by short sweeps of its crescent tail." On the beach, a young woman decides to take an après-love-making swim. The fish, a 20-foot great white shark, rises out of the depths and in a matter of seconds tears the woman to pieces. "Close the beaches," orders the conscientious police chief of Amity after finding what is left of the woman entangled in a clump of weed and kelp. "No, keep the beaches open," respond the town's real-estate interests, fearing for the local economy. So the police chief gives in. The shark attacks again. The plot thickens.
>
> **Other Beasts of Prey**
> And after all, this strong plot is not all that *Jaws* has going for it. A rich thematic substructure also develops. Other beasts of prey threaten the community of Amity. Hooper, the shark expert called in from Woods Hole, is hungry for the police chief's wife: As he makes love to her, his eyes bulge, his teeth grind, and "the ferocity and intensity of his assault [seem] to her a pursuit in which she [is] only a vehicle." The richest local real-estate dealer is struggling to escape the teeth of loan sharks from the mob. The tourists and newsmen who fall upon Amity are garbage-eating scavengers. It seems, in short, that Mr. Benchley is working toward some statement about the way we live—some vision of a society of automated animals who, like the gutted blue sharks that appear in the book's most shocking scene, are just as willing to devour themselves as any other food. And the suspense of this thematic development is almost as strong as the book's plot.
>
> Moreover, Mr. Benchley seems to know what he's doing. Having had the good sense to be born into the Benchley family of writers (his father is Nathaniel,

his grandfather, Robert) and thus, presumably, to have inherited its talent, he then sharpened his story-telling skills by working as a newspaper reporter, a magazine editor, a speechwriter (for President Johnson) and a TV commentator. So he knows the tricks of the storytelling trade; or so it would seem from the skill with which he plants his key information and the cleverly offbeat way he handles the obligatory scenes. (For instance, the consummation of the love affair between Hooper, the shark specialist, and the police chief's wife is dramatized entirely through the preseduction fantasies the two describe to each other over lunch. And significantly, this device is echoed in the climatic shark-hunting scene at the end.) Also Mr. Benchley seems to know all there is to know about sharks.

Caught in the Undertow

But unfortunately, he fails to deliver half of what he promises. *Jaws* builds to a *powerful climax* all right, but there's also an increasingly strong undertow that drags it down. This undertow is Mr. Benchley's inclination to get carried away by dramatic effects. It first shows up in the occasionally arbitrary—and therefore phony—way the narrative switches from one point of view to another. Suddenly, out of nowhere, little scenes appear that have no other purpose but to intimate some new development. And every time the narrative takes up the fish's point of view, we know the monster is about to strike again, and we feel prompted to squeal in mock terror the way we used to do when Lon Chaney Jr. grew hairs.

The undertow grows stronger as the climax approaches, and Mr. Benchley seems to lose interest in the themes he's been developing and to grow increasingly enchanted with his fish story. And finally, as the climax unfolds, our attention cannot resist being divided between the excitement and the undertow. As we discover the demonic intelligence of the great white shark; as we get to know the character of Quint, a monomaniacal fishing-boat captain who becomes obsessed with destroying the monster; as the final showdown takes place, as shark attacks boat, and captain's foot gets caught in harpoon line, and boat and captain go down, leaving the story's hero swimming alone in a wide, wide sea . . . we cannot help but think of another fish story, in comparison to which *Jaws* comes off a distinctly second best.

I don't particularly blame Mr. Benchley for getting
seduced by that other fish story. After all, it's a
pretty good one, and if it insisted on retelling itself
. . . why, what the hell, good stories have been retold
before. But I am sorry Mr. Benchley didn't bother to
use that story to resolve the themes he seemed to be
developing. After all, they were interesting too—
are people nothing but garbage-eating machines? Is
the shark's presence some sort of ecological retribu-
tion? And I would have liked to know what they
were leading to.

Read Jaws—by all means read it—and see if you
don't agree.

                                    Christopher Lehman-Haupt

The blurb excerpts don't accurately convey the general opinion
of the review; they are carefully culled from their context in
an obvious attempt to distort.

Is it an unusual or exceptional distortion? No; typical. The
Bantam paperback edition of *Jaws* has five blurbs on the back
cover and nine more on the first four pages inside the front
cover. The conventions of quotation are abused in the crudest
ways: quotes are rearranged, the use of ellipsis and other punctuation violates standards, and deletions are made without any
warning. Any writer who has struggled to cut a lengthy quotation without doing violence to the essential meaning knows
immediately that the publisher has played them false.

For example, one blurb reads:

NONSTOP ACTION
. . . A major novel, one that has created virtually unprecedented . . . excitement . . . A
fascinating story about what happens when a great
white shark terrorizes a Long Island town.

                                              Publishers Weekly

Compare this blurb with its source in the Nov. 12, 1973 *Publishers Weekly* (italics indicate quoted portions):

Grandson of Robert and son of Nathaniel, Peter
Benchley has written *a major novel, one that has
created virtually unprecedented* pre-publication *excitement. Jaws* is *a fascinating story about what
happens when a great white shark terrorizes a* small
Long Island town. The *action is nonstop.* . . .

One can complain about the shuffled word order and the upper
case "NONSTOP ACTION," but that is a trivial distortion com-

pared with the omission of "pre-publication." The review means that the "unprecedented excitement" occurred *before* anyone had read the book, that is, it was generated by the publisher's promotional efforts.

But at least the omission was indicated by ellipses. Another backcover blurb shows a worse abuse:

> Taut and exciting . . . Peter Benchley has scored a palpable hit with this first novel . . . a fine thriller.
>
> *Christian Science Monitor*

This cut-and-snip collection of quotes comes from a review in the Feb. 6, 1974, *Monitor*. Compare the following sentence from that review:

> Grandson of Robert Benchley, the humorist, and son of Nathaniel, the good all-purpose writer, *Peter Benchley has* already *scored a palpable hit with this first novel.*

The silent deletion of "already" skews the meaning of the review which is discussing the *financial* success of the novel (the sales to book clubs and the movies), rather than the *literary* success implied by the blurb.

I see these blurbs as valuable educational materials. Their study is certainly helpful in demonstrating the duplicity of a major industry; they also furnish a meaningful way to give instruction to accurate citation, and in basic bibliography and research. The following are some activities for various levels of instruction, from junior high to college:

1 (College and high school) Have students select books with blurbs and then locate the reviews from which the blurbs are taken. Does the excerpt accurately reflect the review? Distort it? Are the conventions of quotation followed? (This is difficult to do unless a large library is available; even then the lack of dates in blurbs, and unindexed periodicals and newspapers may frustrate students. In that case, warn students to choose blurbs from periodicals available to them in back editions.)

2 (All levels) Offer students copies of blurbs and the reviews they are taken from; have them locate the blurb in the review and report on the degree of honesty and accuracy.

3 (Secondary levels) As an exercise, give the students reviews and have them excerpt blurbs. Can a negative review be transformed into a rave blurb?

4   (Secondary levels. A number of variations are possible.)
Have students write blurbs instead of book reports. Or write
reviews and then excerpt (or have other students excerpt)
blurbs as advertisements for their book.

Related and Extended Activities:

1   Have students investigate the "history" of a best-seller.
Much of the information on advances, size of printings, TV and
personal appearances, and so forth is in trade magazines, and
author interviews appear in various periodicals, but the students
might also write to authors, publishers, editors, and agents.

2   Examine book cover illustrations in terms of their appeal.
Do they appeal to sex? The macabre? Do they emphasize these
matters to the same degree that they are emphasized in the
text?

3   Interview book store employees and book distributors. Who
determines which books are given prominent display space?
Who orders new releases, and on what basis are they chosen?

4   Investigate analogous industries such as the record industry.
What sort of appeal is made by album covers? How does the
phonograph industry market its product?

Approaches to the Study of Public Lying

Howard Livingston
Pace University

In 1971 the National Council of Teachers of English passed two resolutions which, among other things, gave rise to the Committee on Public Doublespeak. The resolutions indicated NCTE's recognition that (1) our present semantic environment is thoroughly polluted, (2) Orwell's prediction in his novel, *1984*, that language could be used to convince people that "war is peace" and "ignorance is strength" has been realized more than ten years ahead of schedule, and (3) that language study in the English classroom should concern itself with the language environment outside the English classroom. Despite this fact, teachers are still asking "Specifically, what can I do in my English class?" Let me offer a few very specific suggestions.

We might begin with the familiar. All of us are familiar with the way poetry works, the devices and mechanisms that the poet employs. Moreover, I'm sure we'd all agree that poetry utilizes the resources of language to a greater degree than any other mode of expression. Then why not use the very same analytic tools that enable us to determine tone—that is, attitude—*and* nuances in meaning for a semantic analysis of expository material, a political speech or a radio commercial, for example. I am suggesting that you bring the language behavior of the world outside the English classroom into the English classroom, and use a competence you already possess. Let me illustrate: We are able to take a poem and demonstrate how metaphor, images, and connotation *contribute* to tone and meaning. Do the same thing with the political speech. Is the literal sense of the speech consistent with the attitude expressed? Examine the speech for connotative effects. What metaphors are employed? What images are used? Is there an abundance of projectile adjectives? Does the selection of detail uncover a particular focus? Is ambiguity intentional or unconscious?

For advertisements and commercials: how much of the message is purely emotive, i.e., connotative? How much is denotative? It might be interesting to delete all the connotative elements from the advertisements and see what, if anything, is left. Do the same with newspaper editorials.

It might also be productive to have the class bring in magazine and newspaper advertisements for another type of analysis. In addition to examining the advertisements for content, examine them with reference to the assumptions the advertisements make about you, the reader. This should prove most revealing.

Some of you might want to use what you know about rhetoric to detect public doublespeak; some of you might draw on your knowledge of syntactic structure to uncover public lying. Others may find that semantics as a branch of linguistic study seems to be eminently suitable as a way of analyzing public utterances.

Let's illustrate with this Associated Press headline (Oct. 13, 1974) concerning Rockefeller's financing of an anti-Arthur Goldberg book:

> Ex-Justice in Book Hassle Gets Rockefeller Apology.

Changing the syntax and defusing the connotative elements, one might come up with the following:

> Rockefeller apologizes to former Supreme Court Justice in Book Controversy.

Quite a difference, and that difference could provide several periods of class discussion.

In semantics, the focus is on the abstractive nature of language; the confusing levels of abstraction; the discrimination among facts, inferences and judgments; multiple meaning confusion; such considerations as these, when applied to public language, will be most instructive and revealing. For some, it might mean taking a course such as "Language and Meaning," or "Language and Behavior." Good, why not?

Examine the mass media from a larger and different perspective. With newspapers, for example: Who owns them? What else do the owners own? Approximately 80% of the stories reported do not appear in the paper. Who are the censors? What are the criteria for selection? Are certain stories buried? What kinds of news stories are highlighted? Why?

One might want to focus on the accuracy of newspaper headlines vis-à-vis the story itself. Distribute the news stories without the headlines; have the students write their own headlines and compare for accuracy. Discuss the implications. Also, one might go through a news story and make a list of all the adjectives, verbs, and adverbs that contain a judgment. Is there slanting? There are limitless language activities that will foster critical thinking. One can move into other media by comparing the treatment of a story in the newspaper with the treatment on television news. I'm sure some students who may be turned off by what has been going on in their English classes might turn on again if asked to watch a basketball or football game on television and compare their observations with the newspaper account of the same game.

Almost everyone watches talk shows on television. Why not have your students list all of the opinions voiced by the guests on such programs and then discuss each guest's competence or expertise in that field. It might also be productive to see how and for what purpose the camera is used—close-ups, camera angles, panning. This is an excellent exercise for analyzing television news stories and television documentaries.

All of these activities are part of the study of meaning, an area that is primarily the responsibility of the English teacher.

The Doublespeak Committee at NCTE headquarters in Urbana, Illinois has bibliographies and other material. Get in touch. Get involved. Surely, if we don't bring the study of meaning in human contexts into our curricula and classrooms, we are all going to drown in the verbal effluvia that is rising around us.

Elementary

Propaganda Techniques via Children's Literature

Frances B. Cacha
City University of New York

Starting at an early age, when children are introduced to TV, they are bombarded by commercials. Ads in supermarkets, newspapers, magazines, and billboards, depend on attracting attention by some visual effect, but the delivery of the message requires reading ability. Radio commercials, on the other hand, must rely completely on auditory effects. Such ads, using just one modality of learning, either visual or auditory, probably have little influence on young children, but can we make the same assumption about TV commercials?

Television is a powerful medium of propaganda, even for adults. The interaction of both the visual and auditory modalities are used most effectively to capture and sustain the attention of the viewer. The impact comes not only from the use of the two modalities but also from the methods used to combine them. The interaction of the rapid changes in the visual sequences combined with sound effects, timing, as well as the writing and delivery of the auditory message can produce a forceful, emotional impact; one which cannot be achieved in ads which rely on only stationary visual messages. In the TV commercial, the entire presentation can be controlled, while in other ads only part of the message may be noticed. The TV ad can be most mesmerizing for all ages, but particularly for youngsters.

Unfortunately, young children are exposed to and manipulated by the propaganda strategies of advertising long before they study such methods formally in school. Therefore, they need to identify, understand, and be able to verbalize these propaganda techniques, methods which appeal to their pride and shake their self-confidence.

Using methods of affective education, young children can learn about propaganda strategies by having discussions about how they feel in certain situations, by role playing, and by socio-drama. They can analyze interactions between people and ex-amine tactics which manipulate people into doing what some-one else wants. Analogies can be made between examples from children's literature and advertising ploys. After the discussions, children can role play the incidents followed by another dis-cussion for further insight into the problem, which then may lead to additional role playing. Where feasible, a variety of end-ings should be encouraged. Finally, a series of cartoons can be drawn to summarize the sociodramas created.

As an example of the technique of persuasion, discuss with your students their feelings about different kinds of animals; be sure to include spiders, rats, and pigs. Then read *Charlotte's Web* to your class. Do they still have the same feelings about those animals? Most likely the book will elicit great empathy for the characters. If so, this is an example of persuasion where the author was able to change negative attitudes to positive ones. Analyze with your class how the author, E. B. White, was able to do this. Role play some incidents from the book.

At this point, explain to your class that manufacturers want people to think well of their products so that they will buy them. Therefore, they advertise their products on TV, in mag-azines, newspapers, etc. The purposes of advertisements may be to create a need for a product, to convince consumers that they need it, or that it is being sold for the lowest price for the highest quality. Since most manufacturers have competitors, the problem is to convince the buyer that a certain brand is the best.

Children can identify easily with the animals found in stores. Aesop's fables, in particular, are excellent sources for making analogies between the problems encountered by the animals and dilemmas of people in TV commercials. Here are two sugges-tions as to how these fables may be used.

In the fable, "The Cock and the Jewel," the rooster finds a jewel while he is pecking for food. Being a sensible cock, he appreciates and admires its luster but knows that the jewel will not satisfy his hunger. A comparison can be made between this fable and ads which try to create a need for a product. Show ads to your class and discuss with them how the advertiser tries to make a potential buyer feel inferior or unpopular if he or she doesn't have the product. In the role playing, encourage your students to think of ways to resist the sales pressures.

In "The Porcupine and the Snakes" a porcupine, seeking shelter, prevails upon a family of snakes to let him live with them. After they agree, the snakes realize that the porcupine's quills are sharp and unpleasant. Since the porcupine is satisfied, he insists that if the snakes are unhappy, they must leave the nest.

An analogy can be made between this fable and customers who buy things they don't need or want because they don't wish to offend the sales person. Again, in the role playing, encourage children to learn to say "no" when they don't really want something.

These are only two of many fables which can be used for this purpose. Other examples from children's literature will occur to you besides Aesop's fables and *Charlotte's Web*.

Of course, the whole concept of limited resources and unlimited demands creates complex problems. With constant reminders on TV, it may appear to children that resources are unlimited and for reasons which may seem capricious to them, they can't have what the children on TV seem to have. A child needs to learn not only that it is not possible to have everything but that there are, nevertheless, choices that he or she can make. Adults can help by giving children reasonable choices and by providing them with sufficient information so that they can make their choice independently without being manipulated.

One Approach to Teaching Critical Listening

Daniel J. Tutolo
Bowling Green State University

Since the early 1960s, and indeed even before that time, there has been a movement to open another frontier in learning—listening. Technological advances in electronic devices for communication including radio, television, and other electronic media have emphasized the need to improve listening. Rapid progress has been delayed because of the current inability to answer some basic questions about listening, but partial answers have been found for some of the fundamental questions.[1]

Waiting until research is definitive before teaching listening seems unfair to our present generation of elementary children who need facility in this skill. The search for instructional strategies continues for critical listening, a skill requiring analysis and synthesis of information, does not appear to be a skill acquired through random learning.[2]

Lundsteen defined critical listening as a three-step process including: 1) having a standard of highly conscious criteria present in the mind of the listener; 2) sifting the evidence and making a critical judgment; 3) drawing a conclusion or acting on the judgment made. This paper, which suggests a way to teach critical listening to elementary children, is concerned primarily with a method applicable to fifth and sixth grade levels, yet some ideas would be practical with other children.

Since many of the listening skills presently taught to children are the result of logical thinking rather than empirical fidelity, validation of the existence of these skills awaits scientific study. The present lack of validation, however, should not discourage attempts to teach listening, for enough is known about auditory learning to suggest that significant strides can now be made. What is presently needed are some worthy strategies for teaching listening skills which are clear, specific and relatively easy to employ.

To help in this matter, Kellog listed a compendium of listening skills divided into two general categories: 1) listening to get information and 2) critical listening.[3] The critical listening skills are listed below:

1   Relating heard material to own experiences
2   Making use of contextual clues to determine unknown meanings
3   Discerning between fact and opinion
4   Recognizing that which is relevant
5   Making logical inferences from what is heard
6   Keeping an open mind before forming opinions
7   Developing skills relating to the analysis and judgment of propaganda.

This report provides a format for teaching the skills relating to the analysis and judgment of propaganda. The oral discourse is divided into constituent parts (analysis)[4] and a judgment is made of the message (evaluation).[5] These particular skills were selected because the other skills of critical listening are subsumed here, i.e. to analyze and judge propaganda the other skill competencies of critical listening seem to be essential.

Another reason for focusing attention on these skills is the availability of almost unlimited examples to elementary teachers. Selection of appropriate messages for analysis takes little effort. Radio advertisements bombard our ears daily. Normally we do not think of advertising as propaganda, yet by definition it is a kind of propaganda. Propaganda is any systematic, widespread dissemination or promotion of particular ideas, doctrines, practices, etc. which further one's own cause. Radio advertising can be defined as spoken matter that publicly describes or praises a product, service, etc. so as to make people want to buy. Thus, by definition, advertising is a kind of propaganda.

Within the present century the popular image of propaganda has undergone change, and the word has come to acquire sinister overtones.[6] This change can be dated from World War I when the official use of propaganda was employed as a weapon in warfare to attempt to influence results. Advertising, too, has been accused of manipulating mass opinion and controlling individuals' minds. Although advertising may not be regarded as sinister, it too often seems filled with puffery to be taken as fact. In the minds of some people, Madison Avenue exemplifies the devil's symbol.[7]

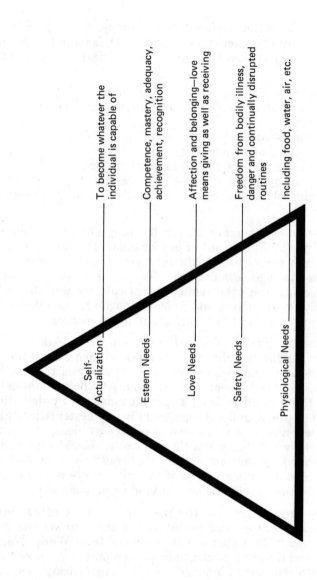

Figure 1. Maslow's Hierarchy of Needs.

On the other hand, several claims of the social benefits of advertising have been made and are worthy of note. It is claimed that advertising lowers prices by increasing the sale of an item. Secondly, it is claimed that advertising justifies itself economically by bringing knowledge of desirable goods to the customer. Finally, it is claimed that advertising brings about an improvement in the quality of goods because the advertisers' reputations are, in the long run, their livelihood.

Probably the truth of the matter lies somewhere between these opposing points of view. Advertising and propaganda are neither inherently good nor inherently bad. Our task as teachers is to help children to make intelligent judgments about a message. The three steps enumerated in the definition of critical listening provide an appropriate vehicle for making judgments: (1) setting a standard of highly conscious criteria in the minds of the listener, (2) sifting the evidence and making a critical judgment, (3) drawing a conclusion or acting on the judgment made.

Step One
As an aid in this step, Maslow's Hierarchy of Needs shown in Figure 1 provides criteria in an easily comprehensible fashion. These criteria are delineated in *Motivation and Personality,* chapter five.[8]

A facsimile of these needs can be reproduced on a transparency for use with the overhead projector and they can be projected on a screen for study purposes. Maslow theorized that when one need is satisfied, another need emerges. It is a false impression, however, that one need must be satisfied *completely* before another need emerges. In point of fact, most normal members of our society are partially *satisfied* in all their basic needs and partially *unsatisfied* in all their basic needs. Radio advertisements could and most often do appeal to more than one need at a time.[9]

As another dimension of the first step, encourage a small group of pupils to tape four or five radio advertisements heard over local radio stations. Cassette recordings are particularly appropriate because they are practically child-proof. The advertisements should be replayed while the transparency of the hierarchy of needs appears on the screen. The pupils are encouraged to determine to which basic needs the message appeals. There need not be complete agreement during this discussion, and varied points of view might even be encouraged. In the interchange of ideas, it is likely that those children whose interpretations were narrow might benefit from the alternatives presented. In many advertisements the appeal is subtle. Later it will be seen that appeals to emotional motives are more subtle than appeals to rational motives.

While discussing these things with sixth-grade children, I found the classes very responsive. Because they enjoyed debating the relative merits of the message in appealing to certain needs, I occasionally had to remind the pupils that differences of opinion were expected. This concludes the first step in the process of critical listening: setting a standard of highly conscious criteria in the mind of the listener.

Step Two
In the second step of the critical listening lesson, it is necessary to sift the evidence and make a critical judgment. For this step the advertisement should be reduced to writing. It is much easier to analyze verbal data through reading than through listening. Reading imposes a helpful constraint of a relatively permanent medium.[10] Perhaps the possibility of reviewing the printed message with no time pressure, the possibility for clearer organization and the absence of personal influence are important here. A small group of eager children can play the advertisement several times and write it out without much difficulty. The teacher then can type the ad on a master and run off copies for the class.

This second step involves analyzing the advertisement to determine the techniques of persuasion being used. Harter and Sullivan delineate seventy-seven propaganda techniques.[11] We recommend reducing this number to a workable minimum of seven, sometimes called the ABCs of propaganda analysis.

1 Name-Calling. Giving the idea a bad label to encourage rejecting or condemning the idea without examining the evidence. A variation of this technique is "glad words" where the intent is to associate a good feeling or idea with the products without examining the evidence.

2 Glittering Generalities. Sweeping and meaningless statements which appear to prove a point with an air of finality.

3 Transfer, sometimes called Favorable Association. A catch-all technique which associates a plea with a socially acceptable principle, individual, or object.

4 Testimonial, sometimes called Endorsement. Well-known people are used to endorse the merits of a product. If the big name thinks it is good, it must be good.

5   Card-Stacking. A device which misuses statistics. Statistics often add an aura of unimpeachable sanctity to the argument. Few people are in a position to contradict the statistician.

6   Identification, sometimes called Plain Folks. An effort is made to get the listener to identify with the message or product. "This is a product for you and for me."

7   Bandwagon. A suggestion that "everyone is doing it. Why don't you?" The inference is made that you are out of step if you are not doing whatever is suggested.

If the advertisement is double-spaced when typed, it is easier to record the persuasion technique being used. In step one, establishing in the minds of the listener a standard of highly conscious criteria, a great deal of flexibility was permitted. Here less flexibility is advised. The children should be encouraged to make a judgment that a particular persuasion technique is being used. Small groups of children ought to be able to agree that a word or group of words represents a stated persuasion technique.

When the children have analyzed one advertisement, they are ready to make a judgment about that advertisement. This is a synthesis process where a plan is produced. Lundsteen suggests three criteria to judge propaganda and advertising.[12]

1   It is bad if it adds up to a deliberate lie or if it encourages people to do things harmful to mental or physical health.

2   It is harmless if it advises some harmless product. (Most advertising falls into this category.)

3   It is good if it tries to get people to believe or do something of generally recognized worth or to aid people. (The public service announcement is regarded as persuasion toward a goal considered "good" by society.)

Step Three
A decision is made to buy or not to buy the product. Note that while steps one and two involve analysis and synthesis, step three calls for evaluation. This evaluation is difficult for children, yet seems to get easier with practice. The advertiser is appealing to different buying motives. Directly, the appeal may involve rational buying motives or considerations of the full, long-range cost of the article. Less directly, the advertiser may be appealing to the emotional buying motives which are far

more difficult to detect. Figure 2 is a checklist to aid in making a decision to buy the product or to defer to another product. A small group of pupils can talk about the choices and decide on appropriate markings. The final decision to buy or not to buy can be an individual decision.

Although it is hoped that consumers will use rational buying motives when making decisions, such is not always the case. Too often emotional buying motives which serve one end—the gratification of ego—are determining factors. Emotional buying motives include security, ego comfort, recreation, emulation, pride, sex, and many others. Any attempt to develop a complete classification of emotional buying motives is doomed to failure. Earlier it was suggested that appeals to emotional buying motives are very subtle. Many people are ashamed to admit their

Write the name of the product on the line. _____

Read the questions carefully and check the best answer.

Question	An outstanding purchase	A good purchase	A questionable purchase	Not a good purchase	Not applicable
Is the price what you would expect to pay for a comparable item? (price)					
How much will it cost to use? (cost in use)					
Will it hold up against repeated use? (durability)					
How often will it need servicing? (servicing)					
Is it dependable? (reliability)					
Will it last as long as it should? (length of useful usage)					

Figure 2. Checklist helpful when rational buying motives are employed.

real reasons for buying certain items. An advertiser might appeal directly to rational motives and quite indirectly to emotional motives. It is beyond the scope of this paper to explore emotional buying behavior in detail. As long as children understand that emotional buying motives affect rational buying motives, the end is served.

Notes

1 Stanford E. Taylor, *Listening, What Research Says to the Teacher Series* (Washington, D.C.: National Education Association, Association of Classroom Teachers, 1964).

2 Sarah Lundsteen, "Critical Listening and Thinking: A Recommended Goal for Future Research," *Journal of Research and Development in Education,* 3 (Fall, 1969), 119–120.

3 R. E. Kellog, "Listening," chapter 4 in *Guiding Children's Language Learning,* ed. Pose Lamb (Dubuque, Iowa: William C. Brown & Co., 1971), p. 120.

4 Benjamin S. Bloom et al., eds. *Taxonomy of Educational Objectives, the Classification of Educational Goals: Handbook I, The Cognitive Domain* (New York: David McKay Co., 1956), p. 145.

5 Bloom, p. 188.

6 James A. Brown, *Techniques of Persuasion* (Baltimore: Penguin Books, 1963), p. 11.

7 M. Bressler, "Mass Persuasion and the Analysis of Language: A Critical Evaluation," *Journal of Educational Sociology,* 33 (1959), 17.

8 Abraham H. Maslow, *Motivation and Personality* (New York: Harper and Row, Publishers, 1954), chapter 5.

9 Maslow, p. 100.

10 Sarah Lundsteen, "Critical Listening and Thinking: A Recommended Goal for Future Research," *Journal of Research and Development in Education,* 3 (Fall, 1969), 121.

11 D. L. Harter and J. Sullivan, *Propaganda Handbook* (Philadelphia: 20th Century Publishing Company, 1953), p. viii.

12 Sarah Lundsteen, "Outline of a Lesson in Critical Thinking—Propaganda Tricks," in *Listening Readings,* ed. Sam Duker (New York: Scarecrow Press, 1966), pp. 291–301.

Consumerism

Sandra Schurr
Administrative Intern, Bloomfield Hills, Michigan, School
District

Author's introduction: Too often one finds such subjects as
economics, consumerism and comparative shopping strategies
omitted from the basic elementary social studies or humanities
program. This is not commensurate with the needs and interests
of children who operate in a realistic world. Elementary school
children, as much as secondary students, should have an exposure
to and an awareness of the basic economic concepts around
which our country functions.

The following set of activities shows how consumer economics
can be taught to a class of fourth-, fifth-, or sixth-graders. The
vehicle for getting across some very simple but basic economic
concepts is toys. Topics covered answer such questions as:
What makes a good buy? What is a quality product? How does
one budget to get the most for one's money? What advertising
strategies are aimed at the children? How can we protect ourselves against unfair consumer practices? How do businesses
compete for customers? How does specialization help the
consumer?

Since children of elementary school age spend a considerable
amount of time with toys of various kinds—games, sports equipment, crafts, hobby materials, books, building toys—they represent an effective device for introducing the children to economics.

In this unit, sessions are short and can be covered in a two- to
three-week unit. The activities suggested are varied and stu-
dent-centered and include discussions, interviews, surveys,
role playing, creative projects, simulation games and the use of
community members—parents, local businessmen, local stores,
etc. Critical-thinking skills stressed in the activities include ob-

100

serving, comparing, summarizing, classifying, interpreting, criticizing, imagining, collecting and organizing of data, and finally applying facts and principles to new situations.

All in all, using the child's natural love for and interest in toys to provide some basic understandings in consumer economic principles almost insures the teacher success in dealing with these materials. As Voltaire, the great French philosopher once said: "Remember, play is the work of children!"

Session 1: Pretest
Objective/Concept: It is important to determine what makes a "good buy" in toys if one is to receive full value for money spent.

Procedure: Duplicate the following questions so that each student has a copy of them. Provide space after each question for children to write in their answers. This pretest will serve as a discussion starter and motivational device.

Questions for Pretest

1 What toys have you received as gifts that you especially enjoyed? Give some reasons why you especially liked them.
2 What toys have you received as gifts that you did not enjoy? Give some reasons why you were disappointed.
3 When you shop for a toy, what things do you consider before you buy?
4 In your opinion, what makes a "good buy" in a toy?
5 Interview your mother and ask her what she considers a "good buy" when purchasing a new dress?
6 Interview your father and ask him what he considers a "good buy" when he purchases a new suit?
7 List the following factors in the order of their influence on your buying in the toy department (most influential on top of the list, least influential at the bottom): Price, quality, material used in construction, labels, sale or bargain item, wide selection available, advertising, recommendation from a friend, appeals to personal interest or hobby, unusual in design or application.

(End of test)

Give students time to think and write out the answers to these questions as well as time to interview their parents. You may want to use all of these questions or only those few which are most appropriate to your students.

When students have completed the questions, go through them

in a total group discussion looking for a list of items that one considers when getting a "good buy" whether it be toys, dresses or suits. Also, compile a group list of toys that are most popular among the children in the class. Both of these lists will serve as a point of reference later in the unit.

Session 2: Selecting a Toy

Objective/Concept: One of the things a parent needs to learn is how to buy toys. Parents in the United States spend more than two billion dollars annually on toys. Unfortunately, too much of this money is wasted.

Procedure: Outline the criteria for a good toy. List on the board and have students take notes or copy list for future reference. Discuss each item as you go along using students' own toy experiences as much as possible. Here are the criteria I use:

1 A good toy is safe.
2 A good toy is durable.
3 Ninety percent of the play should be in the child and 10 percent in the toy. (Compare a push-button battery-operated toy with a set of wooden blocks.)
4 A good toy is fun.
5 A good toy must be suitable to the age and stage of development of the child as well as the special interests, hobbies, and skills of the child. (This list of criteria and the discussion idea that follows have been adapted from material in *Toy Review*, Vol. 1, No. 3, Christmas 1972, published by Toy Review, Newton, Mass.)

Next, discuss the value of a cardboard box as a good toy for a child. Point out that a large cardboard box is big enough for a child to crawl into. It is abstract rather than specific so it can be many things—a fort, a boat, an igloo, a computer. It stimulates and enriches a child's powers of inventiveness. Children can use it as it came originally. They can cut holes in it where they wish. They can paint or crayon it any color they like. There are few toys which you can buy in a toy store with the play value of a large cardboard box.

Assignment: Ask students to think of a toy that they now have which best fits the five criteria outlined above. In a good paragraph, they are to justify their choice. Follow up with a small or whole group discussion on the childrens' choices. Do the same toys come up again? Can the children agree with one another? Do they own many toys of this caliber?

Session 3: Consuming

Objective/Concept: Children are a big market for toy advertising. Television commercials, comic book advertisements and cereal box offers sell toys through a variety of techniques.

Materials: Supply of comic books. Supply of cereal boxes. Scripts of TV commercials from Saturday morning shows.

Procedure: Ask students to name at least three different television advertisements that are aimed at children. Discuss these choices. Review scripts of some of the commercials to refresh the children's memories.

Ask the students to identify the techniques used that are especially appealing to children (language, cartoon figures, music in background, price, display of the toy features, etc.).

Next, ask the children to examine the back of a variety of different cereal boxes. Have them cut out and clip one of the backs to a piece of paper and use it to identify and list advertising techniques cereal manufacturers use to sell their products. The children can compare lists for similarities and differences.

Ask students to go through a comic book and list the many different kinds of things advertised for sale to children. Have them try to classify the items and evaluate their appropriateness in some organized fashion.

Have students role play or act out a variety of commercials or advertisements from television, radio, cereal boxes or even comic books. The rest of the class must guess what product is being sold. How do they know? What clues give away the products?

Session 4: Toy Reviews
Objective/Concept: It is important that children learn to recognize the elements of a good toy and to act as responsible citizens by recommending good toys to others or by writing to toy manufacturers. It is equally important that they act in some constructive way to eliminate toys of poor quality from the market.

Procedure: Have the children use the five criteria learned in Session 2 to choose an extremely good or an extremely bad toy which they currently have. Each child is to write an original toy "review." Toy reviews should include the answers to the following questions:

1 Were you satisfied? (Was the price fair? Did you get what you thought you were buying? Were the advertising and packaging honest?)
2 Does the toy work? (Do the parts fit together? Is it washable? Does the motor work?)
3 Is the toy suitable for the child's age and abilities? (Is it too complicated or too simple?)
4 Is the toy open-ended? (Is it too realistic? Can a child use it in many different ways?)

5   Does the toy teach? (Does it develop some skill, such as hearing, touching, seeing, or tasting? Does it promote coordination, dexterity, creativity, independence, social awareness, self-confidence, understanding?)
6   Is the toy durable?
7   Is the toy appealing, interesting and fun?
8   Is the toy safe? (Check for sharp edges, poor construction, etc.)

Have the students write finished toy reviews on masters—after they have been checked for accuracy and writing skills, of course—and compile them in a classroom Toy Consumer Reports. Each child can take one home to share with the family so that they, in turn, can improve their buying habits when shopping for future toys.

Session 5: Competition and Profit
Objective/Concept: Competition is a contest among producers of goods and services to win the consumer's money. Producers compete with each other in many ways.

Materials: Several sheets of plain and colored construction paper. Glue, crayons, scissors.

Procedure: Divide the class into several small groups of 4 or 5. Teacher begins activity by stating that he or she owns a successful toy shop, and explains to the students that they, too, are owners of toy shops all competing with one another. "Now as you know, store owners watch very carefully what other store owners who sell the same thing as they sell are doing. Why do you think this is so?" Discussion.

Teacher says, "In playing this game, you are to watch very carefully what my business does and what you would do to stay in business."

Teacher starts game placing a sign made of oaktag or cardboard on front of desk. Sign reads: TOYS FOR BOYS SHOP. Students respond by thinking of company names and making signs for their groups. Give students time to share their signs with other groups and award gumdrops (or some noncalorie toy) to the makers of the best and most creative sign. Students may use any of the materials to make their signs.

Teacher puts out another sign that says: TOYS FROM AS LOW AS $1.00. Again student responses may vary with prices that are lower, higher, or a combination of values. Give students time to share once more and reward makers of signs where economy and value of items for sale are in the best balance.

Proceed with similar signs such as: TOYS MADE OF STURDY MATERIALS; TOYS GUARANTEED NOT TO BREAK; BUY ONE TOY AND GET ANOTHER AT HALF PRICE; OUR SLOGAN: BUY A TOY FOR YOUR FAVORITE BOY AND WATCH HIM JUMP FOR JOY!

Follow Up: Discuss the following questions: Is competition good or bad? Why? How do businesses compete with one another?

Prepare a survey questionnaire with which each student can interview the owner of a business: mother or father, neighbor, friend, relative. Questions should include:

1 What made you go into your business?
2 Do you employ other people? How many?
3 Did you have any special aptitude, training or experience that has helped you succeed?
4 Would you like to expand your business? How?
5 How do you compete with other businesses?

Session 6: Interviewing a Toy Store Owner
Objective/Concept: Learning how to interview experts in the toy field is an invaluable aid to analyzing consumer buying habits in the area.

Procedure: Have students—in small groups or in total groups—design a questionaire for purposes of interviewing people connected with the sale of toys. This might include owners of local toy stores, managers of toy departments in large stores or owners of toy businesses.

Sample questions might include:

1 What types of toys do you have that sell best in the following categories? Sports equipment, active games, constuction toys, science toys, preschool toys, board games, dolls, mechanical toys, others.
2 What are some ways you advertise your toys?
3 Do you ever run specials or sales on your toys? If so, when and what determines the sale items and price?
4 How do you decide what toys to sell in your store?
5 Do you think toys are made as well today as they were several years ago? Please explain.
6 What toy manufacturers do you represent?
7 How do you compete with other toy stores or departments?

Have each child interview some person in the field and then report and compare findings with the other children.

Consumer Education and the English Teacher

Mildred D. Berkowitz
Dartmouth Middle School, Massachusetts

Consumer education taught by the English teacher? Why not? Consumer education for seventh graders in an open classroom? Again, why not? When I came across some excellent materials published by the Consumer Education Services of Sears, Roebuck and Company, I saw limitless possibilities for the use of reading, language, and communication skills in a very practical way.

Goals and Objectives

The first task would be to state clearly the objectives. Open classrooms are frequently the misunderstood targets for educational guerrilla sniping, and we have learned to be our own severest critics, to be certain that our ideas are educationally sound and defensible. My statement of goals and objectives follow.

Goal

To provide the opportunity for the students to apply the basic skills learned in school to practical situations. To demonstrate the direct relationship of the skills of reading, writing, math, and critical thinking to everyday life.

Objectives

At the end of this unit, the student will be able to:

1 Compare prices on specific items by reading from printed material furnished by several types of retail outlets: catalog order houses, department stores, specialty shops, and discount stores.

2 Compare specifications of quality, maintenance, size, and additional costs by analyzing product claims.

3   Interpret critically product claims for fabric performance, care requirements, guarantees, and warranties.

4   Interpret critically product information presented to the consumer through advertising.

5   Handle the mathematics of shopping, purchasing, and income management: figuring sales taxes, shipping costs, credit charges, income taxes, etc.

6   Interpret written material on several types of credit plans and be conversant on the advantages and disadvantages of each.

7   Fill out printed forms correctly: order forms, receipts, credit applications, job applications, checks, deposit and withdrawal slips.

8   Experience several kinds of writing: letters for job applications; letters of customer complaint; classified ad for position wanted; classified ad for goods or services to be sold.

9   Use the telephone and the telephone directory in the most efficient way possible to obtain maximum information.

10 Use effectively and properly terms and terminology commonly used in the marketplace, in family management, and in newspaper items related to consumer education (include multi-meanings).

11 Employ the use of graphs and charts in analyzing data and statistics.

18 "Families"

The ninety-six students in the three classes were divided into five-member and six-member "families." I made up the groups, juggling personalities for strengths and weaknesses. The most dependable and creative of the boys and girls were designated as "heads of families," and the strongest pairs got the larger number of "children."

Now I used caution. To avoid the stickiness of seventh-grade boy-girl attitudes, although I *had.* served as marriage broker, we always used the term "heads of families," not "mother and father" or "husband and wife." Immediately, as the families were announced and grouped, each chose a family name, again to avoid personalities. They came up with such appellations as: the Schmidlaps, the Aquarians, the Bunkers, the Schwinebackers, and the Kung Fus. By doing this almost at once, we avoided the snickering and rib-poking which might have deflected us from the business-like atmosphere which we retained throughout the month-long unit. We had marvelous moments, but it was all related to the business at hand.

Each family was given an imaginary income of $10,000.00 a year, a monthly rental of $175.00, and utilities budgeted at $50.00 per month. As a group they could choose four items from a list of things like bikes, tape recorders, big-ticket appliances, clothes, or musical instruments to use for comparison shopping. They could also plan out-of-school field trips in pairs or in families to visit stores.

The heads of families were given a performance chart to keep records of each member of the family as assignments came due, and each individual was given an individual performance checklist, and a list of suggestions for more intensive, optional activities. The teacher received weekly reports from the family heads.

The individual performance checklist looked like this: Each member of a family is responsible for the following:

1 Write at least one business letter: proper form, first draft, final copy.
2 Know the list of 60 BUSINESS TERMS and their meanings (spelling counts) and be able to use them in evaluation.
3 Complete the sheet of 25 ABBREVIATIONS OFTEN SEEN. (Example: FTC, HEW, CPA, FCC, HUD, IRS, EOM.)
4 Fill out satisfactorily: credit application, job application, check and stub, receipt, bank forms.
5 Write a classified ad.
6 Make a chart of comparison shopping: item, features, prices, stores, attitude of salespeople.
7 Bring in examples of garment and products tags, labels, trademarks, warranties, and guarantees.
8 Demonstrate the ability to handle the mathematics of money management.

In addition, each family was responsible for a monthly budget plan beginning with gross income, subtracting FICA taxes, state income taxes, and withholding taxes to arrive at take-home pay. On this form were also listed expenses, such as rent, utilities, food, clothing, lunches, gasoline, and savings. This was a real eye-opener as they watched their gross income melt away. One worried young family head with four "children" came to me and said, "Mrs. Berkowitz, I'll never make it unless my wife goes to work."

The Team and the Community Cooperate

The social studies teacher took on the question of critical reading and listening in advertising. Which ads are misleading? What claims are false? How are words used to influence the buyer? Does a picture tell a story? Students brought in examples of ads and the classes discussed their features, making judgments as to the quality of each ad. Each student created a television commercial, complete with an original product, costumes, script, and sound effects. Meanwhile, our local newspaper, the *Standard-Times*, sent us without cost a week's supply of newspapers, one for each student, and I, the English teacher, taught them their way around a newspaper, including news stories and what is believable in what we read. We studied the newspaper sections, noted how graphic sports headlines can be, comparison shopped grocery and classified ads, and skimmed for specific items of business and human interest.

The Internal Revenue Service sent us actual tax schedules from which the students had to figure their tax deductions. They had to be able to skim and scan to find the section and column which applied to their particular tax deductible situation (married, three children, etc.). Since we were working with converting yearly, monthly, and weekly figures, the math teacher was a handy person to know. A knowledge of percent came into play in computing sales taxes, carrying charges, and interest rates. Terms for mathematical operations had to be read with comprehension.

An executive of a supermarket chain spoke to the classes about operating costs from the business point of view, including the serious shrinkage from pilfering. The students took notes on his lecture. He also brought canned and packaged food samples for comparison by looks and taste. (To his surprise he had 96 willing tasters. They even ate the corn and stringbeans, as his talk was given just before lunch!) He spoke about truth in packaging, urging his youthful audience to "read the fine print."

The father of one of the students, a tax attorney, came another time and told the classes why taxes are needed and the purposes for local, state, and federal taxes in our society. The Bell Telephone Company furnished a free film on the use of the telephone in business. Our local Sears store was most cooperative, giving us a number of current Sears catalogs for the classrooms, booklets on credit information, job applications, and credit applications. The home office of Sears in Chicago sent a number of their basic Consumer Education books for handy reference for all three teachers on the team.

This year (our second time out) a student's father, head meat cutter of a First National Store, brought in a side of beef and cut it up for us. Another father who owns a fleet of overland trucks brought a 34-ton truck to school and we climbed all over it while he lectured. Another father, a retail merchant of books and office and school supplies, toys, art goods, told us about the trials of being in business these days.

Conclusion

We were a smash! It was so gratifying to see seventh-graders poring over the catalogs, seriously discussing the relative merits of different washing machines, stoves, and refrigerators by reading the details of each item. Terms like *credit bureau, value received, cash reserves, net profit,* and *gross income* from our list of business terms were used freely in discussing assignments. Eyes lit up in recognition when they came across HUD, HEW, C of C, or ICC in newspaper headlines. Some clever games and quizzes were produced by creative students and we used them all. They gasped in disbelief when they saw prices of $1.35 for a pair of shoes and 50¢ for a man's shirt in the 1897 Sears catalog. Our movement from a rural to an urban society was emphasized by the items advertised in the same early catalog, items which are now obsolete or much changed in form and efficiency due to technological advances. We had many small-group and large-group discussions, both planned and spontaneous.

In retrospect, we honestly feel that we fulfilled our stated educational objectives. We related language skills to everyday family life in a way that had meaning to the students and showed them the value of what they were being taught.

Consumer Education Evaluation: Unedited Student Comments, November, 1973

In the Consumer Education Unit I learned a lot of things that I never knew before. I feel I got a lot out of it. The unit wasn't like any other unit that I had before. I liked pretending that our groups were familys and that we lived in our own homes.

I was always busy and I was never bored. We had guests come in to talk to us. I especially enjoyed listening to the meat cutter. I also liked listening to a boy's father who is a truck driver. This whole unit was very exciting and I enjoyed being a part of it.

Stephen Marshalek

I think I learned alot more than I think about it. Prices, inflation, commercials, TV programs, vocabulary, advertising, taxes, you name it. We were taught to write checks, receipts, and job applications. We were also shown that a steer is not all steak, and a pig is not all pork chops. A boy's father actually came in and showed us how to butcher a steer and a pig. Fantastic, it is. So many ways to look at things and to learn things. I think it's a new way to realize if you tried you could use everything. Just start from scratch.

It's really surprising what they'll do to things on a commercial to make it look good. It's really the best way to learn, because Consumer Education made me climb the ladder one more step. I tried my best, but I did the work first so I could get into detail. I did research at home. It's funny what they did years ago, from today. I did my best and it ran very well.

Carol Manley

I think that the Consumer Education Unit is a neat thing. I've never experienced anything like it before, I like it a lot.

I learned how hard it is going to be a mother with kids and everything. I learned how ten thousand dollars isn't much. I have the funniest kind of feeling that in years to come there is going to be a deppression. I liked the way Mrs. Berkowitz set up the families. I learned alot, and I liked it, too.

Christie Carr

I think that the consumer ed. unit was run very well. It was nice and loose. You can take things home and have fun while you are doing it. I like the idea of living like a family and doing things like check receipts, job applications, etc. The idea of having a father and learning all about the problems parents and children have.

Peter de Silva

I think the Consumer Education Unit was very interesting. I learned alot from the new business terms, and the newspaper terms. I feel that I have done very well in this unit, and I hope that I will keep this knowledge.

Now that I have learned new words about business, I can understand some things on TV and the radio. It was very interesting watching Mr. Ledoux cut all the special pieces of meat from a pig and also when Mr. Fusaro talked about all the diferent kinds of rules a truck driver must obey. I hope I will have this unit again in my future grades.

Tim Cassell

I liked our consumer unit because we had guests come in and tell us about their jobs.

I also thought the commercials were a lot of fun. Doing the commercials and talking about them, taught me the good and bad points of any ad.

Also, doing the comparison shopping taught me: If you want something at a store, compare at other stores: It could be less expensive!

Kim Lenling

Materials Used

Bell Telephone Company, "If an Elephant Answers," 26-minute, 16 mm color film on handling the phone in different business situations.

Israel, Fred L., editor, *1897 Sears, Roebuck Catalogue.* New York: Chelsea House Publishers, 1968.

Perkins, Terry William, *Understanding the News.* New York: Scholastic Book Services, 1970. (Skills Book SW15)

Perkins, Terry William, "Values/Advertising," A TAB Creative Teaching Unit, New York: Scholastic Book Services, 1971.

Sears, Roebuck Company, Consumer Education Booklets (1972– 1973): *Age of Adaptation, A Department Store in the Classroom, Using Retail Credit* (for students of low reading ability).

Evaluating Advertising

Charlene W. Smith
California State University, Fresno

Advertising is with us, and there are no indications that techniques to "sell the public" are fading. Television commercials, radio commercials, billboards, and newspaper and magazine ads abound. Oral, visual, and written commercials originate not only from Madison Avenue but from local sources, including the hastily written notices on the community bulletin board in the supermarket. Advertising gives a variety of information about new products and techniques, available public and private services, and numerous cost, barter, or trade possibilities.

Television is one of the main ways in which children are influenced by advertising designed to meet or create needs and desires (and dare we say values?). The double input of sight and sound of TV reaches children before they can read. The creative children's television series, "Sesame Street," has utilized the repetitive qualities of the conventional TV commercial by including several segments involving specific letters and numbers throughout each program and by proclaiming at the show's conclusion that the program was "brought to you by the letters b and r and the number 7" (or whichever letters and numbers were featured during that program).

There are indications that children, as well as adults, are becoming more sophisticated in evaluating some of the superlatives used and the claims made in advertising. While we are interested most particularly in the listening aspect of modern advertising, just ask an 8-year-old, 12-year-old, or 17-year-old to tell you his or her idea of the funniest, weirdest, most stupid TV or radio commercial. The beauty of the mimicry and the additions to the commercial text in pointing up ludicrous aspects are very revealing. When you start a discussion about commercials, you get remarkable feedback from children.

The following examples can help you begin work in evaluative listening with your class. It won't be long before you'll have some lively discussions concerning honesty in ads, ads that seem to help people, and gimmicks that are used for an appeal of one kind or another. You'll find that some of your best original ad writers and deliverers are the eight- and nine-year-olds. The sky's the limit with them! Older children are sharp in these aspects, also. Their expertise in researching unfounded ad claims can be a boon.

The evaluative listening experiences of this section have been broken into three categories: public service ads; local ads; and commercial advertising.

In using the evaluative listening experiences, consider your children and consider their past background in evaluative thinking, and start from where they are. Add to your own collection of ads from all the media. The children can help you by citing other ads and bringing in examples. Then, as you and your students begin to work through the various kinds of ads, commercials, and announcements, the types and classes will begin to fall into place. In this inductive approach, the decision on terminology will be the children's, with your assistance offered as necessary. The precise terminology is not important, for the emphasis is on the children's recognition of the different aspects of presenting product and service information through the various media.

Simply stated, the study of announcements, advertisements, and commercials leads elementary school children into the following basic analysis of the wide variety of input they receive each day: Who is presenting the message or information? For what purpose or reasons is the information transmitted? What are the responsibilities of the receiver (both the listener as receiver or the reader as receiver)?

Public Service Ads
1   Bill was listening to the radio when he heard the announcer start to talk about safety at home. Listen with him to find out why the announcer is talking about safety. Is he trying to get his audience to buy any particular kind of product?

"Now that spring is here, it's time for cleanup, paintup, and fixup inside and outside of the house. Before you start your outside work, here are a few tips. Are you about ready to trim some high bushes? Will you paint your house? Our station suggests one of the first things you need to check is your step-ladder. Get it out now and be sure that it is firm and steady. Be sure to see that metal parts are strong and not rusted. In short, our station wants you to stay well and healthy. Take your transistor radio outside and while you work, listen to our latest news, weather, and music."

2   It was Friday the 13th, and Pete was watching a special TV show about superstitions called "Bad Luck Day." There was a master of ceremonies talking with some people about old superstitions, where they had come from, and if they were really true. Listen with Pete to the concluding statements of the master of ceremonies. Ask yourself if the master of cere- monies is trying to sell a particular product, or trying to make you think in a particular way?

"So, my friends, as you walk out on the street today and start toward home, don't be worried about the black cat that runs in front of you. No one believes that cats have any magic prop- erties. That cat is probably in a hurry to get home, too. And as you walk down the street, forget the old rhyme, 'If you step on a crack, you break your mother's back.' It's just not so! You might walk around a painter's ladder instead of under it—not because it's bad luck to walk under a ladder—you might avoid getting some paint splatter on your coat. So Friday the 13th is not a bad luck day. It's just another day when you can think of all the superstitions that people used to worry about long ago. Oh, yes! If you get home and break a mirror, don't worry about seven years of bad luck for that's not true either. All you have to worry about is picking up the pieces without cut- ting yourself and then saving some money to buy a new one."

Local Ads
1   Outside the local hardware store Jenny stopped to look at the bulletin board where everyone was invited to put up ads for things to buy, sell, and trade. One ad was particularly in- teresting to her for it told a pretty good story about a person who wanted to make a trade. Listen to the ad to see if you can tell why this person wants to make a trade and why the ad was placed on the bulletin board.

"After some winter mishaps and some time in the hospital, I have decided to take up a hobby more suited to my athletic talents. Complete girl's ski equipment available—new skis, clamps, wax, the whole business. Boots (size 7) and three new girl's ski outfits (size 8). Will trade for modern stereo equip- ment in excellent condition. Call 498-7432."

2   Mr. Jatta was looking through the ads of the shopping

newspaper that was delivered to his door. One ad was very interesting to him and made him wish that, just this one time, he didn't live in a small apartment. He loved pets very much. See if you can tell something about the writer of the ad.

"Fella, our two-year-old collie, needs a new home. We are moving and cannot take him along. Fella is playful, but very gentle with children. He loves a big yard to play in and lots of people for company. He is a good watchdog. We don't want any money for our dog. We just want to be sure he has a good home. We will be leaving for New Jersey in August. Please call us, the Jones family, at 669-7321 if you have the home and love that Fella needs. Then you come over and meet our fine pet."

Commercial Advertising

1 Ms. Jenny Jacobs heard a commercial on her car radio one morning as she drove to work. In the background there was lively, happy music. As Ms. Jacobs heard the commercial, which was about buying new clothes, she decided to go shopping during her lunch hour. Then she thought, "There were so many interesting words used in that clothes commercial. That's why I want to shop for clothes!"

Here is the commercial she heard. You listen for some of the special words that might make someone want to go shopping.

"Y brand clothes for young career women with something new! We have picked the newest colors for your spring wardrobe. The sun rises and sets in our new shades for you. After the long, drab winter we have selected the warmest, softest, most vibrant colors for your clothes. Our colors have been taken from the sky, the earth, the sand, and the sea to give you their glowing vibrant warmth. The sun rises and sets this spring in the new colors of brand Y clothes."

2 Sam called his friend Todd on the telephone. Laughingly, he read an ad to him. Both boys like to fish. You listen to the ad that Sam read. It was about a very special bait for catching fish. See if you can find out why the ad seemed so funny to Sam and Todd.

"Catch more fish, better fish, and bigger fish. Our new, specially treated worms help you catch more fish whether you are fishing in a small pond, a rushing stream, or a big lake. Our special soil and feeding procedures make our worms yummy to any fish. Fish just can't stand it until they capture our delectable worms. Come in and price our buckets of irresistable worms. They're worth the price when you find out that you can haul in limit catches of fish in no time! Hurry in, while the supply lasts."

3 In the fifth-grade classroom, the boys and girls were evaluating a television commercial that several of them had seen. They set up questions that they wanted the other boys and girls to consider after they heard the commercial. The commercial was about a new breakfast cereal. The questions were: How might mothers feel about this commercial? Are there any reasons why people should eat breakfast? Do children do poorly in school because they don't eat this particular cereal? Listen to the commercial so that you can participate in a discussion as these children planned.

"Attention, mothers! Do your children get the 'drags' or the 'blahs' at school? In the morning, do you think they may be missing out on math or reading lessons because of improper diets? Boys and girls who are bringing home Ds and Fs on their report cards may be showing that they need Breakfast Tune-up, our new breakfast cereal. Breakfast Tune-up is the fastest growing cereal on the market. Since Breakfast Tune-up has more nutritional value than any other breakfast cereal, shouldn't you be a good mother and give your child the very best breakfast cereal?"

4 Mrs. Williams was talking about an ad she had read. Her friend wanted to hear it; so Mrs. Williams read the ad. The two women felt that the ad was not truthful regarding the toys it was advertising. You see if you feel the ad is believable or not believable. Why or why not? Here is the ad:

"Parents, do you want your child to have a good start in school? Toys-By-Us are the toys for you. Our games teach your preschoolers to count and to read the newspaper headlines. Here is one of our many letters from happy parents:

> Dear Company that makes Toys-By-Us,
>
> Your number games are terrific. After having gone through game six of *Numbers* by Toys-By-Us, my five-year-old is now in charge of distributing the lunch money and weekly allowances for his four older brother and sisters.
>
> Signed,
> Mr. and Mrs. R. L. B., Chicago

"Help your child find success. Buy Toys-By-Us at your local department store."

Detecting and Dealing with Doublespeak

Jane M. Hornburger
Boston University

Language manipulation is becoming a way of life and children need to be taught to detect and cope with the increasing flow of doublespeak. At present we face language pollution in most of our daily activities and it does not appear that the future will provide any relief from this worsening situation. Consequently, it behooves us as teachers to help our students develop coping techniques—to react critically, question, evaluate, and then formulate opinions and plans of action based on facts derived from considered judgment.

One of the most important factors in teaching critical reading is the teaching/learning climate. A classroom atmosphere that encourages inquiry and evaluation is the best kind of setting for the development and advancement of analytical skills. Teaching critical reading is not a formidable task, neither does it require any special methods or materials. Some of the most effective materials are free, and students are very good reference sources. They may be asked to bring in various printed reports, magazine and newspaper ads, editorials, and clippings from old textbooks.

Intermediate-grade children seek reality and objectivity in the world outside themselves and many of them are avid readers. They are eager to know and to do, and this desire is satisfied by the mass media. They are hip to figurative language and they can repeat most of the popular TV commercials. Youngsters enjoy discussions involving controversial/political issues and readily check on conflicting reports, theories, etc. Because of the nature of the intermediate child's developmental characteristics, these kinds of materials will prove to be effective sources for teaching about doublespeak.

Through participation in discussions, games and activities involving propaganda and doublespeak, children will learn to clarify concepts, make more discriminating choices, and arrive at increasingly sophisticated generalizations. It is true that these activities help to develop and improve analytical skills, but more important, they provide for relevant and enjoyable learning. The following are practical suggestions to assist elementary teachers in preparing children to cope with public doublespeak.

1   Prepare transparencies from appropriate pictures, handbills, ads, clippings from the text of newspapers and magazines, and use them in discussions to give children practice in identifying the basic propaganda techniques.

2   Ask the children to bring in advertisements to share with the class and tell which propaganda technique they think has been used in each. Later they might make individual scrapbooks or contribute their advertisements to a class scrapbook on examples of propaganda devices.

3   Provide two reports of the same sports event—one written by a reporter who is loyal to the home team and the other written by a reporter who is sympathetic toward the visiting team. Have children decide which reporter supports each team, and then determine which words and sentences might be changed or deleted if the reporters were to change sides.

4   Have children evaluate an article for the purpose of separating fact from opinion.

Ask a group to analyze a speech for emotional words, rewrite it without the emotional words and then compare it with the original.

5   Have the class write TV jingles/commercials and assign them to each of the seven basic propaganda techniques.

6   Prepare transparencies containing statements representing the basic propaganda devices and have children identify the statements with the appropriate device.

7   After children have gained an understanding of doublespeak, ask them to participate in a doublespeak contest. Provide the facts of an incident and have them write (create) a doublespeak selection to share with the class. The class may decide openly or by secret ballot the winner of the doublespeak award. (*Adaptation:* Groups could then convert the winning paper into a well-written factual report and win an award for unpolluted language.)

Since public doublespeak seems to be increasing at a rapid rate, critical reading is needed as never before. Our most important task now is to prepare children to judge the validity of information presented in spoken statements and in printed materials. The foregoing activities should prove helpful in accomplishing this task.

Secondary

Surveying Your Information Environment

Robert Cirino
University of Hawaii

In the United States, all representative viewpoints—from the radical left to the far right—have freedom to publish. But, since the publications of some viewpoints are unpopular, attract little advertising, or are poorly distributed, not all citizens are exposed to them.

In order to find out whether you are being exposed to a competitive marketplace of ideas, you need first to be aware of what information products you are consuming.

How to Make Your Own Reading Chart
On the following chart, list every publication that you read regularly, classifying it in two ways. First, decide what kind of a publication it is. Is it national or local? Does it deal primarily in news and public affairs or in other topics of general or special interest? Second, decide how liberal or conservative each publication is by asking what, in your opinion, seems to be the overall bias, message, or orientation—radical, very liberal, liberal, conservative, very conservative, or far right?

At this point, it doesn't matter whether anyone else agrees with your classifications or whether you can justify them fully. If you are not sure what the overall viewpoint is, make an approximate choice anyway. You are merely surveying the opinions you *now have* about the publications you are presently reading. Use your own idea of what a radical, liberal, conservative, or far-right viewpoint is—not somebody else's.

After entering the name of the publication in one of the columns, add in parentheses the approximate number of minutes per week that you spend reading it.

This chart is not meant to be a test of any kind. The only thing you should be concerned about is how accurately it re-

What I Read

The Spectrum of Political Viewpoints

Publications Read Regularly	Radical	Very Liberal	Liberal	Conservative	Very Conservative	Far Right
National weekly or monthly news and public-affairs magazines						
Local weekly school, college, "underground," or community newspaper						
Daily newspapers						
Other publications of general or special interest (on literature, fashion and homemaking, humor, history, science, sports, personal relations, hobbies, etc.)						

Figure 1.

veals to you your current reading habits and information consumption.

How to Make Your Broadcast Consumption Chart
Most Americans spend much more time watching television and listening to the radio than they do reading. The average household has the television on seven hours a day, and the average adult listens to the radio (at home, at work, or in the car) four hours a day. Today, 64 percent of Americans of voting age depend on television as their major source of news and, by a wide margin, they find it more believable than newspapers, magazines, or radio.

Using the following chart, figure out how much time, on the average, you spend watching TV or listening to the radio. If you watch one movie or football game a week, divide the time of that one program by seven to get the daily average.

You may have some difficulty trying to determine the political

viewpoint of some types of programs. In classifying entertainment or music, ask yourself what the overall message was and
how it made you feel about society or politics. For instance,
the pregame or half-time ceremony at a football game may
make you feel that America is great the way it is and should

Broadcast Consumption		
Type of program	Average amount of time per day (in minutes)	Range of political viewpoints expressed
Local TV news programs		
Local TV public affairs programs (documentaries, interviews, or specials)		
Network TV news programs		
Network TV public affairs programs		
Local or network TV entertainment programs		
Local or network TV sports programs		
Total TV time per day		
Local or network radio news		
Local or network public affairs		
Local or network radio entertainment (including music)		
Local or network radio sports		
Total radio time per day		

Figure 2.

be left alone. You might classify it as "moderate to conservative." On the other hand, a folk song program may make you feel that the American system has some faults and that radical change is needed. You might want to call this "liberal to radical."

Remember, there is no right or wrong judgment about the range of political bias that you find expressed in certain types of programs. This is merely a survey of your own opinions.

Looking at the two surveys, you can see that your information consumption falls into certain patterns. If you wish, make out charts for your parents, brothers and sisters, or classmates, so that you can compare your patterns with theirs.

You can now decide whether you are receiving all of your information from just one or two viewpoints, or whether you are being equally exposed to the entire spectrum—from the radical left to the far right. Have you made up or are you making up your mind about important issues without having heard or read what every representative viewpoint has to say?

If you answer yes to this last question there are probably two reasons why. First, people naturally tend to read or listen to ideas that reinforce what they already believe or want to believe. Second, the extremes on the political spectrum do not have as much communications power as the moderate viewpoints. In order to get some points of view, you would have to go to the library or subscribe to a special weekly newspaper or magazine. Since many people do not have enough time, money, or reading ability to do this, they depend on the cheapest, most easily consumed, and most powerful information agencies—television, radio, daily newspapers, and mass-circulation magazines. Most of these agencies tend to be moderate in their political orientation.

Community Information Survey
Who has communications power in your community? To find out, form a small group to investigate the major information sources in your area.

1   Who owns the daily newspaper or newspapers, local weekly newspapers, radio stations, and television stations? Are the stations affiliated with any network or are they independent? Does the newspaper subscribe to any nationally syndicated features? (A syndicated article is one that is used by many newspapers the same day.) Most of this information can be obtained by asking the stations or newspapers themselves.

After you find out who owns the mass media agencies in your community, try to find out if the owners own other businesses. For example, does the newspaper owner also own a radio or television station, a paper mill, or a book-publishing house?

You will probably discover some interesting patterns of ownership. Many recent observers have noted a nationwide trend toward monopoly in the mass media. Fewer and fewer companies are owning more and more newspapers and stations. As reported in the December 1972, *Columbia Journalism Review*, only 4 percent of American cities had competing daily newspapers in 1972. More than 60 percent of daily newspaper circulation is held by chain publishers (publishers who own more than one newspaper). One-fourth of the total revenue of daily newspapers (approximately $2.2 billion) is earned by the ten largest chains.

Those who own both print and broadcast agencies (cross-media owners) control 36 percent of daily newspapers, 25 percent of TV stations, 8.6 percent of AM radio, and 9.5 percent of FM radio. Chains, cross-media owners, conglomerates, and firms related to mass media control a total of 58 percent of daily newspapers, 77 percent of TV stations, 27 percent of AM radio, and 29 percent of FM radio.

The eleven largest cable TV companies have half of all cable television subscribers. Broadcasters and newspapers own 37 percent of cable television.

2   Although it is not part of the mass media, another important element of the information environment—especially for a student—is the libraries. How many are there in the community? Which daily newspapers, local weekly newspapers, and national news and public-affairs magazines do they subscribe to? Make a spectrum chart for the library's newspapers and magazines like the one you made for yourself. In your opinion, or in your group's opinion, does the library offer publications from the entire spectrum of viewpoints? Are you taking advantage of the diversity that the library does offer?

3   In the future, Community Antenna Television (CATV)— usually referred to as cable television—will become an important part of your information environment. Cable TV has the potential of offering a clearer picture, two-way communication (enabling the viewer to participate in a program or shop for groceries via TV), reception of stations from other towns, and as many as eighty-four channels.

You or your group should investigate the present situation regarding cable television in your community. Find out if the franchise to operate cable has already been granted to a cable company by your city council. What does the franchise agreement say? Who owns the company? How many other businesses or cable systems does the company own? Are there any channels set aside for citizens to use ("public-access channels")? How much does it cost to subscribe? How many and what percent of households subscribe?

If the franchise has not yet been granted, which cable companies are competing for it? Who owns them? What kind of cable service are they offering?

Community Taste Survey

The final factor to survey is your own media likes and dislikes. Answer the following questionnaires for yourself, and then go on to collect answers from your parents, classmates, neighbors, and other members of the community.

Television and Radio Questionnaire

1　On the average, how many hours per day do you spend watching television? listening to the radio?
2　What are your three favorite programs?
3　Are you satisfied with the variety and quality of entertainment programs?
4　Is there too much violence in entertainment programs?
5　Should the amount of violence in entertainment programs be restricted?
6　What news program do you like best?
7　What newscaster do you like best?
8　What commentator or editorializer do you like best?
9　Would you like to see more public-affairs programs during prime time television (7:30 P.M. to 11:00 P.M.) and early morning or late afternoon radio time?
10　Do you think newscasts and public-affairs programs, together, represent fairly all viewpoints on the political spectrum?
11　Does the total programming provide enough information to enable viewers or listeners to make intelligent decisions on major issues?
12　Do you think the overall effect of advertising on viewers is good or bad?
13　How often do you watch or listen to "public" or

"educational" television or radio as opposed to commercial stations?

14 Should public noncommercial television and radio programming be decreased, kept the same, or increased?

15 Are you satisfied with the quality of children's programs?

Newspaper Questionnaire

1 How many days a week do you read the daily newspaper?

2 Which section do you like best (news, sports, comics, personal interest, family, etc.)?

3 Which section do you read first?

4 Is there too much or too little coverage of trivia (stories or pictures about animals, pretty girls, unusual but unimportant happenings, etc.)?

5 Is the newspaper providing enough information to enable readers to make intelligent decisions on local issues? national issues? international issues?

6 Do you think the newspaper fairly presents information and opinions from the entire spectrum of possible viewpoints?

7 Would you like to have two or three competing newspapers in town instead of just one?

8 Which source of news do you trust the most: television, radio, the daily newspaper, or a news magazine?

9 Which of the above sources do you think is the most biased?

Going over your own, your neighbors', and your classmates' answers to the questionnaires, do you find that you are basically satisfied with the information and entertainment you are getting? Do you think that citizens in your community are being adequately exposed to the kind of information that will enable them to make the best choices on important issues? Is it possible to like television, radio, and newspapers because they are entertaining, but at the same time feel that they do not present enough information or diversity to best serve the public need and interest?

Recognition of Doublespeak in Local Politics

Clare E. Barkley
Urbana High School, Illinois

Coping with doublespeak at the secondary school level is probably not much different from coping with it anywhere else, inside of school or out. First doublespeak must be recognized and its effects seen, for only then can we deal with it. I prepare my students to cope with doublespeak in a course entitled "Communication—Community as Classroom." The course, open to sophomores, juniors, and seniors, is an interdisciplinary course in communication and political behavior, and is designed to introduce students to their community as participating citizens, not isolated members of the high school environment—a little community all its own.

In this course, which is conducted outside the high school building and outside of regular school hours entirely, the students are required to do four things: attend designated public meetings, read our three local newspapers each day, keep a daily journal, and participate in a weekly seminar.

The first requirement—to attend public meetings—provides the course's content. We all attend our two city council meetings each month and many of the other thirty or so regular public meetings of legislative and administrative bodies connected with our city government. The students attend two or three of these meetings each week because it is here that decisions are made which immediately affect the lives of all citizens of the community. The results of these decisions are seen and felt directly by the students while many of the decisions made by state and national governments seem remote.

Before a month is over, the students understand the structure of the city government and the relationship between city government and other policy-making and governing bodies within

130

the community, such as the school board and the park board. Students usually begin to have a particular interest in special issues quite early in the course and tend to spend most of their time following these issues on appointed bureaucratic rounds. In order to keep up with everything which will eventually affect the outcome of an issue, they find it necessary to broaden their view of communication. Of course, they have to observe people talking together, making speeches, deliberating, and so forth. But they also have many opportunities to read legal notices in the newspapers, use newspaper files, read zoning ordinances, observe public hearings, read by-laws of various boards and commissions, observe parliamentary procedure, read maps, attend court sessions and watch public opinion as it forms and changes.

After I have described the course even as briefly as I have, it may be obvious where the students encounter doublespeak. (Incidentally, I do not refer to it as doublespeak, nor is the course specifically a language course, but the students quickly see the relationship of language to action.)

Since they do attend the public meetings, students are keenly aware that only very few of the people affected by the decisions made at these meetings are present and that most of the people depend on the news media for their information. In their journals students write their own notes on the meetings they attend. Then they compare their notes with the news reports given in the two competing daily newspapers in our area as well as in the University of Illinois newspaper, and with the reports given in the newscasts on our three local television stations. They eventually become quite discerning in their assessment of distortion, bias, and completeness of news coverage. Since there isn't time for all of us to attend every meeting we want to—and sometimes it is even impossible because two or more meetings are held at exactly the same time—it is clear to us that we must depend a great deal on the news media for information, and that people act on the basis of that information, right or wrong.

Probably the most dramatic doublespeak examples are the ones that affect the students as they follow their special interest as citizens. One evening at seminar, a student described his experience in an office where he asked to see a public record. The secretary in the office told him he was asking for a "limited access" document. He came away without seeing it and wondered where he might find the information. There was no other place, so he returned to the same office and asked what a "limited access" document is. At the next meeting, he reported that "limited access" meant simply that he could not remove the document from the office. It was only after he went back to have the words interpreted that he could in fact read the document. This is an example of doublespeak which the student thought was deliberately designed to put him off the track—in effect, taking away his right as a citizen to investigate and speak out.

A controversial project is now under consideration in our city. An effort is underway to replace an obsolete community swimming pool with a new one in some other location which will serve most of the population in the most convenient way and which can be used by the schools for swimming classes. The tentative year for completion of the project is 1976. A group of people who favored the project referred to it in a series of public hearings stretching on for almost a year, as "The Independence Bicentennial/Educational Recreational Center"—a patriotic label. The Park District Commissioners call it "a community recreational facility centrally located relative to population density." A group of objecting neighborhood residents call it "a public swimming pool right in the middle of a quiet residential area." The students observed that the amount of fruitful, specific discussion increased as the wording described the project more specifically. While the pool was "The Independence Bicentennial/Educational Recreational Center," the discussion was in abstract terms and little progress was made toward approval or rejection of the project.

Other instances of doublespeak and its effect on decisions regarding the community occur in city planning activities and zoning matters. What the Public Works Commission announced as "street improvements which will increase traffic flow" was almost accepted as a desirable and progressive move until someone pointed out that it really meant widening the streets, which would destroy a number of trees and tear up brick streets which many people wanted to preserve as a charming bit of our past. That project was not carried out because of citizens' objections, but there were no objections at all until people understood what "street improvements" meant in this case.

In our zoning ordinances, the term "usable open space" occurs frequently, and the students apparently thought they and everybody else knew what that meant, or that it didn't matter. But they attended a city planning meeting one night when a man came to apply for zoning variance. He thought the term was merely a formality tolerated by the citizens, because to him "usable open space" meant *his* space to *use* to build a garage on. The intent of the ordinance, however, is that usable open space must be unoccupied by buildings, usable for drainage by means of ground permeation, usable for vegetation, recreation, and light and air circulation. The students observed with fascination the drafting of a new and clearer definition of the term "usable open space" over a period of several weeks. Students also encountered many other examples of technical language and jargon which affected decision-making. These decisions ultimately had an impact on their physical surroundings, as in building construction, landscaping, and industrial development that did or did not occur during the semester.

One of the girls in the class investigated volunteer services within the city. She reported that a great deal of volunteer time is spent with "underprivileged," "the disadvantaged," "lower income families," and "senior citizens." As the girl described her week's activities, she talked about "senior citizens" without any difficulty, until she tried to tell us about a friend she had made. She couldn't quite refer to an individual as a senior citizen. She couldn't say, "I was talking to this senior citizen. . . ." Finally she admitted that he could be described as an old man— that there *are* old men and old women in the world—though we hardly ever say that.

This matter of euphemistic labels comes up frequently. High school students give themselves labels. The labels seem to change from year to year (*jock* is the only one with any durability), but they don't seem to mind. What they say they do mind is having their school labels changed or taken away from them. A boy in the class said he didn't know where he stood at the high school. He was gifted in grade school, accelerated in junior high school, and now he is heterogeneous; he thinks he needs an identifying label because he has always had one.

These students certainly understand that their academic potential hasn't changed—only the school labels and perhaps a teacher's view of them, if teachers depend on labels of this kind to identify and categorize students. They understand, as well, that the labels by which city officials are identified are no more valid than their own school labels. The mayor and the district representatives are identified as Republicans or Democrats, liberal or conservative, but these labels have little to do with describing how they act. They imply a vague sort of expectation of how they *might* act, but have little relationship to reality.

The students follow and sometimes work in the campaigns of candidates running for city government positions or of local candidates running for state government. They hear the campaign rhetoric of someone they've actually watched in action or of a candidate running for the first time who is talking about doing a job he or she has never done before. The students know, at least, what the job is and whether or not the new candidate, if elected, will actually be able to make changes, or deliver on promises made to constituents. They are in a position, too, to compare the past actions of an incumbent with campaign promises for the future.

One student followed the campaign of a man who referred to blue collar workers as "the working people" when he wished to indicate they were not a part of the academic community, and as "the *real* working people" when he wished to distinguish them from unemployed welfare recipients—an interesting use of language.

As you might suspect, students like to attend school board meetings. After each meeting their journals reflect their distrust of such words as *alternative, innovative, career-oriented, individualized,* because they can interpret the words that are used to describe programs in their school; the school board members who take action on the basis of this language often cannot.

The students study the long school board budget printout each week; they found recently that a cut in the coaching staff was quietly restored after dozens of people had objected to that budget item and had gone away from the budget hearing thinking it had indeed been cut. The next budget printout carried the item "Contractual services athletic dept." Thus the coaching position had been restored without discussion.

This kind of course helps students achieve new awareness by introducing them to the reality of politics and the power in their own city—a manageable situation that allows them to watch decisions being made largely on the basis of language, and to see the results of these decisions. It also helps them to recognize and use their own power as citizens.

A Student-Centered, Process-Oriented, Interdisciplinary Non-Unit on Doublespeak

Nancy McCracken
Youngstown State University

> Generals, clergymen, advertisers, and the rulers of totalitarian states—all have good reasons for disliking the idea of universal education in the rational use of language. To the . . . authoritarian mind such training seems (and rightly seems) profoundly subversive.
>
> Aldous Huxley

This article began as a formal unit on semantics for use in senior high school. I have since discovered that the success of the approach I want to describe depends upon the very fact that it cannot be put into the standard unit plan form. So, out of respect for semantic precision, I will call this a description of an approach to teaching semantics which I found very fruitful in my own class. I offer it in hopes that it may be of use to others whose backgrounds are more firmly grounded in the study of literature than in the philosophy of language, and who are disillusioned with existing units on semantics found in so many high school texts.

One of my main teaching concerns has been that too often we teach "semantics" in a vacuum—as though it were something separate from the regular English curriculum—a kind of gimmick thrown in between grammar review and stort stories. A common underlying philosophy has been: Arm the kids with a list of propaganda techniques with catchy names, prove to them that those are bad things done by bad people out to get their money or their votes, and then move on. The students' involvement seldom lasts beyond the unit, and even more seldom beyond the classroom. It's not just that this approach is insufficient to prepare students to deal with language in our culture; much worse, it is a disservice, because it perpetuates a falsehood

135

about communication (only bad people manipulate language for their own ends), and it prevents students from applying the language skills we teach all year to the areas where they most need them. With this in mind, I planned a year-long study of semantics with three vital components: 1) the study of semantics was to be integrally related to the traditional, literature-centered, senior high English curriculum; 2) students were to be afforded opportunities to examine those language environments which directly affect their lives; and 3) students were to conduct investigations of language use outside the English classroom and over an extended period of time.

The first component is essential because it allows us to teach semantic discrimination through the medium we know best. We need to know much more about general semantics, but in the meantime, we are all somewhat expert at literary analysis, and we can apply those skills immediately. I began with poetry. It has always interested me that novice students of poetry find it so difficult to accept ambiguity—it takes so long for them to stop asking what a poem finally *means;* yet when confronted with nonliterary language, they readily accept not only ambiguity, but gobbledygook, blatant propaganda, and general vacuous nonsense. There are a few reasons for this. We teach students that their interpretations of poetry are important—they will be graded. We don't do this with nonliterary language even though ability to interpret it may be the most important skill we can teach. Further, students are so inundated with the language of "authority" that they turn it off. They come to believe that persons in authority seldom say anything worth translating or that there is a magic key to their language which they will get somehow when the need arises. Finally, I'm afraid that much of what we do with language in the classroom results in the students' loss of faith in their own interpretive abilities, and they are eager to accept someone else's interpretation. If we can get students to respond to the art of poetry, and to trust their own responses, we have them dealing with language manipulation in the hands of masters.

Poetry works in several ways toward developing semantic discrimination in interpreting nonliterary language. In the first place, poetry uses many of the same devices that propagandists use. In teaching poetry, we teach analogy, imagery, symbolism, ambiguity—in short, the techniques of propaganda. Although the critical terms differ, the difference between language manipulation by poets and propagandists is often only one of purpose. In the hands of a poet, literary devices are used to communicate

the most intense personal response to the reader. In the hands
of a propagandist, they may be used to thwart that communication. An illustration may be useful. In our class, we began with
MacLeish's dictum: "A poem should not mean, but be," and
contrasted it with another: "A public statement must mean,
not just be." There are some very instructive pairs to be made
of poem and public statement. The Marine Corps "Rifleman's
Creed" and Randall Jarrell's "The Death of the Ball Turret
Gunner" make one such pair. To some students' initial frustration, Jarrell's poem subverts attempts at purely intellectual
analysis of meaning.

> From my mother's sleep I fell into the State,
> And I hunched in its belly till my wet fur froze.
> Six miles from earth, loosed from its dream of life,
> I woke to black flak and the nightmare fighters.
> When I died they washed me out of the turret with a hose.

The language here bypasses logic to create in the reader a more
immediate sense of the subject (war). In contrast, while the
Rifleman's Creed also subverts attempts at logical analysis, it
does so to create a greater distance between the reader and the
subject (also war).

> My rifle is human, even as I, because it is my life.
> Thus, I will learn it as a brother. . . . We will become
> part of each other. . . . Before God I swear this creed.
> My rifle and myself are the defenders of my coun-
> try. . . . We are the saviors of my life.

Here are poetic devices used to create a personal response, but
surely *not* to the real business of war.

On another level, e.e. cummings' poem "Next to of course god
America i" and almost any one of Ron Zeigler's statements to
the press during the Watergate period make another instructive pair. In both cummings' poem and the press statements,
the language is gibberish punctuated with patriotic slogans, but
while the poem could be termed "inoperative" (we frequently
ask of a poem, "does it work?"), the press statement cannot be
so termed. The public statement termed inoperative is a lie.
The tag line of the Watergate administration, "Will it *play* in
Peoria?" supports the notion that the language of literature is
usurped by public speakers in authority to subvert communication. Students comfortable with the language manipulation devices of literature are one step closer to recognizing propaganda
when they hear it.

Another way literature study works to develop semantic discrimination is to counteract the numbing effect of the sheer verbosity of our culture. The language of poetry is concentrated; while that of public speech is often inflated to the point where meaning is entirely obscured. In our class we read some Flannery O'Connor and portions of James Joyce's *Portrait of the Artist as a Young Man* to have students deal with language which reveals character at its most essential level. Coming to know Hazel Motes or Stephen Dedalus from the inside out, and reading language of interior monologue, language stripped of conventional filler, is good preparation for analysis of much public language. The contrast is so startling that it reawakens the students' sense of impatience and dislike for political jargon and commercial hyperbole. Finally, poetry works as an antidote to the antiseptic abstractions of much public language. While public speech dulls our senses with phrases like: *peace with honor, benign neglect, protective reaction strikes*, and *satisfactory levels of unemployment*, poetry continues to keep us sensible of the loss of human life and dignity, bigotry, pain, and hunger. There is a memorable illustration of this principle from the Senate Watergate hearings. Consider the impact of Erlichman's *poetic* statement about Patrick Gray: "Let him twist slowly, slowly in the wind." That one lyric line cut through all the faceless bureaucratese to reveal the depths of inhumanity underlying the whole Watergate affair. It was a fine irony that Erlichman himself used the most effective counter-propaganda device available against his own propaganda.

Regardless of the heightened language awareness and skills the study of poetry can bring to the analysis of nonliterary language, students probably won't make the direct application unless the language of everyday life is actually brought into the classroom for analysis. Past attempts of mine to make students conscious of public doublespeak had failed in part because my analyses centered on politics, when, for the most part, high school students don't feel they have a vital interest in politics. When I centered discussion on advertisements, there had been a great deal of enthusiasm, but most of it superficial—after all, most high school students aren't in a position to be sucked into buying a sexy and expensive new car. While they delight in picking out sales gimmicks and psychological pressure in ads, they know that if they get fooled into buying one brand of jeans over another less expensive but better brand, there will be no major consequences. The study too often becomes a game. If we are to convince students that careful semantic analysis of everyday language is an important thing, then we have to apply that an-

alysis to areas of the students' lives that *they* see as vital.
That is the second component of this non-unit.

I chose *Language In America*, edited by Postman, Weingartner
and Moran (Pegasus, 1969), as the shared classroom text for
discussion of nonliterary language. While this book worked extremely well in my class (Honors English at a private academy),
I do not wish to suggest that it is the best or only good collection for use as a student text. (In fact there are many communities beyond West Virginia which would flatly reject it on
grounds of obscenity, anti-authoritarianism, and anti-American-
ism.) Besides being a funny and sometimes very sad book with
a large variety of examples of public doublespeak, it offers an
approach which I found useful. The first essay in the book,
"Demeaning of Meaning" by Neil Postman, speaks of "language
pollution," and to high school students already tuned in to ecology, the metaphor is intriguing. The book analyzes several different semantic environments in terms of their pollution index.
It is truly subversive, because it says over and over that language has to communicate meaning in a way appropriate to its
context and it offers example after example where it does not.
The primary value of this book is that it shows language pollution occurring not just in the words of the stereotyped "bad
guys" but even in the rhetoric of well-meaning clerks, lovers,
liberals (as well as conservatives), even nice guys like Hugh
Downs and Walter Cronkite. Semantic environments examined
range from the languages of love, politics, and racism to those
of research, economics, and computers. There is even an essay
on the pollution of teacher-language. "The Language of Education: the Great Trivia Contest" by Terence P. Moran is especially useful, because it focuses semantic analysis on the field
of greatest concern to the students—the language of tests.
Moran reminds us of a line by John Dewey: "Education is what
remains after the facts are forgotten," and offers a series of
paired test questions—questions from school tests matched with
trivia game questions. For example:

I   A silver bullet is used as an identifying symbol by (a) Tom
Mix, (b) the Durango Kid, (c) the Lone Ranger, (d) Hopalong
Cassidy.

II   A silver bullet ends the life of the principal character in
(a) *Orpheus Descending*, (b) *The Emperor Jones*, (c) *The
Silver Cord*, (d) *The Great God Brown*.

The similarity between the two sets of questions was obvious
to the students and they recognized many of the questions from

school tests. I assigned most of the essays in the book, and they provided a base for heated classroom discussion for two weeks. What is most significant is that students were encouraged to examine the language pollution index in their own environment, and they did so with an intensity which was surprising.

Some interesting things began to happen in the school—many of them outside my classroom. My students began to get even more "uppity and obnoxious" than seniors are supposed to be. While senior year is a time for rebellion against the school environment in general, this year, the rebellion was taking a different form—one which was not easily dismissed with short answers. The political science teacher was "harassed" into breaking his lecture schedule to allow for discussion of terms previously memorized and bandied about by students as though they had clear single meanings ("Communism," "free enterprise system," etc.). We later invited him to spend two hours in our class discussing the merits of ambiguity in major public documents (e.g. the pursuit of happiness).

The students asked the science teacher the purpose of studying physics, and then pointed out that the kinds of questions she asked on their objective test belied her answer. They boycotted one of her tests, and finally convinced her to give an alternative open-ended problem-solving test to those who preferred it. In my own class, we had begun reading *Anna Karenina* from several different translations. The students pointed out that in several cases it was not possible to come to agreement about even the literal meaning of certain passages, let alone the non-literal meanings because the choice of *language* differed from one translator to another. The student council, led by one of the students in our class, launched the yearly campaign against several school regulations and at least temporarily baffled the administration by taking up the argument that the regulations were at variance with the *language* of the official school philosophy.

The faculty and administration response to all this activity was, at first, resentful, but with only one exception they were ultimately supportive and, in fact, pleased. The students were reexamining the language environment that controls their lives and demanding at least attempts at semantic honesty. The next step was to broaden the students' interest in language beyond the context of the school. And that takes me to the final component of this non-unit on doublespeak.

In keeping with the scientific metaphor introduced in the Postman essay, I assigned students to field work in a semantic
environment of their choosing. They were asked to determine
what they believed to be the proper function of language in the
environment they chose to study, and then to analyze the language used in order to determine whether it performed that
function. At the end of a semester of observation, note-taking,
and recording, they were to report to the class on the pollution
index of their specific language environment. The only restric-
tion I made was that the students had to choose language
environments which had high interest for them and to which
they had frequent access. Some of the language environments
the students chose to investigate and their conclusions are worth
sharing here.

One student brought a tape recorder to three of the homes
where she regularly babysat. With the parents' permission, she
taped the conversations of three- and four-year old children
under several different conditions (anger, solitary play, and
anxiety). She found that much of the children's language was
used to express an inner reality quite distinct from observable
reality—and that the children were aware of the distinction
while often the listening adults were not. She concluded that
communication is thwarted when the adult language does not
take into account the function of child language.

Another student, formerly a budding radical feminist, began to
analyze the language of popular feminist publications and found,
to her deep regret, that the language used was often highly
sexist. She concluded that since the function of feminist journals should be to minimize faulty discrimination between sexes,
their use of sexist language indicated a high level of language
pollution.

A student who had recently buried a grandparent reported on
the language of funeral directors. She interviewed several funeral directors in the neighborhood and examined copies of their
professional journals. (One was happily entitled *Sunnyside and
Casket*.) Going on the premise that the function of funeral
director language should be to provide assistance to a mourning
family and a clear explanation of technical services offered and
their costs, she concluded that that semantic environment was
grossly polluted. She reproduced pages from the journals which
openly stated ways for funeral directors to obscure language for
the purpose of playing on a family's grief while making a
greater profit.

Another student "forced herself" to begin watching the local television news station regularly. She perceived a blatant editorializing in the drawings which were flashed behind the anchorman to illustrate each news item. One of the most dramatic examples she reported was a news item on Arab-Israeli peace talks, accompanied by a drawing of a sheik complete with cloak and dagger. The student called the television station to make a complaint, but noted that she was then thwarted by the language of bureaucracy.

Other students looked into the language of Watergate, sermons, college applications, book reviews, local newspaper editorials, advertisements, and televised political speeches. The interest in semantics remained high throughout the year and continued to influence other classes and language environments outside the school. The students became adept at recognizing doublespeak when they heard or read it, and even began to recognize it when they spoke it themselves. In our class, analyzing the language of literature and that of everyday language continued to have a reciprocal benefit for interpreting both.

My students convinced me that given a chance to apply skills they learned through literature study to other semantic areas, and the freedom to explore the languages that they see as vital to them, they could become more discriminating semantically than I had hoped. But I remain convinced that separate units on semantics will not have their desired effect unless they can be incorporated into an entire curriculum aimed at semantic study. We simply cannot continue to treat it as a mysterious subject somehow outside our province. Given the mass media explosion in our culture and the concurrent increase of public language abuse, semantic study must become the core of our curricula. Something is seriously wrong when we succeed in teaching most of our students to recognize the verbal deception of our favorite fictional villains, and yet fail to prepare them to analyze the deceptive language of political candidates and elected officials.

The War of the Words

Christine Fontenot
Loreauville High School, Louisiana

"Sticks and stones may break my bones, but words will never hurt me" is one of those old saws that all have heard and none believe. The cruel nicknames that are too near the truth to be funny; the ethnic slurs and jokes that are hostile, not humorous; parents' words that ridicule rather than encourage; the half-truth that damages more than any lie; the faint praise that damns; the examples are endless. Yet most people are far more terrified by guns, knives, or sticks of dynamite than by words, "mere" words. Perhaps in a slower, quieter age more conducive to contemplation, people were more—rather than less—aware of the power of words than we are in an age of verbal "overkill," in itself a startling and revealing term. A verse often written in autograph books in the first quarter of this century reads:

> Keep a watch on your words, my darling,
> For words are wonderful things.
> They are sweet like the bees' fresh honey,
> And, like bees, they have terrible stings.

In this last quarter of the twentieth century, teachers of English have an immense responsibility to their students in the area of words. Traditional vocabulary study is fine, and we all hope students learn to distinguish "affect" from "effect," but unless we help them to distinguish words that inform from words that persuade; words that state from words that slant; words that clarify from words that deceive—we will have failed to arm them for "The War of the Words" that they will have to fight competently and knowledgeably if they are to maintain integrity of both mind and soul. (Wells quite likely would allow the pun and approve our tactics.) In "Politics and the Study of Language," H. Thomas McCracken states, "If English teach-

143

ers don't have a mandate to analyze political language with their students, I don't know who does." It is not only political language that must be scrutinized, however, but the whole range of what has come to be called public doublespeak, including as it does statements (and "misstatements") of politicians and government spokesmen; the gyrations of advertisers; and the views of current events and contemporary life as presented—and even created—by the mass media.

The first problem in waging war against public doublespeak is the tactical one of deciding on a battle plan. Language manipulation can be studied within a variety of frameworks, some of which will be sketched briefly here. Furthermore, much of the material needed for one approach is similarly useful for another so that teachers who want students to evaluate ideas from more than one viewpoint can use the same material in more than one study unit.

I   An Introduction to Semantics and Logical Fallacies
A workable way to get into semantics is to assign a dictionary lesson on such terms as etymology; etymologist; semantics; semanticist; linguistics; linguist; jargon; euphemism; gobbledygook; inference; judgment; report; objective; and subjective. Ask students to prepare answers to questions like these:

1   At this point in your life, how do you feel when you are called a *child?* a *kid?* a *teenager?* an *adolescent?* a *young adult?* If these terms cause you to react differently, can you explain why?

2   If you possessed little or no money, would you prefer to be called *poor, needy, indigent,* or a *person of low economic status?* Why?

3   Are the intentions and interpretations the same for *Negro, nigger, black, colored, a person of color?* How much depends on who the speaker and the listener are?

4   If you were 65 years old or older, would you prefer to be called an *old person,* an *elderly person,* or a *senior citizen?* Explain your preference.

5   Do *cop, pig, policeman, patrolman* say the same thing? If not, why not?

6   Do *shameful* and *shameless* have the same meaning? Explain.

7   Does *termination of pregnancy* sound the same as *abortion?* If not, why not?

8   Do words like *grace, charm, wit* sound masculine or feminine to you? Explain, giving sample sentences.

9 Figure out what "purr-words" and "snarl-words" are and
   give examples of each. Discuss the reasons for your choices.
10 Guess at the meanings of one relatively new term, *newspeak*, and one very recently coined term, *public doublespeak*. Give examples.

Good class discussions of these questions should amplify students' understanding of their own attitudes and those of others
toward the same words. Following the discussions, let students
practice writing straight reports; deliberately complimentary accounts full of purr-words; deliberately derogatory descriptions
full of snarl-words. Lead them to see how straight reporting
differs from judgments and inferences. Having students write
paraphrases of a variety of selections, from fairly simple to
more complex ones, is a useful way to determine how much
they have learned about what words do and how they do it.

Discovering emotional overtones and word shadings and color-
ings is most effectively accomplished inductively. Likewise, students learn more about semantics, its methods and objectives,
from working with semantic problems than by reading about
them or hearing lectures. At this point, it is also helpful to
review or study logic and logical fallacies. Most students react
enthusiastically to "puzzles" like

> Nothing is better than freedom.
> Prison is better than nothing.
> Therefore, prison is better than freedom.

and

> All rabbits like carrots.
> You like carrots.
> Therefore, you are a rabbit.

Once they know the importance of establishing the definition
and the distribution of terms, students can analyze other forms
of equivocation. The witches' prophecies in *Macbeth* are an
excellent example. Ask students to write the prophecies in a
left-hand column and in the right-hand column the events or
statements that finally show Macbeth he's been had.

They will also profit from a study of the *non sequitur*. Television commercials are a particularly rich lode to mine: a "problem" is dramatized, a certain brand of beer is hawked, and a
voice proclaims, "Beer X—because we're all in this together."
A closely related fallacy, *post hoc ergo propter hoc*, likewise is
staple fare: taking a patent medicine will make a wife more

dearly loved and cherished by a husband who looks out at us and says, "My wife: she takes care of herself, and I love her for it."

Another device that should be studied is *argumentum ad hominem*. "The fact that Senator Gruening is 81 years old will not be an issue in this campaign," Mike Gravel said when he ran against and defeated Gruening in 1968. More serious personal attacks like mud-slinging sometimes boomerang, although the smear tactics and hate sheets used by some Nixon supporters in 1972 did not elect Humphrey or Jackson.

A trap students need to recognize and avoid is the *false analogy*. Students are especially fond of dismissing advice from elders by insisting that parents and other oldsters cannot possibly understand how students feel. Young people looking for excuses to experiment with drugs, for example, often say, "You can't judge it if you haven't tried it." Married couples argue from shaky ground when they say that an unmarried person cannot possibly be a good marriage counselor. A little reflection, however, reveals that it is not necessary to break one's leg to know that a broken bone is painful. A little thought also shows that although no man has ever given birth, an obstetrician can be male, and an obstetrician is usually more of an expert on pregnancy and delivery than the most fruitful mother.

If we succeed in helping students to understand *rationalization*, we may very well be doing them a lifelong favor:

a   I failed Miss Prim's algebra test. She never liked me anyway.
b   Boys only go out with girls who go all the way, so I have no choice but to give in.
c   Nobody in my family ever went to college. Besides, I'd really rather drive a truck.

The person who goes through life being fooled and manipulated by others is a pitiful object, of course, but the person who never learns to overcome self-deception is a fool indeed.

II   Political Fact and Fiction
Going from an introduction to semantics and to logical fallacies to the study of political language is both easy and sensible. If students have really learned how to detect deliberate language manipulation, they are ready to tackle something like this:

> Since the Supreme Court's decision twelve days ago,
> I have ordered my counsel to analyze the sixty-four
> tapes, and I have listened to a number of them my-

self. This process has made it clear that portions of
the tapes of these June 23 conversations are at variance with certain of my previous statements. (First
two sentences of the fifth paragraph of a statement
issued by Richard Nixon on August 5, 1974.)

The convolutions of the second sentence are truly marvelous.
What "process" has made *what* clear? Does Nixon mean that a
Supreme Court decision on July 24 was necessary before he
could know that one statement was "at variance" with another?
Was the "variance" made clear because his counsel analyzed
sixty-four tapes? Or was his listening to "a number" himself
the "process" that "made it clear that portions of the tapes of
these June 23 conversations are at variance with certain of my
previous statements"? What is the meaning of "since" in the
first statement? Is it a reference to a passage of time, or is it
a way of stating cause? In the second statement, what does
"at variance" mean? If "portions of the tapes" are "at variance
with certain . . . statements," has he admitted that he lied?
How powerful a smokescreen is the sheer bulk of words? (Later,
students can compare newspeak negatives like *uncold, unlight,*
and *ungood* with "untrue," "not entirely candid," and "at
variance.")

Students will be intrigued to discover what they can make of
this:

Objective considerations of contemporary phenomena
compel the conclusion that success or failure in competitive activities exhibits no tendency to be commensurate with innate capacity, but that a considerable element of the unpredictable must invariably be
taken into account.

Give them copies of this rewriting by Orwell with instructions
to "translate" it. Let students compare what they have managed to do with it, and then give them copies of the Biblical
passage:

I returned and saw under the sun, that the race is not
to the swift, nor the battle to the strong, neither yet
bread to the wise, nor yet riches to men of understanding, nor yet favor to men of skill; but time and
chance happeneth to them all.

Students will now be in a better position to appreciate Orwell's
"Politics and the English Language."

The next reading assignment should be *Animal Farm.* If we
can help students see something more in this classic than "a

satire on Communism," a sort of inevitable reaction, they can do a great deal of exploring and learning about language. What kinds of words are used by the leaders of the revolution? Compare the speeches of Major and Napoleon. What actions does Napoleon take to insure the effectiveness of his public speaking? Study the song and the commandments. Compare the original commandments with the revised version. Define the evolution of "equal." If all are "equal" but some are "more equal" than others, then what does "equal" mean? Finally, ask students to compare the quality of life before and after the pigs and their comrades have replaced the farmer. What has actually happened? Has life changed for any of the animals? Which ones? How? Can we draw any generalizations about human life from this fable?

If students have become real fans of Orwell, and most will have, proceed to a study of *1984*, a future that is uncomfortably close at hand. Other obvious reading choices here include *Brave New World; A Clockwork Orange; Childhood's End; Space Odyssey: 2001; I, Robot; Fahrenheit 451;* and *We,* all of which deal with devastating changes in every aspect of human life. A study of what happens to language and what happens because of language focuses on social and political changes and makes a study of these fictional worlds more manageable. However, a study of Orwell's "newspeak" is the single most helpful step to take now.

Before reading *1984,* give students a list of selected terms, asking them for sample definitions and sentences:

Newspeak	doublepluscold
doublethink	uncold
speedwise	unlight
pluscold	undark

One of the first word forms students will spot as familiar is "speedwise," since they have become accustomed to hearing such novelties as "price-wise" and "time-wise." Furthermore, a Madison Avenue creation like "Uncola" renders "uncold" and "undark" more accessible. Language mutation and mutilation are facts of life students must learn to deal with in very practical and realistic terms. Help them see that while "speedful" or "unlight" may be awkward, backward ways of thinking and speaking, such word forms are fairly innocuous. The danger lies in the fact that such tampering prepares the way for other, far more ominous changes like:

ungood   (bad)

goodthink	(orthodoxy or to think in an orthodox manner)
crimethink	or thoughtcrime ("All words grouping themselves round the concept of liberty and equality . . . were contained in the single word *crimethink* . . . .")
thinkpol	(Thought Police)
Minipax	(Ministry of Peace, i.e., Ministry of War)
joycamp	(forced-labor camp)

By consulting a source like *Vital Speeches*, students can compare what politicians, government spokesmen, and other public figures have said over the past few months and years with what has actually come to pass. Few pronouncements are as sobering in retrospect, for example, as statements of the past decade about American involvement in Viet Nam. It's depressing as well to review the words, words, words about our economic situation. Students cannot fail to respond to the doubletalk and doublethink of phrases like "protective reaction," "de-escalation," "Vietnamization," or "cautious optimism." We must accept the fact that we live in the age of the instant cliché. (Today what woman in her right mind would believe the fellow who promises a "meaningful relationship"?) Nonetheless, tags and slogans must be recognized and dealt with for what they are: noise—noise that may be deliberately created to be diversionary. Simply hearing or reading "War is Peace" or "Some are more equal than others" or "The economy is on the upswing" or "This billion-dollar weapon will preserve world peace" does not make it so. We must remember with full horror that if Winston Smith can come to love Big Brother, any "impossibility" can become a reality.

Other selections which focus on politics and/or power-plays are *All the King's Men, Babbitt, Elmer Gantry, Catch-22, The Butterfly Revolution, Lord of the Flies*, and even *A Farewell to Arms*, useful for Henry's recognition that words like "sacred, glorious, and sacrifice and the expression in vain" are embarrassing, even obscene. *Johnny Got His Gun* likewise pits the individual human being against the monstrous concretions of "glory" and "honor." And if ever a group of words deserved the closest kind of study, it is Doc Daneeka's explanation of the twenty-second catch to Yossarian in *Catch-22*. If your students can find the logical loopholes here, congratulate yourself on having done a superior job with the syllogism.

We ought to capitalize on the nostalgia craze before it dies out and give our students a healthy dose of early twentieth-century

history, especially of Nazi Germany. Whether or not they read
all or part of *Mein Kampf, The Rise and Fall of the Third Reich,
The Diary of Anne Frank, Inside the Third Reich, Night,* and
Man's Search for Meaning, use filmstrips and photographs to
help them see that Hitler, et al., relied as heavily on nonverbal
language as they did on the big lie to manipulate people. The
language of the uniform lines and clothes, the goose-step and
"Heil Hitler" salute, the red and black flag, and the symbolic
power of the swastika all contributed to the mass hysteria that
became the Germany of the '30s and '40s. This is also the
time to study traditional propaganda. Students need enough
background concerning the Institute for Propaganda Analysis
to know that it defined propaganda, classified it into seven
types, and began issuing bulletins in 1937. Making posters and
scrapbooks of political cartoons, speeches, campaign strategies,
editorials, and advertisements, accompanied by analyses, offers
students valuable experience in dealing with conventional propaganda devices.

III Madison Avenue and All That
Studying propaganda techniques and power politics is the finest
sort of preparation for a study of modern advertising. It becomes harder, justifiably so, for the Joe Namaths of the world
to make students believe in the sincerity of their commercial
pitches once students know something about the testimonial,
and it doesn't take students long to recognize that eating cereal
("organic," yet) *alfresco* in what appears to be "the country"
is a variation on the old theme of plain folks. Students, in fact,
are authorities of a kind on the television commercial, the electronic folklore they've grown up with. Give a word association
test and you'll probably discover that "case" makes them think
of "Coke" which in turn makes them think of "the real thing."
A Sunday school teacher I knows swears that some years ago
at a church picnic when she asked a five-year-old, "What'll you
have?" the little girl's reply, as instantaneous as an involuntary
reaction, was, "Pabst Blue Ribbon."

Student parodies of commercials produce real gems, like seeing
Mr. Wipple and a couple of giggly housewives squeezed to
death by giant packages of Charmin or watching a finally ex-
asperated housewife strangle the chanter of "Ring-around-the-
collar" with a large, visibly dirt-ringed "Rope-around-the-neck."
Don't tell your colleagues to whom Wordsworth and his every
word are sacrosanct, but substituting "Television" for "The
World" in his "too-much-with-us" sonnet produces clever parody and valuable insights:

Television is too much with us; late and soon,
Lounging and glaring, we lay waste our hours;
We have given our integrity away, a sordid boon!
The Screen that bares its face to us goons;
The Noises that will be crackling at all hours;
For this, and the loss of conversation, we are in doom;
We move not—Great God! I'd rather be
Too poor to own a TV—innocent born
Of this invention, enjoying talk and tea,
Seeing real sights that would make me less forlorn;
Smiles and tears I could feel and see;
Laughter—not audio difficulty to make me mourn.

> Ramona Mullican, English 401
> Loreauville High School

But in addition to the fun and games of techniques like these, we need to offer students a more serious approach to a serious problem.

Vendors today are not content simply to sell their wares; they are creating and attempting to sell life styles. The Ancient Greeks created gods in the image of man; today we create men and women and children in whatever images we choose. An old and respected cosmetics firm has allowed one of its perfumes to be used as the vehicle to sell the "new man" and the "new woman," perhaps in the hope that these new people will sell the perfume. We hear from the screen (or read from a magazine ad): "I used to think that being more of a man meant having fifteen-inch biceps. Today I think it means being strong enough to be gentle," and "I used to think being more of a woman meant acting hard to get. Today I think it means not acting at all." The *coup de grace:* "Want him to be more of a man? Try being more of a woman," juxtaposed neatly against the perfume being sold. The problem is not with the perfume, which we may or may not find pleasant to smell, but with the creation of these "with-it" people. If viewers know their own minds, if they know what basic considerations concern them in choosing a product, that's fine. It's the uncritical, unsophisticated, uninformed, unarmed viewer we must educate. Decisions on what to eat, what to wear, what to drive, what movies to see ought to be made with full knowledge of the battle the manufacturers and advertisers are waging. We don't want to be like the man in a cartoon some years ago who sat before the television set trying to explain to his wife, who'd just come in carrying bags of groceries, what had happened to him. The remains of a home permanent were on the floor and his hair was

set in curlers. The caption: "I don't know what came over me."
Our students need to know so that they *won't* be overcome.

Recently the selling of floor-care products has been adjusted
to the fact that more women, once housewives only, are now
working outside the home as well. "But I promised myself,"
one bright-eyed young thing says, "that when I went back to
work, home still came first so I use Brand X and my floors are
still beautiful." *What* is being sold, the necessity to keep the
floors as beautiful as though she could spend all day doing
them, or a particular brand of cleaner? *How* is it being sold?
Is fear of being "less" of a woman because she is working outside the home created and exploited?

What groups of people are the targets of advertising campaigns?
How can they defend themselves? A helpful approach here is
to adapt the 5 W's of reporting to the analysis of television
commercials:

Who is doing the selling?
What is being offered for sale?
How is it being offered?
What is the setting?
To whom is the product being offered?
What appeals are being used to gain favor with this group?
How can we recognize what is happening?

These last two are the most crucial and difficult questions to
answer.

Ask students to find out about the designing, producing, and
financing of television commercials; to study marketing research techniques; and to discover the salaries of people like
Madge the Manicurist. How do students feel when they
compare the earnings of performers in commercials with those
of professional people like doctors, professors, college presidents,
even elected officials like governors and senators? What does it
say about our sense of values when we learn that the model, as
"THE GIRL" for a particular brand of cosmetics, earns as
much as the President of the United States?

Use the emergent expertise of your students to increase everyone's awareness of what happens in commercials. For example,
the musicians among them can listen to the musical background
of several different car commercials and help us hear the economic quality of music as used by ad-merchants. A car whose
chief appeal is its miles per gallon is not backed up by the
same kind of music that accompanies the selling of admittedly

luxurious cars designed for those of "discriminating taste." Let
the home economics major analyze food commercials and do
comparisons of "convenience" foods and dishes made "from
scratch." Other students will be interested to know the differences in nutrition, price, and preparation time. Business
students can test their shorthand ability by trying to take
verbatim accounts of network and local news programs. Journalism majors and others who volunteer can become class television monitors and reporters. Divide them into groups of CBS,
ABC, and NBC watchers. Students who have tape recorders
can use them to record the audio portion while writing reports
of what they see. Comparing these accounts in class will demonstrate quite plainly that: (1) we don't always see the same
thing even when we look at the same thing, and (2) the same
event reported by different news agencies often appears to have
varying degrees of significance. A few examples of optical
illusions presented in class will also show that we don't always
see what we think we see:

There

Was An

An Old Woman

Do this up as a book cover and show it on an overhead projector. Most students are startled to discover that they do
not, at first, spot the double determiner. Then hand out copies
of the illustration, because students will want to measure the
lines to prove the truth to themselves.

Which line is
longer, a or b?   a   b

After students have analyzed why they buy one brand of blue
jeans, shirt, record, toothpaste, car, pizza, etc., and not another,
introduce them to Fromm's theory of "personality packaging"
in today's marketplace society as he develops it in *The Art of
Loving*. People ought to know if they are being made into
Barbie and Ken dolls or their black counterparts.

Try to scrounge up enough copies of two or three different

daily and weekly newspapers so that each student has a set. Study the headline, lead story and editorial of a small town daily and compare the same features in a metropolitan paper of the same date. How can differences and similarities be accounted for? Can students begin to see "vested interests"?

An essay that every student should have a copy of is Marchette Chute's "Getting At The Truth." It is the truth, not the triteness, of a saying like "He has an ax to grind" that must be impressed on our students.

But the mass media are here to stay. Furthermore, we have no quarrel with producers and editors who respect the power they wield and make special efforts to get at the truth. In order to appraise television fairly, we must study and analyze its positive aspects as well as its weaknesses. Divide students into debating teams and stage a series of "Great Debates about Television." Have the student audience decide, by secret ballot, which teams are more persuasive and why. Have other teams debate the pros and cons of magazine and newspaper reporting and the advertising techniques of these two, as well as radio and billboard advertisements, paying particular attention to word forms and changes. Ask students to begin keeping lists of abbreviated or telescoped words. Such a list will probably include *home ec, PE, phone, TV*, and *bus*. They need to know that these word forms limit the possibility of word association and thereby thought association. *Home ec*, for example, has a single, specific, quite limited meaning, while the complete "home economics" can make us think of many ideas other than studying sewing and cooking in school. *Home* can make us think of "Home is where the heart is" and "Home is where when you go there they have to take you in" and "Home sweet home" and "Home at last." All these thoughts connote warmth, love, peace, family, security. *Economics* can make us think of economical, saving, conserving, using short cuts, the economics of the free enterprise system, and the intrusion of economics upon our way of life.

Making critical listeners and viewers, and responsible thinkers, readers, and writers out of our students is a formidable task, but the need to perform this task and the rewards for accomplishing it are equally great. Although we will never have absolute freedom of choice, the less manipulated we are by language deception, the nearer we come to being free to control our own lives. As one of my students said in a class discussion recently about the ethics involved in high-pressure selling, even when what is being sold is something we approve of: "But it's the truth that's important. That's where it's at, man."

The War of the Words: A Reading List

Asimov, Isaac, *I: Robot.*
Bradbury, Ray. *Fahrenheit 451.*
Burgess, Anthony. *A Clockwork Orange.*
Butler, William. *The Butterfly Revolution.*
Clarke, Arthur C. *Childhood's End.*
————. *Space Odyssey: 2001.*
Chute, Marchette. *"Getting At The Truth."*
Frank, Anne. *The Diary of a Young Girl.*
Frankl, Viktor. *Man's Search for Meaning.*
Fromm, Erich. *The Art of Loving.*
————. *Escape from Freedom.*
Golding, William. *Lord of the Flies.*
Hayakawa, S. I. *Language in Thought and Action.* (2nd ed.)
————. *Symbol, Status, and Personality.*
Heller, Joseph. *Catch-22.*
Hemingway, Ernest. *A Farewell to Arms.*
Hitler, Adolph. *Mein Kampf.*
Huxley, Aldous. *Brave New World.*
Lewis, Sinclair. *Babbitt.*
————. *Elmer Gantry.*
McCracken, H. Thomas. "Politics and the Study of Language," *English Education,* V (December, 1973—January, 1974), 73–78.
Orwell, George. *Animal Farm.*
————. *1984.*
————. "Politics and the English Language."
Shirer, William. *The Rise and Fall of the Third Reich.*
Speer, Albert. *Inside the Third Reich.*
Trumbo, Dalton. *Johnny Got His Gun.*
Vital Speeches of the Day. Semi-monthly since 1934.
Warren, Robert Penn. *All the King's Men.*
Wiesel, Elie. *Night.*
Zamyatin, Yevgeny, *WE.*

The Language of Advertising Claims

Jeffrey Schrank
Learning Seed Company

High school students, and many teachers, are notorious believers in their immunity to advertising. These naive inhabitants of consumerland believe that advertising is childish, dumb, a bunch of lies, and influences only the vast hordes of the less sophisticated. Their own purchases are made purely on the basis of value and desire, with advertising playing only a minor supporting role. They know about Vance Packard and his "hidden persuaders" and the adwriter's psychosell and bag of persuasive magic. They are not impressed.

Advertisers know better. Although few people admit to being greatly influenced by ads, surveys and sales figures show that a well-designed advertising campaign has dramatic effects. A logical conclusion is that advertising works below the level of conscious awareness and it works even on those who claim immunity to its message. Ads are designed to have an effect while being laughed at, belittled, and all but ignored.

A person unaware of advertising's claim on him or her is precisely the one most defenseless against the adwriter's attack. Advertisers delight in an audience which believes ads to be harmless nonsense, for such an audience is rendered defenseless by its belief that there is no attack taking place. The purpose of a classroom study of advertising is to raise the level of awareness about the persuasive techniques used in ads. One way to do this is to analyze ads in microscopic detail. Ads can be studied to detect their psychological hooks, they can be used to gauge values and hidden desires of the common person, they can be studied for their use of symbols, color, and imagery. But perhaps the simplest and most direct way to study ads is through an analysis of the language of the advertising claim.

The "claim" is the verbal or print part of an ad that makes some claim of superiority for the product being advertised. After studying claims, students should be able to recognize those that are misleading and accept as useful information those that are true. A few of these claims are downright lies, some are honest statements about a truly superior product, but most fit into the category of neither bold lies nor helpful consumer information. They balance on the narrow line between truth and falsehood by a careful choice of words.

The reason so many ad claims fall into this category of pseudo-information is that they are applied to parity products, products in which all or most of the brands available are nearly identical. Since no one superior product exists, advertising is used to create the illusion of superiority. The largest advertising budgets are devoted to parity products such as gasoline, cigarettes, beer and soft drinks, soaps, and various headache and cold remedies.

The first rule of parity involves the Alice in Wonderlandish use of the words "better" and "best." In parity claims, "better" means "best" and "best" means "equal to." If all the brands are identical they must all be equally good, the legal minds have decided. So "best" means that the product is as good as the other superior products in its category. When Bing Crosby declares Minute Maid Orange Juice "the best there is" he means it is as good as the other orange juices you can buy.

The word "better" has been legally interpreted to be a comparative and therefore becomes a clear claim of superiority. Bing could not have said that Minute Maid is "better than any other orange juice." "Better" is a claim of superiority. The only time "better" can be used is when a product does indeed have superiority over other products in its category or when the better is used to compare the product with something other than competing brands. An orange juice could therefore claim to be "better than a vitamin pill," or even "the better breakfast drink."

The second rule of advertising claim analysis is simply that if any product is truly superior, the ad will say so very clearly and will offer some kind of convincing evidence of the superiority. If an ad hedges the least bit about a product's advantage over the competition you can strongly suspect it is not superior— maybe equal to but not better. You will never hear a gasoline company say "we will give you four miles per gallon more in your car than any other brand." They would love to make such a claim, but it would not be true. Gasoline is a parity product, and, in spite of some very clever and deceptive ads of a few years ago, no one has yet claimed one brand of gasoline better than any other brand.

To create the necessary illusion of superiority, advertisers usually resort to one or more of the following ten basic techniques. Each is common and easy to identify.

1 The Weasel Claim

A weasel word is a modifier that practically negates the claim that follows. The expression "weasel word" is aptly named after the egg-eating habits of weasels. A weasel will suck out the inside of an egg, leaving it appear intact to the casual observer. Upon examination, the egg is discovered to be hollow. Words or claims that appear substantial upon first look but disintegrate into hollow meaninglessness on analysis are weasels. Commonly used weasel words include "helps" (the champion weasel); "like" (used in a comparative sense); "virtual" or "virtually"; "acts" or "works"; "can be"; "up to"; "as much as"; "refreshes"; "comforts"; "tackles"; "fights"; "come on"; "the feel of"; "the look of"; "looks like"; "fortified"; "enriched"; and "strengthened."

Samples of Weasel Claims

"Helps control dandruff *symptoms* with *regular use."* The weasels include "helps control," and possibly even "symptoms,"

and "regular use." The claim is not "stops dandruff."

"Leaves dishes *virtually* spotless." We have seen so many ad claims that we have learned to tune out weasels. You are supposed to think "spotless," rather than "virtually" spotless.

"Only half the price of *many* color sets." "Many" is the weasel. The claim is supposed to give the impression that the set is inexpensive.

"Tests confirm one mouthwash *best* against mouth odor."

"Hot Nestlés' cocoa is the very *best.*" Remember the "best" and "better" routine.

"Listerine *fights* bad breath." "Fights" not "stops."

"Lots of things have changed, but Hershey's *goodness* hasn't." This claim does not say that Hershey's chocolate hasn't changed.

"Bacos, the crispy garnish that tastes just *like* its name."

2   The Unfinished Claim

The unfinished claim is one in which the ad claims the product is better, or has more of something but does not finish the comparison.

Samples of Unfinished Claims

"Magnavox gives you more." More what?

"Anacin: Twice as much of the pain reliever doctors recommend most." This claim fits in a number of categories but it does not say twice as much of what pain reliever.

"Supergloss does it with more color, more shine, more sizzle, more!"

"Coffee-mate gives coffee more body, more flavor." Also note that "body" and "flavor" are weasels.

"You can be sure if it's Westinghouse." Sure of what?

"Scott makes it better for you."

"Ford LTD—700% quieter."

When the FTC asked Ford to substantiate this claim, Ford revealed that they meant the inside of the Ford was 700% quieter than the outside.

3   The "We're Different and Unique" Claim

This kind of claim states that there is nothing else quite like the product advertised. For example, if Schlitz would add pink food coloring to its beer they could say "There's nothing like new pink Schlitz." The uniqueness claim is supposed to be interpreted by readers as a claim to superiority.

Samples of "We're Different and Unique" Claim

"There's no other mascara like it."

"Only Doral has this unique filter system."

"Cougar is like nobody else's car."

"Either way, liquid or spray, there's nothing else like it."

"If it doesn't say Goodyear, it can't be polyglas." "Polyglas" is a trade name copyrighted by Goodyear. Goodrich or Firestone could make a tire exactly identical to the Goodyear one and yet couldn't call it "polyglas"—a name for fiberglass belts.

"Only Zenith has chromacolor." Same as the "polyglas" gambit. Admiral has solarcolor and RCA has accucolor.

4 The "Water is Wet" Claim

"Water is wet" claims say something about the product that is true for any brand in that product category, (e.g., "Schrank's water is really wet.") The claim is usually a statement of fact, but not a real advantage over the competition.

Samples of "Water is Wet" Claim

"Mobil: the Detergent Gasoline." Any gasoline acts as a cleaning agent.

"Great Lash greatly increases the diameter of every lash."

"Rheingold, the natural beer." Made from grains and water as are other beers.

"SKIN smells differently on everyone." As do many perfumes.

5 The "So What" Claim

This is the kind of claim to which the careful reader will react by saying "So What?" A claim is made which is true but which gives no real advantage to the product. This is similar to the "water is wet" claim except that it claims an advantage which is not shared by most of the other brands in the product category.

Samples of the "So What" Claim

"Geritol has more than twice the iron of ordinary supplements." But is twice as much beneficial to the body?

"Campbell's gives you tasty pieces of chicken and not one but two chicken stocks." Does the presence of two stocks improve the taste?

"Strong enough for man but made for a woman." This deodorant claim says only that the product is aimed at the female market.

6 The Vague Claim

The vague claim is simply not clear. This category often overlaps with others. The key to the vague claim is the use of words that are colorful but meaningless, as well as the use of subjective and emotional opinions that defy verification. Most contain weasels.

Samples of the Vague Claim

"Lips have never looked so luscious." Can you imagine trying to either prove or disprove such a claim?

"Lipsavers are fun—they taste good, smell good and feel good."

"Its deep rich lather makes hair feel good again."

"For skin like peaches and cream."

"The end of meatloaf boredom."

"Take a bite and you'll think you're eating on the Champs Elysées."

"Winston tastes good like a cigarette should."

"The perfect little portable for all around viewing with all the features of higher priced sets."

"Fleishman's makes sensible eating delicious."

7   The Endorsement or Testimonial
A celebrity or authority appears in an ad to lend his or her stellar qualities to the product. Sometimes the people will actually claim to use the product, but very often they don't. There are agencies surviving on providing products with testimonials.

Samples of Endorsements or Testimonials

"Joan Fontaine throws a shot-in-the-dark party and her friends learn a thing or two."

"Darling, have you discovered Masterpiece? The most exciting men I know are smoking it." (Eva Gabor)

"Vega is the best handling car in the U.S." This claim was challenged by the FTC, but GM answered that the claim is only a direct quote from *Road and Track* magazine.

8   The Scientific or Statistical Claim
This kind of ad uses some sort of scientific proof or experiment, very specific numbers, or an impressive sounding mystery ingredient.

Samples of Scientific or Statistical Claims

"Wonder Bread helps build strong bodies 12 ways." Even the weasel "helps" did not prevent the FTC from demanding this ad be withdrawn. But note that the use of the number 12 makes the claim far more believable than if it were taken out.

"Easy-Off has 33% more cleaning power than another popular brand." "Another popular brand" often translates as some other kind of oven cleaner sold somewhere. Also the claim does not say Easy-Off works 33% better.

"Special Morning—33% more nutrition." Also an unfinished claim.

"Certs contains a sparkling drop of Retsyn."

"ESSO with HTA."

"Sinarest. Created by a research scientist who actually gets sinus headaches."

9 The "Compliment the Consumer" Claim
This kind of claim butters up the consumer by some form of flattery.

Samples of "Compliment the Consumer" Claim

"We think a cigar smoker is someone special."

"If what you do is right for you, no matter what others do, then RC Cola is right for you."

"You pride yourself on your good home cooking. . . ."

"The lady has taste."

"You've come a long way, baby."

10 The Rhetorical Question
This technique demands a response from the audience. A question is asked and the viewer or listener is supposed to answer in such a way as to affirm the product's goodness.

Samples of the Rhetorical Questions

"Plymouth—isn't that the kind of car America wants?"

"Shouldn't your family be drinking Hawaiian Punch?"

"What do you want most from coffee? That's what you get most from Hills."

"Touch of Sweden: could your hands use a small miracle?"

Suggestions for a Unit on Advertising Interpretation

1 Collect, categorize, and analyze advertising claims according to the ten techniques presented in this article. Remember that there may be some other types of claims and that some are difficult to classify completely in any one category. Look for advertising claims that fit "category 11"—honest and useful consumer information.

2 Compare product claims with the product. Construct a

series of tests to verify the claims made about a particular product.

3   Rewrite ad claims so they give information that would help a customer make a wise buying decision. Write honest ads that correct ads you consider misleading.

4   Write manufacturers and ask them to back up the claims they present in their corporate advertising. A college class in marketing tried this and found that many companies did not respond and very few took up the challenge.

5   Find the emotional hooks in ads. This would include appeals to status, security, acceptance, patriotism, happiness, etc. Vance Packard is still a most useful source of ideas.

6   Select some parity product and write advertising claims for it, illustrating each of the ten techniques explained in this article. For example, if you select a mousetrap as your parity product (not the "better" mousetrap, just an ordinary one) your ad claims might include:

   a. Weasel "Often helps control your rodent problems."
   b. Unfinished "Kills rats better and faster."
   c. We're Unique "Only Imperial mousetraps have the unique Imperial craftsmanship behind them."
   d. Water is wet "Spring action mousetrap."
   e. So what? "Made with finest knotty pine and tempered steel. Uses any kind of cheese as bait and comes in a variety of sizes."
   f. Vague claim "Imperial mousetraps are easy to operate, effective, and can make you feel like a new person again without that annoying gnawing fear of being eaten alive by a hungry mouse."
   g. Endorsement "None of my friends will ever go near an Imperial mousetrap. Believe me."—Mickey Mouse
   h. Scientific claim "Works 33% faster than another popular brand under normal conditions."
   i. Compliment "For the man whose time is too important to to spend hunting mice."
   j. Rhetorical question "Shouldn't your family have the feeling of Imperial safety?"

Advertising Bibliography

I Can Sell You Anything by Carl Wrighter (Ballantine, $1.25) is aptly subtitled "How I Made Your TV Commercial with Minimum Truth and Maximum Consequences." The book is useable for student reading in spite of the sloppy writing and almost nonexistent research. He manages to draw on his own vast experience as an ad writer to explain how claims in ads are made to sound like they promise the world, when, in fact, they merely declare it to be more round then square. The book changed my approach to advertising and enables the readers to distinguish the phony ads from those which announce a superior product. The classification of the claims in this article is partly based on Wrighter's ideas. *I Can Sell You Anything* is especially good in communications units, since it concentrates not on the emotional or psychological manipulation but on the very careful wording of ads. Thousands of examples, fifth-grade reading level, and an eye-opener. Far from perfect but very likely the best student book on advertising currently available.

The Hidden Persuaders by Vance Packard (Pocket Books, 95¢) is practically a classic and still useable in spite of its age. Packard's look at the emotional and motivational side of the ads is a nice contrast and supplement to Wrighter's linguistic approach.

Down the Tube by Terry Galanoy (Pinnacle Books, $1.25) is an "adman gives a behind-the-scenes tour of the making of commercials" book. *Down the Tube* reads like a novel and relies heavily on anecdotes about the making of TV commercials. Certainly not as instructive as either Wrighter or Packard but fun to read and with redeeming social value. A fascinating glimpse into the world of TV commercials.

The Permissible Lie: The Inside Truth About Advertising by Sam Sinclair Baker (Beacon Press, $2.95) tells how ads distort the truth, yet it defends the institution of advertising. The book is dated but more comprehensive than *I Can Sell You Anything*. Baker devotes chapters to advertising research, program ratings, government regulations, and even to how to improve what you don't like and how to get the full value from your purchase.

Subliminal Seduction by Wilson Bryan Key (Prentice-Hall, $7.95) is an outrageous book that could serve as the basis for one or more fascinating classes on advertising values.

Remember a few years back when some movie houses experimented with flashing subliminal messages like "Eat popcorn" on the screen so fast they were registered by the eye but not consciously noticed? Angry editorials decried the new technique as an "insidious threat to our privacy." The messages reportedly did have some effect on the audiences but the technique quietly faded from public attention. But subliminal advertising is still very much alive, according to Key. His thesis is that subliminal "embeds" and symbolism have been used secretly in magazines and TV ads for the past fifteen years.

Thousands of ads in major magazines have the word "sex" and four letter words secretly embedded in ice cubes, shadows, and backgrounds. A Hilton Hotel room-service menu has "sex" embedded from breakfast through dinner; the word "sex" saturates the paper cover of Eldridge Cleaver's *Soul on Ice* and even the Sears Catalog is loaded with "fascinating subliminal perversities."

In *Subliminal Seduction*, Key tries to blow the cover on the secret use of subliminal techniques designed to influence readers below the level of awareness. Not only are words camouflaged into ads, but symbols are used with the skill of a Freudian poet. "Commonly used phallic symbolism includes neckties, arrows, flagpoles, automobiles, rockets, pencils, cigars, and cigarettes . . .—the list is endless." Key finds full page color ads (especially for liquor and cigarettes) in major magazines filled with hidden words and sexual symbolism.

To accept all of Key's book requires a highly active imagination and complete suspension of disbelief. The book contains numerous examples; some prove Key frighteningly correct, while others seem little better than interpretations by a college freshman who has just discovered a dictionary of symbolism. But Key's analysis is provocative, never dull, and does serve to alert readers to the fact that magazine ads have quite a bit going on that is missed by 99% of their viewers on a conscious level.

Key is at his best interpreting magazine covers as advertising for the newsstand sales of the publication. He sees a number of *Playboy* covers symbolizing castration and a nursing mother. He analyzes *Cosmopolitan* and *Vogue* as advertising pieces playing to the needs and desires of their intended audiences.

In spite of occasional brilliance, Key is carried away with his own theory. A true believer of *Subliminal Seduction* is probably someone who was also convinced that Beatle Paul McCartney is dead and that Marilyn Monroe was killed by the CIA.

It is difficult to read *Subliminal Seduction* with an open mind and not gain at least an increased awareness of advertising symbolism. A class presentation, complete with slides of some subliminal embeds, is never dull and usually provokes a far-reaching consideration of advertising values.

Speaking of People:
Teaching about Sexism in Language

Sidney J. Hormell
Head, Language Systems, Hawaii English Program

We use language to label everything in our environment, including other people. The study of how we do this may help students better understand how language works and how it is affected by their biases and prejudices, both conscious and unconscious.

How accurately does language reflect reality? How does it change to meet changing reality? How does language determine people's perceptions of reality?

One of the many ways the Hawaii English Program* tries to get at these questions is to study what we call the "language of stereotyping." What do we mean by that?

By its nature, language involves generalization and abstraction, to varying degrees. As the semanticist will tell us, this aspect marks the usefulness, as well as the problems, in using ordinary language for communication. We can "overgeneralize," fitting people or things into oversimplified categories. If they share one trait, it is assumed they share more. This is the "If you've seen one, you've seen 'em all" way of thinking. It's what we call stereotyping.

Individuals are locked into molds much as was the type set

* The Hawaii English Project is an attempt to develop a comprehensive K-12 language arts program for the public schools. As part of the junior high school curriculum we have twelve 4-week units under the rubric "Aspects of Human Communication" which deal with various ways we use language to find our identity and communicate with ourselves, others, and our total environment. One of these units, "Speaking of People," deals directly with questions of language stereotypes.

for a page of a newspaper, from which the term "stereotype" comes. The molds are labeled "girl," "white," "nigger," "hippie," "kid," "old codger," etc.

The heroine of one of our units is an individual who is a young, Hawaiian, left-handed girl. Everyone stereotypes her according to these categories. She is unjustifiably relegated to the bottom of the social heap. She cries out, "Why won't people just let me be *me*?"

Stereotyping is a subtle form of "doublespeak," or deception in language, that permeates all of our communications. Since these "overgeneralizations" often have some general truth in them, they are not recognized as outright "lies." Yet they are concrete examples familiar to students. Therefore, they are excellent subject matter for the exploration of deceptive (and self-deceptive) uses of language.

Let's look at some ideas for classroom activities which explore one type of stereotyping, or deceptive languaging: "sexism." We have found that students, particularly those in the intermediate grades, respond quite dramatically to this issue, for sex identity is a crucial problem they are facing in their lives.

The teacher should be careful not to end up *teaching* stereotypes: reinforcing old ones and adding to the students' repertoires. Once stereotypes are brought into the open and identified, students should examine where they came from, why they are used, what is accurate and inaccurate about them, and how individuals can be identified and described more realistically.

As starters, students could be asked to "brainstorm" descriptions of "boy" or "girl," "man" or "woman." List descriptions in words or phrases. You might try "All girls are _____." Sugar and spice and everything nice? There may be no single activity which would create such passionate discussion (or debate) for a mixed classroom of students. When they do calm down, each sex will be more than ready to poke holes in the negative stereotypes suggested by the other sex. There will be some labels each sex is proud to wear (e.g., boys are "strong," girls are "sexy"). These need to be questioned, as well, through other activities, such as a project of finding examples in stories, newspapers, etc. of individuals who do not fit such descriptions.

Students might draw or write a "profile" of the ideal boy or girl. (A male is strong, handsome, has a good job, likes sports, has a pretty wife or girlfriend?) All of these initial responses can be recorded and used later, after other activities, so that students can compare their initial responses to their later ones. You might try some kind of "semantic differential" questionnaire to get at the feelings and connotations associated with labels. Students would rate "girl" or "boy" on scales of strong-weak, good-bad, heavy-light, hard-soft, active-passive, loud-quiet, hot-cold, etc. Or, you might have students identify mannerisms, behaviors, styles of speaking, clothing, hairstyles, etc. which they feel "symbolize" boys or girls. The fact that clothing and hairstyles are not as "identifying" as they used to be can point up how symbols change and may no longer be useful generalizations.

A fun activity is having girls and boys exchange roles in short plays or role-play situations, observing the exaggerated stereotyping they produce spontaneously, similar to the one-act comedy of some years ago titled "If Men Played Cards As Women Do." A more serious role-play activity would be one which focuses on why one sex negatively stereotypes another. Some reasons are economic, and the protection of a social role. You could have the students role play a hiring situation, in which one sex applies for a job usually held by the other sex. (A boy can play a principal and a girl can apply for a coaching job. The boy must think of reasons why not to hire her, while the girl must counter these reasons.) Students can hunt for examples in newspapers, magazines, or from their own experience of women who have jobs formerly the province of men, and vice versa.

Generate lists of job titles. How many are sexless? Some may not distinguish, such as "engineer," "nurse," "truck driver," "pilot," "minister." Why do people usually say "male nurse" or "lady truck driver?" Some labels suggest sex. Others actually mark it: "waiter" and "waitress," "host" and "hostess," "salesman" and "saleslady." Have students play with possibilities: "ministress?" "carpentress"?

Merchandising and advertising are rich with visual and verbal appeal to sexual stereotypes. Have students hunt for brand names and images and explore their meaning. Why would "Brut" and "Right Guard" deodorants appeal to men, "Virginia Slims" and "Eve" cigarettes appeal to women? What images do advertisers associate with them. (A good side-activity would be identifying our use of pronouns "he" and "she" with inanimate objects or animals. What qualities cause some people to refer to ships as "she" or cars as "he," or refer to all dogs as "he" and all cats as "she.")

You can move in your study of nouns, adjectives and pronouns to the more subtle sex biases of language, which many women's consciousness groups argue reflect male dominance. Why are both sexes referred to as Mankind or Man? Why are business letters usually addressed Dear Sirs, or Gentlemen? Encourage students to find more instances. What could they suggest to defuse generic terms? Personkind, Gentlepersons, etc.? Addressing business letters years ago "Dear Sirs" may have reflected reality more than it does today. Dear SOM (Sir or Madam) may reflect better today's situation. But how strange, radical, or phony does that sound? Is there a different feeling to "bachelor" than there is to "old maid"? They both describe an unmarried adult. Should "unmarried person" be substituted for both?

Language changes to fit changing reality. Revolutionary changes like this could lead students into a discussion of language change and the whole area of euphemisms. What is euphemistic, glossing over difficult issues, and what is conciliatory, redressing imbalance in sexual bias in language?

As with race or ethnicity and age, the language of sexism subtly reflects bias and prejudice. It reinforces a "status quo" in which males, as well as females, are locked into social roles. Those in the less powerful roles are rebelling. The women's movement is one such liberation thrust.

Students have looked at name-calling or labeling, euphemism, and conciliation. Another type of languaging they need to be aware of is that of protest. "Male chauvinist pig" is only one dramatic example. Students should be made aware that in times of revolution, we find not only correctives, but overcorrectives, which become new stereotypes. The image of the passive housewife is suddenly changed to the image of Superwoman. Even the image of God is changed from the Great Father to the Great Mother. The class can hunt examples of visual and verbal stereotypes representing both extremes of bias, and again discuss the accuracy of overgeneralization in describing individual reality. Advertising again, is a perfect resource for such discussion.

A dramatic user of stereotype language is the stereotyped antihero, Archie Bunker. His words have been reproduced on records and in paperback books. They are obviously a popular source for clear-cut sex stereotypes and reverse-stereotypes. Sex stereotypes can readily be found in popular literature, including children's books. If you are so bold, you can encourage your students to hunt for them in school textbooks! But the richest sources for stereotype material are the mass media of radio, TV, movies, magazines and newspapers. The nature of mass media is to condense information into simplified forms or formats.

Informational contents, as well as ads, not only convey stereotypes, but appeal to "stereotypes" in the audience as well. Students should bring to class not only ads which supposedly appeal to males or females, but magazines such as *Argosy* or *Woman's Day*. Examine not only the ads, but the table of contents. What is supposed to be of interest to one sex and not another? Art, cooking, child-rearing for women? Sports, adventure, money-making for men? A parallel activity would be to get students to designate which topics of conversation are most likely among boys, and which among girls. The generalizations may be fairly accurate in describing the situation. Get one sex to read some interesting material from the other's magazines. Some students may admit they found the other material interesting. If so, pursue the point that stereotypes shut each off from opportunities for growth.

You can also explore the "jargons" or styles of writing supposedly appropriate to each sex audience. Students can write their own "spoofs" on how a reporter would write about the same event for a male and for a female audience. (A politician might be described "as quite handsome in his knit suit which fits his trim, 30ish figure.") Such activities could lead to discussion of how we select features of our environment according to cultural biases.

Until recently female viewers of TV had only the extreme models of the "dumb blond" or "sexy chic" or "passive housewife." Now they have the female "super cop" as well. Have students analyze movie and TV characters and discuss what other or alternative models might be needed to better reflect reality. Or, are people just too complex to be represented by *any* hero or heroine?

The newspaper, from whose jargon we got the word "stereotype" in the first place, may be the richest single source for material. Have students examine stories written by and for males or females, general stories and photos which emphasize a person's sex, cartoons, letters to the editor, etc. Where you can find a story about a woman, check that epitome of shorthand generalization, the headline!

To demonstrate the time and space pressures of mass media, which encourage stereotyping, you might assign students to write about sex roles in various formats within a time deadline. Urge them to try to steer clear of stereotyping. Peer evaluation of the efforts will lead quite naturally into a discussion of the inevitability of generalizing in language, the difficulty of avoiding stereotypes, inaccuracies which often arise out of stereotyping, and with luck, some examples of more fair and accurate reporting. We say "more" fair and accurate, for language can never fully describe or encompass the vast dimension and complexities of reality.

The teacher's job is not to foist his or her set of values or biases upon students, but to help the students' awareness and consciousness. Such an exploration into the subtle biases of language use can and should be growth experience for the teacher, as well as an opportunity for students and teacher to better understand sexism in language and the complexities of human nature.

College

The Stylistics of Belief

Julia P. Stanley
University of South Dakota

In theory, at least, language is the possession of every human being on earth. In fact, language remains, to a large extent, the preserve of the powerful who control and affect our lives with their decisions. Through their access to the media, these people have the power to change English as they use it for their own ends. The Madison Avenue copywriters who write advertisements for corporations use our language as it suits them to influence our choices at the store. Politicians use English to convince us to vote for them, or to disguise their motivations and manipulations. Writers of fiction and nonfiction use language to persuade us, their readers, of the validity of their hypotheses and interpretations. Anyone who has access to the media, including television, newspapers, radio, books, and movies, is in a position to control and influence our decisions and opinions. This paper is one approach to beginning to understand how we are manipulated by the powerful through their use of English, and provides us with a method of analyzing what is happening to us.

First, it is necessary to emphasize that language is a social contract. Whenever we speak to another person or to a group of people, whenever we agree to listen to someone else, we have entered into a social contract with that person or persons. Social contracts are arbitrary and subject to change only, presumably, with the agreement of the individuals involved in the contract. English is an arbitrary set of symbols, and, whether we are using that set of symbols as speakers or listeners, we are engaged in the act of carrying out a social contract in which

Editor's Note: This is a revised version of a paper delivered to the Conference on College Composition and Communication, Anaheim, California, April 4-6, 1974. That version is available through the ERIC system: ED 091 693.

the parties to that contract feel justified in assuming certain
"givens." For example, when we participate in a speech act,
either as speakers or listeners, we usually assume that parts of
speech will occur in a predictable order depending upon the
type of sentence necessary for communication. Likewise, we
also assume that those listening to us will understand the meaning of the words we use. As listeners, of course, we can ask
the speaker for clarification if we are unsure of the intended
meaning, but this situation doesn't hold true when we are
readers or members of passive audiences. (By "members of
passive audiences," I mean those situations in which we are
listening to a speaker but do not have the prerogative or the
means to ask questions regarding "intended meaning." Such
situations include: watching television, listening to the radio,
attending large public lectures or debates, or watching a movie.)
When we are in one of the communicative contexts in which we
cannot question the writer or speaker, we are left to our own
devices in trying to make sense of what has been said. Because
of the nature of the electronic and printed media, we are daily
placed in a passive position; that is, we are being talked *at*, not
to, and the range of responses available to us is not very wide.
For example, if you disagree with something that I've said in
this article, or if you aren't sure what I mean by a certain
phrase or sentence, how can you question me? You could write
to me, if you could find me, but would I answer? If I did
answer, you might be even more confused than you were when
you first decided to write to me. Whenever we are members of
a "passive audience," we lose much of our power as agents in
the social contract of language.

The stylistics of belief is the study of the ways in which writers
and speakers manipulate the English language in order to convince us that what they are saying is true and/or meaningful,
or to avoid committing themselves on specific issues. My use
of the term *stylistics* presupposes that there is always more than
one way to express any given idea, that we have available to
us many possible choices for expressing just those meanings we
wish to express. Stylistics is the study of *choices* made by
speakers and writers. My use of the word *belief* refers to the
underlying belief systems of speakers which determine their
choices of language. By analyzing the ways in which English
has been manipulated by the powerful, I hope to make us, the
members of the "passive audience," more powerful than we
are at present.

Two areas of language use will be the focus of my analysis in the pages that follow: 1) syntax (sentence structure); 2) diction (word choice). The use of certain syntactic constructions that deceive or prejudice the judgment of the unwary reader I have elsewhere called *syntactic exploitation*. *Syntactic exploitation* is the use of sentence structures that permit (or require) the deletion of linguistic information, when such deletion occurs in contexts where the reader is unable to recover the deleted information, or in contexts where the recoverability of the deleted information is dependent upon the reader's agreement with what the author is saying. There are two types of syntactic exploitation: 1) The use of deletion to repress information required by the reader or hearer for complete understanding of the message; 2) The use of sentence structure so complicated and involuted that the reader or listener is convinced that there is a message when, in fact, the utterance is meaningless. (I use "meaningless" here to refer to utterances that the audience cannot interpret in context because the utterances fail to satisfy minimal criteria for coherence. My use should not be misconstrued as an atomistic approach to language, which defines language as a sequence of "units" strung together in a linear fashion, and which further assumes that each "unit" has a unique and unchanging "meaning.") Within this second category of syntactic exploitation, there are two additional subcategories of meaningless utterance, although the distinction between the two may not always be clear out of context: 1) Emotional uses of language that occur when the speaker feels the pressure of anxiety or hostility; 2) Utterances that occur when the question put to the speaker involves information to which both the speaker and the hearer have access, although it is usually the speaker who has the most information. This particular type of meaningless utterance is especially favored by those in power, and we know it more widely as THE LIE, that utterance in which there is a discrepancy between what we are told and what we know (or think we know).

Diction is perhaps the most obvious area of language use in which we might expect to find opportunities for manipulation and deceit. However, other writers have explored the possibilities in more detail, and I will examine just two of the several kinds of word choice that are exploitative. The first type of word choice I will discuss is sexist language, terms for women in the vocabulary of English that are derogatory and degrading. Such terms are most often used for their emotional effect, their connotations, the attribution of qualities, stereotyping, and labeling. The second area of word choice to which I will devote some discussion is one that most of us look for only when we are dealing with literature. As I will show, this kind of diction, metaphor, is more widespread, and its effects are more subtle. Metaphors, which involve the underlying assumptions of the speaker, are constructs in which one thing is compared to another for the purposes of exposition, clarification, definition, or emotional effect. [A writer or speaker's choice of metaphors reveals the way in which that writer approaches and interprets the world.] Neither sexist terms nor metaphors are used for deception, although that may be the result of such usage for the uncritical or careless reader. [More often, the selection of derogatory terms and metaphors is made in an effort to persuade others that our opinions are the only "right" ones.]

Up to this point, I have briefly sketched and defined two levels of language use, sentence structures and diction. Certain syntactic structures provide the clever speaker or writer with devices for deceiving listeners or readers, while diction provides a means of presenting a lopsided version of events. Both levels of usage enable the skillful speaker or writer to intimidate an audience or silence opposition by convincing us that statements of opinion (theirs) have the weight of universal consensus behind them or are "facts" that we could verify by our own investigation if we took the time.

The syntactic constructions that permit or require deletion of the agent or experiencer of the predicate include the passive, passive adjectives, nominalized passives, experience predicates (seem, appear), and attributive adjectives (appropriate, inappropriate, proper). According to linguists, the passive and its related constructions permit the deletion of the agent only in contexts where the reader can ascertain the deleted agent from the immediate context in which the sentence occurs. However, the agent can be deleted in contexts where the agent is not specified (as I've just done) without making explicit the agent of the action. In such uses of the passive, deletion of the agent has the effect of either appealing to universal consensus or creating a "generic person," someone or somebody, everyone or everybody, so that the major proposition of the sentence appears to have more validity than it does. In other contexts, deletion of the agent enables the writer to protect those who are responsible for a given action. The examples that follow illustrate uses of the passive to obscure responsibility, to insinuate the existence of a conspiracy, and to shift responsibility to an unnamed "someone."

1 a   Faculty members have to be treated as if they were cogs
        in a machine.

b   Alas, many husbands *are* now *being emasculated* via cig-
    arettes and possibly female hormones *fed* to chickens and
    cattle to tenderize their meat.

c   It is apparent that attention needs to *be given* to com-
    munications, and roles need to *be* more clearly *defined*.

d   You *are authorized* to urge the RLG to begin air attacks
    against Viet Cong infiltration routes and facilities . . .

Note, in particular, the impersonal, authoritarian tone that use
of the passive gives these sentences, making it difficult, if not
impossible, to consider questioning the propositions.

Passive adjectives function in much the same way as the more
familiar passive, but passive adjectives occur immediately before a noun in a modifying position. Their syntactic position
makes them more subtle, because we often do not give them
the scrutiny they should have. The agent *cannot* appear in this
type of nominal construction and we are more likely to miss
the implications of such usage. By using passive adjectives,
writers can slip uncontested assertions past us and force these
propositions on us without having to argue their validity. The
following sentences illustrate how passive adjectives are used by
writers in order to get us to accept an assertion that we might
otherwise reject if it were stated explicitly.

2 a   Men regard as amusing this *exaggerated* fad of trying
       to substitute the "Ms." for "Mrs."

   b   The policy memorandums discuss ways to move these
       audiences in the *desired* direction, through such tech-
       niques as the *controlled* release of information and ap-
       peals to patriotic stereotypes.

   c   Too often we rebel against *accepted* patterns of behavior.

   d   We learn (or should) that to live in an *ordered* society
       we must accept and comply with the laws of Man and
       Nature.

In these examples, the authoritative tone of the passive is increased and the "appeal to authority" implicit in the construction becomes more difficult to question. Sentence 2a is an especially interesting example of the power inherent in a syntactic
construction. The author (Dr. Crane, in his "Worry Clinic")
makes an unsupported claim that substituting "Ms." for "Mrs."
is a "fad," and included as part of this claim is another assertion that the "fad" is "exaggerated." The phrase is nonsense,
although only a few of us would realize this as we were read-

ing. But how does one exaggerate a fad? The phrase sounds even more ridiculous if we begin to question the proposition itself. Bearing in mind that the phrase *exaggerated fad* is an example of the passive adjective, we can ask "by whom" the fad is being "exaggerated," and I give you the possibilities that I can think of.

2 a 1 Men regard as amusing this fad which *women* have exaggerated. . .

　　2 Men regard as amusing this fad which *feminists* have exaggerated. . .

　　3 Men regard as amusing this fad which *someone* has exaggerated. . .

　　4 Men regard as amusing this fad which *everyone* has exaggerated. . .

　　5 Men regard as amusing this fad which *they* have exaggerated. . .

　　6 Men regard as amusing this fad which *Dr. Crane* has exaggerated. . .

This sentence exemplifies the "profundities" to which we expose ourselves when we open a newspaper or turn on the radio.

The nominalized passive, another construction related to the passive sentence, is more complicated than the passive adjective, although deletion of the agent is optional. In nominalized passives, the verbal element of a proposition becomes a noun through the process of nominalization, e.g., *refuse/refusal, destroy/destruction, enjoy/enjoyment, close/closure,* but *use/ use, experience/experience.* The sentences that follow illustrate some of the types of nominalized passive, both with and without the agent.

3 a *Impoundment* of billions of dollars of allocated funds represents an unparalleled *seizure* of power *by the White House.*

　b *Our* almost blind *obedience* to the Presidency has acted to sanction each successive *usurpation* of power and authority *by this institution.*

　c What is needed is more 'intentional' *control,* not less, and this is an important engineering problem.

　d The *misuse* of a technology of behavior is a serious matter.

As these examples show, it is often irrelevant whether or not there is an agent explicitly stated, because the nominalized passive is a useful construction for obfuscation, abstraction, and a vagueness that borders on euphemism. For example, in 3a we learn that "the White House" has seized power, while in 3b it is "this institution" that has usurped power and authority, although we know that it is the man who *inhabits* the White House who has committed these actions.

Experiencer deletion, like the passive and its related constructions, also involves the removal of the person responsible for the perception defined by the predicate. In most usage, we understand that the perception belongs to the speaker or writer, and when the experiencer pronoun is explicit it is usually a first person pronoun. However, as in the case of the deleted agent of the passive construction, the deletion of the experiencer imparts to the statement an impersonal tone of authority, giving a personal observation the weight of "universal consensus." For example, I might say to a friend, "You seem *to me* to be getting careless," or " You seem to be getting careless," and the second version of the sentence implies that other people share my observation. The following examples demonstrate the way in which experiencer deletion converts a personal perception or opinion into an authoritative statement.

4 a We *seem* to be interested in judicious use when we call rewards and punishments just or unjust or fair or unfair.

   b By questioning the control exercised by autonomous man and demonstrating the control exercised by the environment, a science of behavior also *seems* to question dignity or worth.

   c Permissiveness is the absence of control, and if it *appears* to lead to desirable results, it is only because of other contingencies.

   d There *appears* to be no threat when the states of mind said to be responsible for behavior are changed, presumably because autonomous man possesses miraculous powers which enable him to yield or resist.

Although, as I said, the deleted experiencer is usually assumed to be the speaker (within linguistic theory), the four sentences above illustrate what Donald L. Smith has called "the therapeutic use of experiencer deletion." [When a writer uses experiencer predicates in this way, as B. F. Skinner does, he is engaged in *projecting* his assertions into the minds of other people as though those people had thought his thoughts. Confusing. Let me call such usage the "psychiatric stance," in which the writer has assumed unto himself the power of mind-reading when he tells us what we are thinking! The effect of this use of deleted experiencers is extremely subtle, for it places us in a defensive position, and we have to agree with the author's assertions or put the book down and read no further. In this way, readers are coerced into accepting a point of view they might otherwise reject if it were stated more openly, a situation similar to that created by the use of passive adjectives.

The next set of sentences contains examples of adjectives that also require experiencers for satisfactory interpretation. As in the case of experiencer predicates, these adjectives define a perception of opinion, but they are also *judgmental* predicates that define positive or negative value judgments on the part of the writer. By deleting the experiencer, the author conveys the impression that the judgment or perception is one that everyone agrees with, thus claiming universal consensus for individual opinions.

5   a   A person who responds in *acceptable* ways to weak forms of control may have been changed by contingencies which are no longer *effective.*

    b   The outlines of an *effective* technology are already *clear.*

    c   A self is a repertoire of behavior *appropriate* to a given set of contingencies.

    d   If our attempts to control are *unsuccessful,* the cause generally lies in our choice of *inappropriate* means.

If we wish to expose the judgmental values attached to such adjectives, we need only to ask *to* or *for whom* is something *effective, clear, acceptable,* or *appropriate?*

So far I have examined the various types of the first category of syntactic exploitation, those in which a writer or speaker uses specific sentence structures to deceive or coerce readers into agreement (or at least, passivity). My next two sets of examples illustrate the second category of syntactic exploitation, the kind of circumlocutions that produce bafflement and frustration for the reader (or listener) who tries to understand them. The use of syntactic structures to give the appearance of meaning, when, in fact, there is no meaning, has been called *gobbledygook* and *somnigraphy* by others concerned with abusive and careless uses of language. Our first reaction to such sentences is to label them "nonsense."

The quotations in example 6 illustrate the kinds of things politicians say when reporters or interviewers force them to make a comment on a specific issue that they would rather not deal with. We should listen closely to such utterances for two reasons: First, the speaker usually says more than she or he *intended* to say; second, the use of familiar sentence structures prompts the reader or listener to search for a coherent meaning that may not be present. As Monroe Beardsley has observed, we tend to give speakers the benefit of the doubt, and assume that where there's syntactic order there's also semantic order. As the following sentences show, such an assumption is often unwarranted, and we are no wiser for having listened to the people who try to pass their statements off as meaningful.

6   a   People who are not so smart may have a better understanding of generalizations but their lack of knowledge prohibits their ability to expound into them. (From a student theme)

     b   They would take more time to solve the solution because of the low level of their knowledge. (From a student theme)

     c   There is a danger of reasoning ourselves into inaction. From a military point of view, the U. S. could function in Southeast Asia about as well as anywhere in the world except Cuba. (From *The Pentagon Papers*)

     d   How do the separate and disparate experiences of individuals lead to a common acceptance of general meaning but which also permit differences of interpretation?

The following examples illustrate The Lie, a common device when the speaker is "up against the wall." In such situations, the speaker *must* reply, and saying nothing is better than saying something, especially when that "something" could be incriminating. The Lie is usually stated in sentences that are so obscure that they are impossible to follow, much less interpret.

7   a   In September, 1972, Spiro Agnew was asked by a television reporter if he had anything to say about the Watergate break-in. He said: "I don't think people should be talking about something that shouldn't have happened."

     b   Homosexuality is a perversion and a threat to heterosexuality.

     c   "One thing that has always puzzled me about it [the Watergate break-in] is why anybody would have tried to get anything out of the Watergate," Nixon said. "Be that as it may, that decision having been made at a lower level, with which I had no knowledge, and, as I pointed out. . . ." (October, 1972)

d   When a reporter pointed out to Ron Zeigler, Nixon's
press secretary, that Nixon's statements were consistently
contradictory, Zeigler calmly replied: "All previous statements are inoperative."

Example 7a, the quotation from Spiro Agnew, provides an excellent illustration of the pseudo-answer that says nothing, because it is not a direct response to the question, but says *more*
than the speaker actually intended to reveal within the context. Superficially, Agnew's answer is not at all to the point,
but to a critical listener it comes close to being an admission
of complicity, if not guilt. (It is worth remembering that at the
time that Agnew made this statement, he and Richard Nixon
were running for their second term of office.) The principle in
all four quotations seems to be something like "say anything
at all, if you have to, but don't say anything at all if possible."
In the strictest sense, none of these statements is an out-and-
out lie, but no one lies anyway. It's much easier to throw some
words together and thereby lose the listener in semantic dead
ends.

Diction, the second level of language in which our world view
determines our usage, is the most familiar area of language misuse. Because it is the easiest to discuss, I will not spend a lot
of time on it. Name-calling and the use of pejorative terms is
an unpleasant situation with which most of us are familiar,
whether we've been called "fat," "ugly," "stupid," "good-for-
nothing," "an egg-head," or "queer." English, however, possesses a set of terms for the sexuality of women that surpasses
in size virtually every other semantic set in the language, except, perhaps, for the words and phrases synonymous with *fuck*.
Only a few of these terms are ever used by women, although
we've all heard them. Women who enjoy sex (with men) are
"easy lays," but women who don't are "frigid." But sexism in
English extends beyond obvious labels into the dichotomized
structure of our semantics. Thus, we find paired sets of terms
that divide the species into *masculine* and *feminine*, *manly* and
womanly, *womanish* and *mannish*. In spite of the apparent sym-
metry of these terms, a glance at the dictionary will reveal that
the terms for males are positive, while the terms for women are
negative. This asymmetry in definition extends to words like
tomboy and *sissy*, where we find that masculine characteristics
in a woman are more positively valued than female characteristics in a male, until the female reaches puberty, at any rate.
In addition, of course, we find *man* and *mankind* as "generics,"
along with the use of *he* to refer to groups in which there may

be only one male, but never the reverse. That our vocabulary is divided up in this way tells us only that the terms exist to express our attitudes, and until our attitudes change, the words will continue to exist. Perhaps they will become obsolete in a few hundred years.

In order to demonstrate the way in which our world-view permeates our choices of words, I have selected, for my discussion of metaphors, several examples that illustrate how women are used as negative referents in metaphors. That is, if we believe that the world is divided into a group of people with negative characteristics, women, and another group of people with positive characteristics, men, our selection of terms for comparisons will reflect this belief. Metaphors, or comparisons, are chosen to express *perceived relationships between objects*, and our choice of objects in our comparisons reveals the real-world hypotheses on which we base our interpretations with the world.

8   a   Integration is good business. Invest your daughter.

    b   Land, like woman, was meant to be possessed.

    c   It's time for the rape of Amerika, but they're trying to respect her! She doesn't deserve respect: She's an Old Whore! But they're trying to treat her like a lady, instead of socking it to her, and paying her off! A Whore?— You just pay her off and you leave!—Just pay her off and take off, and let her sink in her own mire! She's not like a wife that you try to save and take care of! Europe is trying to be married to Amerika, when they should cut her loose like a Whore!

    d   The guards were seldom harsh and never cruel. They tended to be stolid, slovenly, heavy, and to my eyes effeminate—not in the sense of delicacy, etc., but in just the opposite sense: a gross, bland fleshiness, a bovinity without point or edge. Among my fellow-prisoners I had also for the first time on Winter the sense of being a man among women, or among eunuchs. The prisoners were hard to tell apart; their emotional tone seemed always low, their talk trivial.

In each of these examples, the writer exploits one of the popular stereotypes of women, whether we are an item of exchange, an object to be "invested," a piece of property to be owned, a whore to be raped and abused, or cows, the message is the same: Women are not human beings.

Four more examples of metaphors and their relation to world

views will demonstrate that the view of women discussed previously is only one facet of our present cultural milieu. Women, unsurprisingly, aren't the only ones who are less than human. In addition, the examples below contain uses of the passive and other constructions that link them to the types of exploitation I have been discussing in this article.

9   a   Faculty members have to be treated as if they were cogs in a machine.

   b   Freshmen are input to the university mechanism, and the role of the advisor is to program the student so that the output is a socially useful citizen.

   c   American shipping, both in and out, and our sea-going military arm would be successfully bottled up and forced to either pay high tribute or add several weeks to ocean voyages around canals and locks.

   d   Our advertising agency is trying to establish a stockpile of linguists to help us word advertisements to make them more psychologically effective.

As you've read through the examples in this paper, you've undoubtedly noticed that all of them contain additional examples of the misuses of language. I don't think that this is an accident. In fact, I believe that all of the types of language misuse that I've described are characteristic of the belief systems that are prevalent in our society, and I think that these beliefs require, for their expression, syntactic structures like the passive, and metaphors and labels that define people as objects to be exploited and used by the powerful. The only way to redefine ourselves is to develop a hypersensitivity to oppressive uses of language, so that we become aware, critical listeners and readers.

I am advocating "linguistic consciousness-raising" for all of us, because we must begin with ourselves, whether it is in the classroom, or in our personal relationships. In the classroom, there are many ways to increase the awareness of students, but perhaps the most effective way draws upon an aspect of our conditioning that we can use for self-improvement. That element of our lives is the need to compete. ("Need" is not the best word, but so it seems to us living in this culture.) Ultimately, I would hope that other ways might be found, but this one worked for a friend of mine. He assigned point values to the *circumstances* in which a student noticed sexism in language, and it would work equally as well for any of the other uses of language I've talked about. For example, if a student noticed sexism in the language of another student, in one of the textbooks, or in some outside source, she or he received one point toward her/his final grade in the course. If they noticed sexism in their own language, they received two points, and if they spotted sexism in the teacher's use of language, they got three points. In addition to this obvious system of rewards, one could have students keep notebooks of misuses of language that they hear or read, and set aside one day out of the week to discuss and analyze the examples that the students have collected. This method is illuminating and exciting, and many of my examples have come from my students' energetic researches. In composition courses, or in courses that require several papers, I've forbidden my students to use the passive in one paper, passive adjectives in another, and so on. Each use of the "forbidden" construction costs them ten points. A warning, however: At first, the protests of the students are vociferous, an indication of how much we lean on these constructions! When all the noise has died down, usually at the end of the course, many students have thanked me for helping them rid their written style of a reliance on vagueness and confusion. Doubtless, there are many, probably better, ways of raising one's linguistic consciousness in the classroom; I just don't know about them. But the classroom is the place where awareness has to start for most of us. As teachers, as human beings, we have to assume the responsibility for creating a language environment in which none of us is oppressed.

Notes

1   Julia P. Stanley, "Syntactic Exploitation: Passive Adjectives in English," paper presented at the Southeastern Conference on Linguistics, Athens, Georgia, April 1972. See also "Passive Motivation," paper originally presented at the Southeastern Conference on Linguistics, Atlanta, Georgia, November 1971; "Nominalized Passives," paper originally presented at the Linguistics Society of America, Chapel Hill, North Carolina, July 1972; "The Stylistics of Appropriateness: A Redefinition," paper presented at the Conference on College Composition and Communication, New Orleans, April 1973; "What's in a Label: The Politics of Naming," paper presented at the South Central Modern Language Association, November 1974.

2   Donald L. Smith, "Experiencer Deletion," paper presented at the Southeastern Conference on Linguistics, Athens, Georgia, April 1972.

3   Monroe Beardsley, "Order and Disorder in Art," in Paul G. Kuntz, ed., The Concept of Order (Seattle: University of Washington Press, 1968), pp. 198–199.

4   Cited by James H. Sledd, "Doublespeak: Dialectology in the Service of Big Brother," College English, 33(1972), 439–456. Sledd also coined the term somnigraphy in this article.

Practical Applications of Public Doublespeak Teaching: A Crap Detector for the Junior College Student

Francine Hardaway
Scottsdale Community College, Arizona

It has been suggested that the entire subject of public doublespeak is nothing more than old wine in new bottles; after all, we've always taught semantics and propaganda analysis. But in the two-year college we haven't always taught semantics or propaganda analysis, and if we have, we have usually put our students to sleep. Two-year college students are a different breed of cat from the captive audience at the university or the liberal arts college, because they are so inexperienced at learning for learning's sake. They want a degree, they want better jobs, they want social acceptance, they want a new skill—the last thing they want is a theory of language. To make the subject of doublespeak effective for them, we have to demonstrate its use in everyday life. And this criterion of utility may exclude political doublespeak, the common concern of the educated humanist.

Since politics and ideology don't often concern junior college students in any immediate way, what areas of doublespeak *can* be taught effectively in a classroom full of people with different backgrounds, interests, and degrees of intelligence?

First and foremost, we ought to teach a course in doublespeak for consumers. In this course, major emphasis should be on advertising techniques. When I asked my own students to search for ads containing doublespeak, they were horrified by their own findings. Almost every ad contained some identifiable examples of doublespeak—even for the least sophisticated, least perceptive member of the class. I never touched on academic questions like "hidden ideology"; I had all I could do to keep up with their discoveries of false claims, unprovable and misleading statistics, misquoting of authorities, and other super-

ficial aspects of ad copy. When we got into visual doublespeak—
how people *looked* in TV ads, for instance, or how food is photo-
graphed to make it seem appealing—the students were even
more interested. We even discussed the volume of the commercials in relation to the volume of a given program.

My planned unit on doublespeak was a mere two weeks. But
everyone wanted to continue. I had planned to discuss political
promises, campaign oratory, and journalism, but these seemed
less interesting to the students than advertising. Why? I think
because these people are victims most often and most immediately in the area of consumerism. As uneducated consumers,
they are cheated far more often by the supermarket than by
the Secretary of State. Exposed to some techniques for detecting misrepresentation, duplicity, and fraud, they were anxious
to educate themselves further.

As we began branching out, we got into other consumer areas.
I brought in the instruction manual from my new microwave
oven. First we discussed how impossible it was to find out
whether microwave ovens were dangerous. Certainly the instructions made mine sound perfectly safe. But what about
Consumer Reports? Adverse newspaper publicity?

My instruction manual said "It is not recommended that popcorn be popped in the microwave oven." I asked the students
what a sentence like that really meant. I tried it. The kernels
burned before they popped. What little popcorn resulted was
dry and brown. I brought the results into the classroom. We
reworded the instruction manual: "If you try to pop popcorn
in a microwave oven, it will burn." "Microwaves will not pop
popcorn."

Someone suggested doublespeak in real estate. What does APR
(annual percentage rate) mean? What's the difference between
the maintenance fee, a mortgage payment, and a rental payment? What's a half-bath? A five-and-a-half room apartment?
What's the difference between a condominium, a town house,
a patio home, and a garden apartment?

Still another student wanted to know about medical doublespeak. What constitutes intensive care? What's a pre-malig-
nancy? Here's one response to my short class presentation:

> Doublespeak, the act of saying one thing but actually
> saying another, is one of the most effective forms of
> propaganda today. Learning about doublespeak, that
> is, becoming aware of doublespeak, has turned me

away from most advertising. All forms of double-speak are infuriating.

Medical doublespeak angers me the most. Just last night on "Wide World of Entertainment" there was a special on cosmetic surgery. David Frost asked a group of doctors how much it would cost to have a hair transplant. The doctors all agreed that it was impossible to give a monetary figure. Frost went on to ask, "How much per hair plug? Surely you could give me a round figure." But the doctors went on saying that they did not recommend giving an estimate and recommended getting in touch with your own doctor. Certainly if your own doctor can give you an estimate, so can these so-called specialists. (Student was here encouraged to point out that this omission was a way of denying responsibility for the expense involved in the transplants.)

That's just one example; instructions on prescriptions are even worse. "It is not recommended to take more than two pills every eight hours and it is not advisable to take these pills while under the influence of alcohol." It should say, "If you take these pills while drinking liquor, you are going to get sick or die."

Never mind the aptness of the examples; note the tone of great moral outrage and the attitude of increased perception.

Yet another possible area of investigation could be the double-speak of employment agencies, job descriptions, and classified ads: hostess, receptionist, administrative assistant, Gal Friday—what are they? And what are the implications of "Can't find a job? For $30 we will find you one!"

The last area requested by my students was the college catalogue. Here are some representative course descriptions:

GL 104
Environmental Geology. The study of geology in relation to the environment with an overview of the interaction between man and the natural systems. Topics will include such areas as fossil fuels, geothermal exploration, and mining industry. Emphasis will be placed on geology-related environmental problems concerning Arizona.

Is there a way of studying geology unrelated to the environment? What is the difference between an overview of the interaction between man and the natural systems and any other view?

GT 161

Mathematics for Technology. Study of applied mathematics designed specifically for students in technology curriculums other than those in the electronic technology.

How revealing!

How is the student to distinguish between "credit by examination" and "credit by evaluation?" What's the difference between a remedial program, a developmental center, a terminal program, a nontransfer program, a subcollegiate program, an occupational certificate, an Associate of Arts degree?

The conclusion to be drawn from my first effort to teach principles of detecting and combatting doublespeak to community college students is clear: keep it practical. For them, even the newspaper isn't terribly practical: its concern with language is relatively abstract. Politics, too, may be esoteric. Most community college students are victims of society on a more intimate and immediate level than the political. A course in the doublespeak of police departments, credit bureaus, financial institutions, lawyers, divorce courts, doctors, and, worst of all, schools and colleges would be of real utility.

The problem is, those of us in the professions often don't want to realize how much jargon, euphemism and doublespeak we use ourselves. No wonder the average student says, "The most effective idea that came through to me (from the doublespeak unit) was that of 'survival of the fittest.' Meaning that any person with the knowledge of doublespeak can manipulate a person who doesn't look below the surface."

If we teach the art of recognizing and combatting doublespeak as a skill, we'll have no trouble generating interest and enthusiasm.

Training College Students as Critical Receivers of Public Persuasion

Daniel Dieterich
Chair, NCTE Committee on Public Doublespeak

In October 1974, I conducted a questionnaire survey of heads of departments of English and speech in Illinois junior colleges, colleges, and universities to determine the extent to which courses and units were being taught about public persuasion (e.g., politics, advertising, news media, and the like). In March 1975, I conducted a second questionnaire survey of teachers of persuasion in Illinois in institutions of higher education, a survey which attempted to determine the methods, if any, being used to train students to deal with the persuasive messages they received via the mass media. These surveys were undertaken because I strongly suspected that students were receiving extensive training to prepare them as persuaders but were receiving little training to prepare them as "persuadees," critical receivers of mass media persuasion.

The surveys confirmed my suspicions, despite the fact that those devoting the most time to persuasion were most likely to respond. According to the first survey, to which 132 out of 235 department heads responded, only one-third of the departments even offer a course on persuasion and only one-third of those courses are required. However, *units* on persuasion are offered by more than four-fifths of the departments responding and over four-fifths of these units are found in required courses. Five-eighths of these units appear to be offered in introductory courses and nearly half of them last two weeks or less. Only 11% of the units last more than a month.

On the second survey, although over four-fifths of the 102 re-

Editor's Note: This article is condensed from the author's doctoral dissertation, "The Training of College Students in Illinois as Critical Receivers of Public Persuasion," University of Illinois in Urbana-Champaign, January 1976.

sponding teachers of persuasion (out of 315 solicited) indicated that they prepared students as both persuaders and persuadees, these same teachers were nearly three times as likely to emphasize the role of persuader as they were to emphasize the role of persuadee. Of twelve aspects of persuasion which teachers were asked to rate, only three were rated as receiving "major emphasis" by more than half of the responding teachers: argumentation, logic, and logical fallacies. Among the aspects receiving major emphasis by less than half of the responding teachers were: advertising persuasion (37%), ethics of persuasion (42%), and political persuasion (27%). Texts cited as used in the study of persuasion were many and varied and employed diverse approaches to the subject. However, some devoted no space whatsoever to mass media or persuasion *per se*, while others rendered these topics only the most perfunctory attention. Supplementary materials from the mass media themselves were cited as being used frequently in the study of persuasion by less than a third of the responding teachers.

The surveys also revealed that English departments offered fewer courses on persuasion and spent less time on persuasion in the units which they offered on it than speech departments. English teachers were about half as likely to devote major emphasis to advertising persuasion as speech teachers and were also far less likely to devote major emphasis to political persuasion than speech teachers. Despite the reputation of English teachers for concern about language, the survey revealed that they were less likely to make frequent use of newspaper or magazine ads, taped or printed transcripts of political speeches, or televised ads than speech teachers.

Although I cannot claim to have been surprised by these findings, as a teacher of English I did find them somewhat disheartening . . . especially at a time when political chicanery is a widely practiced art and annual advertising expenditures are fast approaching the thirty billion dollar mark. It appears that Richard Lloyd-Jones was all too accurate in his comment that "The functions of language which we (writing teachers) taught were to report accurately an external world and perhaps to persuade, although we often left the latter function for programs in public relations, advertising, journalism or speech."[1]

Perhaps the only bright spot in the otherwise bleak picture painted by the two Illinois surveys is the discovery that considerable emphasis is being given to the study of the rational elements of persuasion (i.e., logic, logical fallacies, and argu-

ment), especially by departments of English. However, one
wonders whether this silver cloud might not have a sable lining.
Does training in logical analysis equip students to analyze
today's public persuasion? In order to discover a logical fallacy in an argument, one must first have an argument which
has a logical form and approach. My own personal perception
of modern public persuasion is that it contains little or no such
logical patterning. If this perception is accurate, it does not
mean that training in logic and logical analysis is wasted on the
study of public discourse. However, it does suggest that such
training should be supplemented if we wish to prepare students
to deal with public persuasion by advertisers and with modern
political persuasion based on the techniques of commercial
advertising.

Cleanth Brooks and Robert Penn Warren draw a distinction
between argument and persuasion in that "the former is based
on logic, the latter on psychology."[2] They go on to say that
"The end of argument, strictly conceived, is truth—truth as
perceived by the operation of reason. The end of persuasion,
on the other hand, is assent—assent to the will of the persuader."[3] While this distinction might be bitterly debated
among those who responded to my surveys, it merits consideration. If this distinction is heeded, the study of truth and how
truth may be arrived at (the study of the rational process, i.e.,
logic) is the proper basis for an understanding of argument; but
the study of the attitudes, motives, and behaviors of individuals
and groups (i.e., psychology) is the proper basis for an understanding of persuasion. Both argument and persuasion are
worthy subjects for students' attention. And, since elements of
argument and persuasion are commonly intertwined in human
communication, it may be well to study them conjointly. However, one should not assume that providing students with training in psychology will prepare them for argumentation. Nor
should one assume, as apparently a great many teachers do,
that providing students with training in logic will prepare them
for persuasion.

This distinction assumes greater importance in light of the fact
that public discourse is becoming increasingly oriented toward
persuasion rather than argumentation. Politicians have assumed
the persuasive strategies of commercial advertisers (see Joe Mc-
Ginniss's *The Selling of the President, 1968*, Gene Wyckoff's
*The Image Candidates: American Politics in the Age of Tele-
vision*, and Dan Nimmo's *The Political Persuaders: The Tech-*

niques of Modern Election Campaigns). And, under pressure by the Federal Trade Commission and consumer groups to put an end to false advertising which made claims which were factually inaccurate or logically invalid, advertisers themselves are relying less on logical argument and more on psychological persuasion. In the words of one advertiser, "Specific claims can be argued on the basis of facts. Logic can be questioned. . . . But, it is difficult to challenge image, emotion, style (whatever you want to call it). Therefore, agencies and advertisers are turning to the image approach because it is 'safer.'"[4] This triumph of persuasion over argument in American advertising is dealt with in some depth in Ivan Preston's *The Great American Blow-Up: Puffery in Advertising and Selling,* which describes how the ordered, sequential, rational sales pitch has been replaced by puffery and simple association techniques.

If, then, the language of the political arena and the language of the marketplace is geared toward persuasion, it would seem appropriate to direct students' attention to public persuasion in the English classroom. English departments are responsible for instructing students in the workings of language and other symbol systems. Because of English teachers' expertise in this area, it is especially appropriate that they acquaint students with the ways in which symbols may be used to mold the attitudes and opinions of others. The complex ways in which visual and aural, verbal and nonverbal symbols may be intertwined in order to evoke a desired psychological response has long been a concern of teachers of language, literature, and writing. The dawning of the age of the mass media serves only to cast a new light on this ageless subject.

The expertise of teachers in other departments ought not be overlooked. Although I recognize the difficulties inherent in interdisciplinary courses and programs, such courses and programs are especially attractive in an area which is the focus of so much mutual interest. If such extensive interdepartmental cooperation is impossible, English departments would do well to at least acquaint themselves with the offerings in related disciplines and benefit from whatever contributions teachers in other departments can make to English courses and units on public persuasion. In envisioning the direction in which the teaching of English should develop, I keep recalling a remark which Walker Gibson made at the 1973 annual convention of the National Council of Teachers of English in Philadelphia. In describing the need which he saw for changing and enlarging the role of the English teacher at all levels, Gibson said "If we are to survive as a profession, if we are to serve our society in a useful way, it will not be because we've refined our teaching of Walter Scott or even William Faulkner. It will be because we've directed our attention, as experts in symbol systems, to the ways language works in the society."[5] I wholeheartedly agree, both with the warning that to ignore the needs of our students is to condemn our profession to stagnation, and with the contention that we can make our greatest contribution to our society and to our students through the study of the ways people use symbol systems and the ways people are used by others through symbol systems. I can envision no loftier goal for the English teaching profession than to help students understand the conscious and unconscious ways in which people manipulate symbols in order to communicate information, produce works of aesthetic beauty, attain greater self-understanding, and bring others to think and act as they do.

I see in this goal a far broader responsibility for English teachers than that of literary *arbiter elegantiae.* I see instead a discipline which would encompass the study of reading and writing, speaking and listening, and the production and viewing of visual and audiovisual materials; which would, in fact, unify all aspects of the symbolic process, both productive and receptive. I see a curriculum which would provide for the real needs of the students taking it; needs not only for a heightened aesthetic sensibility but for a heightened capacity to understand the production and reception of symbolic communication. And I see future students better informed about how symbolic processes influence their attitudes, beliefs, and actions.

Such a shift from traditional "literacy" to a new "media literacy" is not a simple one, nor am I attempting to oversimplify the matter. It involves more than just the joining of oral, aural, and pictorial literacy to print literacy. As Annelle Houk and Carlotta Bogart pointed out, the new literacy may be defined as "the individual's assertion of his power over his behavior— his refusal to permit his behavior to be modified without his conscious acquiescence. Literacy is independent behavior consciously shaping and being shaped by media of all kinds."[6]

In order to facilitate the shift from literacy to media literacy, future teachers of English at all levels should be trained about public persuasion. Much of this training would merely involve implementing guidelines which have already been drawn up regarding the training of English teachers. For example, the training of elementary and secondary English teachers would benefit enormously were all teacher training institutions to implement guideline four of the "Guidelines for the Preparation of Teachers of English" drawn up by the English Teacher Preparation Study of 1967. That guideline reads: "The teacher of English at any level should have skill in listening, speaking, reading, and writing, and an understanding of the nature of language and rhetoric."[7] Junior college teacher training would benefit enormously were all teacher training institutions to implement guidelines three and seven of the "Guidelines for Junior College English Teacher Training Programs." These read as follows:

> Successful junior college teachers should be able to:
>
> 3 understand the nature of language and be aware of the ways in which all human beings use language to order their vision of themselves and the world, to manipulate others and allow themselves to be manipulated;
>
> 7 understand the relationship among the various communication skills—reading, writing, speaking —as well as be aware of the necessary differences among them.[8]

However, teachers who wish to concentrate their attention on public persuasion might receive additional training as well. Their study of language might involve coursework in general semantics and linguistics so that they might gain a fuller understanding of the nature and function of verbal language as a system of human origin. It might involve training in psychology, so that they might better understand the processes of attitude formation and motivation. It might involve training in marketing, so that they can understand the techniques employed by the advertising industry. It might involve training in media production, anthropology, or the social sciences. And it might involve training in ethics, so that teachers can help their students achieve a sense of perspective in the study of an area in which the criterion of excellence is customarily effectiveness rather than accuracy.

Such study of language or symbol systems should be joined to a study of the media environment which employs public persuasion. Students of all ages should be acquainted with the several functions of advertising; the many forms which advertising takes; the controls placed on advertising by manufacturers and distributors, the advertising industry, and the federal, state, and local government; and some of the hidden agendas of public service, ideological, commercial, and political advertisements. The study of the language of politics should be joined with a study of American political institutions so that students might better understand not only *what* is being said in a given piece of political persuasion, but *why* it is being said, and such study should extend not only to the discourse of national political figures but to the persuasion employed in state, local, and student body political offices and contests. Students should examine the myths of objectivity in American journalism and explore the ways that traditional American media systems foster editorials and news reporting which reflect a conservative to liberal range of opinions and exclude opinions of the far right and left. Students might contrast this traditional media bias with the bias of counterculture, radical, and reactionary publications and explore the question of whether such nontraditional viewpoints should or could find expression in the mainstream of American mass media.

One exercise which teachers might employ in the study of public persuasion would involve one student or a small group of students in an in-depth analysis of a single television commercial. The student(s) would be asked to select a commercial, draw up a story-board layout of it, and accompany this with a 16mm film of the commercial or a tape of the commercial's sound track. The student(s) would then be asked to explain to the rest of the class the ways in which the commercial accomplishes (or attempts to accomplish) its persuasive purpose. What psychological appeals are employed? Why did the advertiser select this music, this setting, these particular colors, the particular actors/characters employed in this commercial, the activities depicted here, etc.? Why is the visual composition as it is? What is accomplished through framing, camera angles, transitions, editing, and timing? If association techniques are employed, are they appropriate and effective? What are the dominant symbols and what are the immediate and long-term effects of using such symbols? What is the effect of the commercial as a whole? What is its audience? Is the commercial ethical, tasteful, appropriate? What underlying philosophy does it express? Do you or do you not agree with this underlying philosophy? Does the commercial make any verifiable claims or is it sheer puffery? If it makes verifiable claims, are they accurate claims? Is the commercial persuasive?

Students should also go beyond this analysis of the techniques employed in modern public persuasion to an analysis of the nature and function of public persuasion. In the case just cited, students should also consider why the particular ad chosen for analysis exists and indeed why all commercial advertising exists. Should such ads exist? Are they necessary? If so, for what? Should ads be restricted or controlled? By whom? In what way? What values do commercial ads communicate to their audience? Who pays for ads? Are they cheap or costly? What effect do they have on the media in which they appear? What effect do they have on society as a whole—for good or for ill? These larger questions merit intense scrutiny by students, despite the fact that answers to them will necessarily be tentative.

Similar analytical techniques should be used to study public persuasion in the news media and in political speeches and commercials. Such study might appear in an elective course or mini-course at the secondary school level, in the college freshman English class, or in a college course devoted solely to the study of public persuasion. Its form would vary from situation to situation and the techniques used in exploring the subject would depend upon the preferences of the individual teacher. The aim of such study would always be to extend students' understanding of the ways in which symbol systems are employed in modern society and to better equip students to cope with public persuasion.

In proposing "some central courses in rhetoric" for the college English or speech curriculum, Robert M. Gorrell details the form one such course might take, a course in "Rhetoric and Society." Gorrell's course would be

> . . . a broad study of some of the social implications of different rhetorical choices. It would certainly involve ethical problems in the use of language. It would not be a course in how to make friends and influence people, but it would look at some of the ways in which language is used to manipulate. I would want it to analyze uses of doublespeak and circumlocution, to look at some of advertising's devices for deception, but I would not want it to be a course primarily in propaganda analysis. . . .[9]

Other teachers might employ a linguistic approach, a general semantics approach, or a media-centered approach. Perhaps the approach employed is not as important as the fact that something be done to prepare students for public persuasion. In the words of William D. Boutwell, "If the teacher can make his students aware of those forces which would mold them, would compel them to act without reasoning through the bases for their actions, would demand acceptance without question,

then society, in the final summing up, would find that it owes
that teacher a rather considerable debt."[10]

Notes

1   Richard Lloyd-Jones, "The CCCC-NCTE Language State-
    ments: New Choices for the Teacher of Writing," paper pre-
    sented at the Conference on College Composition and Com-
    munication, St. Louis, Missouri, March 1975, p. 3.
2   Cleanth Brooks and Robert Penn Warren, *Modern Rhetoric*
    (New York: Harcourt Brace Jovanovich, Inc., 1972), p. 181.
3   Brooks and Warren, p. 177.
4   J. R. Carpenter, "Voice of the Advertiser," *Advertising Age*, 19
    April 1971, p. 57.
5   Walker Gibson, "Seeing Ourselves," *College English*, 35 (1974),
    p. 737.
6   Annelle Houk and Carlotta Bogart, *Media Literacy: Thinking
    About* (Dayton, Oh.: Pflaum/Standard, 1974), p. 3.
7   National Association of State Directors of Teacher Education
    and Certification, the National Council of Teachers of English,
    and the Modern Language Association of America, "Guidelines
    for the Preparation of Teachers of English," (Urbana, Ill.:
    National Council of Teachers of English, 1967), p. 8.
8   Guidelines Committee of the Conference on College Com-
    position and Communication, "Guidelines for Junior College
    English Teacher Training Programs," *College Composition and
    Communication*, 22 (1971), p. 305.
9   Robert M. Gorrell, "Ghetoric, Dickoric, Doc: Rhetoric as an
    Academic Discipline," *College Composition and Communica-
    tion*, 26 (1975), p. 18.
10 William D. Boutwell, ed., *Using Mass Media in the Schools*
    (New York: Appleton-Century-Crofts, 1962), p. 12.

Resources

Resources

> Knowledge is of two kinds: we know a subject our-
> selves, or we know where we can find information
> upon it.
>
> Samuel Johnson

Since none of us can yet lay claim to "knowing" all there is
to know about the subject of doublespeak and about how to
teach our students how to deal with it, it is good that there
are other sources to turn to for information and inspiration.
We hope that the many items here, reprinted from the *Public
Doublespeak Newsletter*, Vol. 2, No. 2 (1975), will augment
the information you already have and will provide both the
novice and the experienced teacher with new insights into the
subject of doublespeak. Those looking for further sources of
information on doublespeak are invited to read "A Personal
Reading List" in *Language and Public Policy*, edited by Hugh
Rank.

My thanks to the many people who have written me over the
past months to suggest books which I have overlooked or to
announce new publications dealing with doublespeak. My special thanks to committee member Clare Barkley who wrote
annotations for all of the books contained in the committee
exhibit. Without her help I could never have compiled the
following list:

Books

About Television by Martin Mayer. New York: Harper & Row, 1972.

Intelligent, well-researched, clearly written description of the how and why of TV production, programming and advertising.

Against Misinformation: A Media Action Program for Young People by Jerome Aumente. New York: KTAV Publishing House, Inc., 1973.

About half the book is devoted to making young people aware of the misinformation that surrounds them. The second part is a series of suggestions for young people to get to the truth and to correct the flow of misinformation.

The Age of Communication by William D. Lutz. Pacific Palisades, California: Goodyear Publishing Co., Inc., 1974.

A collection of articles about current language from newspapers, magazines and journals; also contains samples of ads. Each of the three divisions, Advertising, The News Media, and Current Culture is followed by a page of topics for discussion. College text.

Children's Television Commercials: A Content Analysis by Charles Winick and others. New York: Praeger Publishers, 1973.

Describes a study of 236 commercials aimed at kids. Each commercial was coded on a scale to measure the degree to which each of 145 dimensions of content was present. Dimensions covered product information, health/nutrition, sales persuasion techniques, sales pitch delivery, cast of characters, setting/story elements, production techniques, and language.

Coming to Terms with Language edited by Raymond D. Liedlich. New York: John Wiley and Sons, 1973.

A collection of 30 contemporary essays, most of them written for a general audience. Each is followed by suggestions for discussion and writing.

Communicate! by Stuart Chase. Evanston: McDougal, Littell & Co.

A small high-school text which attempts to help the student recognize and gain control of his position in the communication network; a semantic approach.

Coping with Television edited by Joseph Fletcher Littell. Evanston, Illinois: McDougal, Littell & Co., 1973. ($3.27—school price)

A high school text (and teacher's manual) containing sections on: the impact of television, television production, the content of television, television ratings, television advertising, and how you can influence the media.

204   Resources

Don't Blame the People by Robert Cirino. New York: Vintage Books, 1971.

A book filled with specific, documented examples of bias, distortion, and censorship in the media.

Doublespeak: Language for Sale by William Sparke, Beatrice Taines, Shirley Sidell. New York: Harper & Row, Publishers, 1975.

A lower division college textbook (reader/rhetoric) which explores the uses of doublespeak in printed and electronic media, in advertisements, government communications, editorials, store windows, billboards, direct mail appeals, etc. Its three sections deal with doublespeak of the present, past, and future.

The Electric Mirror: Politics in an Age of Television by Sig Mickelson. New York: Dodd, Mead and Co., 1972.

Explores the influence of television on politics and government. Control of the medium by an administration in power or irresponsible direction by owners and operators could destroy the democratic system.

English Everywhere: Meaning, Media, and You by Robert R. Potter. New York: Globe Book Co., Inc., 1971.

A high school textbook divided into an introduction to general semantics, "How Words Work," and words in literature, movies, news, ads, politics. Includes illustrations, classroom exercises.

Ethics in Human Communication by Richard L. Johannesen. Columbus, Ohio: Charles E. Merrill Publishing Company, 1975 (160 pp.) $3.95.

Chapters cover: public confidence in truthfulness of public communication, ethical responsibility in human communication, political perspectives, ontological perspectives, some basic issues, some examples for analysis, etc.

Euphemism by Walker Gibson. New York: Harper & Row, 1974.

A pamphlet which examines euphemisms both private and public and discusses the role they play in human communication.

Exploring Television by William Kuhns. Chicago: Loyola University Press, 1973.

A combination textbook-workbook which is aimed at helping students to understand, analyze, criticize, evaluate, and judge the experiences they have in front of the TV set. Teacher's Guide.

Frauds, Swindles and Rackets by Robert Rosefsky. Chicago: Follett, 1973.

The author, a nationally syndicated financial columnist, describes patterns of fraud and deceit likely to be perpetrated on any of us.

There are examples of swindles in which the author himself became an intentional victim.

Government and Society in Urban America by Jack Allen, Thomas H. DeBolt, and Susan E. DeBolt. New York: American Book Co., 1973.

A high school text about citizenship in American society. Excerpts from interpretive writings, editorial cartoons and picture essays are used because they raise the issues in a way that most active citizens must deal with.

The Great American Blow-Up: Puffery in Advertising and Selling by Ivan Preston. Madison: University of Wisconsin Press, 1975, $11.95.

Contends that advertising puffery (e.g., "You Can Be Sure If It's Westinghouse!") creates an attitude of distrust among American consumers which is harmful to seller and buyer alike, a credibility gap similar to the one which has arisen in American politics.

The Hidden Persuaders by Vance Packard. New York: Pocket Books, 1972, originally published by David McKay Co., 1957.

A popular book which identifies the manipulators of minds by use of symbols and discusses the antihumanistic characteristics of each manipulation.

How to Talk Back to Your Television Set by Nicholas Johnson. New York: Bantam, 1970.

Written by a former member of the FCC, this book deals with the influence of television on our individual lives and on society. Ends with suggestions for institutional changes and for individual citizen's efforts to improve television.

I Can Sell You Anything by Carl P. Wrighter. New York: Ballantine, 1972.

Written by an ad-man who says they've stopped making better mousetraps, but TV commercials are designed to make the consumer believe they're different.

The Idea Invaders by George N. Gordon, Irving Falk, and William Hodapp. New York: Hastings House, 1963.

A book about propaganda, focusing on international propaganda. Part one deals with the historical context into which mass persuasion fits today (1963). Part two deals with the influence on the minds of foreigners exerted by the United States. The authors call it a souvenir of the period.

Influence, Belief, and Argument: An Introduction to Responsible Persuasion by Douglas Ehninger. Scott, Foresman, 1974.

Discusses the role of evidence, warrant, and claim in formulating sound, logical proof. Analyzes sham or counterfeit proofs used by public speakers.

Language and Public Policy edited by Hugh Rank.

A reader on doublespeak containing articles written by over 30 authors. (Available from NCTE for $3.75 to NCTE members and $4.75 to non-members; also available in hard-cover from Citation Press.)

Language Awareness by Paul A. Eschholz, Alfred F. Rosa, and Virginia P. Clark. New York: St. Martin's Press, 1974.

A collection of essays, many written by practicing journalists and TV newsmen. Discussion questions follow each article.

Language in America edited by Neil Postman, Charles Weingartner, and Terence Moran. New York: Pegasus, 1969 ($1.75) 240 p.

Covers the use and abuse of language in politics, in advertising, in education, in the media, in bureaucracy, and in general.

Language in Uniform: A Reader on Propaganda edited by Nick Aaron Ford. New York: Odyssey Press, 1967.

A collection of classic and contemporary writings on propaganda divided into four categories: political and economic discussion, racial and religious considerations, education, and advertising. Discussion questions in each section.

The Language Lens edited by R. Brent Bonah and Sheila Shively. Prentice-Hall, 1974.

An anthology of essays on language, it includes essays by Postman & Weingartner, Hayakawa, Packard, Clyde Miller, Russell Baker, Stuart Chase, Walter Cronkite, Joe McGinniss, and many others.

The Language of Man Series edited by Joseph Fletcher Littell. Evanston: McDougal, Littell & Co., 1971.

Designed especially for students as they progress from junior through senior high school. The six books deal with such topics as semantics for the seventies, coping with television and the mass media, the language of advertising, using the dictionary and encyclopedia, understanding ads and commercials, language and politics, language and race. Alternate books in the series are *Coping with the Mass Media, How Words Change Our Lives, Dialects and Levels of Language, Using Figurative Language.* Teacher's manuals.

The Language of Oppression by Haig Bosmajian. Washington, D.C.: Public Affairs Press, 1974.

Chapters on "the language of" anti-Semitism, white racism, Indian derision, sexism, and war resensitize us to the invidious power of innocuous terms to cover ugly realities.

Making Sense: Exploring Semantics and Critical Thinking by Robert R. Potter. New York: Globe Book Co., 1974.

A secondary textbook which introduces semantics, includes chapters on body language and logic. Classroom exercises.

Mass Communications and American Empire by Herbert I. Schiller. New York: Augustus M. Kelley Publishers, 1970.

A college text which examines the structure and policy of mass communication in the context of its economic and political functions.

Mass Media by Ann Christine Heintz, B.V.M.; M. Lawrence Reuter, S.J.; and Elizabeth Conley. Chicago: Loyola University Press, 1972.

A combination workbook-textbook aimed at helping the student analyze, evaluate, and judge TV, films, radio, newspapers, magazines, and advertising. Teacher's Guide.

Mass Media: A Casebook by Richard F. Hixson. Thomas Y. Crowell, 1973.

Discusses, among other things, the media's responsibility toward ethnic minorities, the press and current events, and myths about the media and about consumership.

Mass Media and Mass Man (2nd ed.) by Alan Casty. New York: Holt Rinehart and Winston, Inc., 1973.

A college text designed to guide the reader to a greater understanding of such significant media matters as the role and influences of the media, their methods and performances, their relationship to political and private life, to the public, and to individuals.

Media Power: Who Is Shaping Your Picture of the World? by Robert Stein. Houghton Mifflin, 1972.

Explores the effect of the mass media on individual and social consciousness. "The World Ends Tomorrow, Details after This Message" discusses the amount and kind of information being disseminated through the media. "McLuhan and Agnew" describes the impact of the broadcast media. Among other chapters is one on "The Truth as Property."

The Media Works by Juan Valdez and Jeanne Crow. Dayton: Pflaum/Standard, 1973.

An activity-oriented text designed to investigate the variety of ways each medium suits itself to our needs, works its way into our lives and directs the way we live. Separate log book to record activities.

No More Lies by Dick Gregory (James R. McGraw, ed.), New York: Harper and Row, 1971.

A survey of American history from the Puritans to recent Presidential campaigns. The author deals with distortions or "myths" of major historical events.

208   Resources

Pacification and Social Process by Russell Jennings. Center for
Communication Research, Dept. of Speech, Southern Illinois University, (1974). Soon to be available through the ERIC system,
30pp.

Pacification is a technique for subverting or negating the problem
solving process by discounting some aspects of it, e.g., the problem
itself, its solvability, the abilities of those involved to solve the
problem. It is based on the exaggeration of the problem through
the use of abstract language, generalizations, stereotyped language,
clichés, or proverbs.

The Pentagon Propaganda Machine by Senator William J. Ful-
bright. New York: Vintage, 1971.

An account of the highly effective and expensive propaganda program carried on by the Pentagon to make citizens believe it is
necessary and desirable to spend more and more—even in dangerous policy areas such as ABM and Vietnam.

Perfectly Clear by Frank Mankiewicz. New York: Popular Library,
1973.

Chapter four is a discussion of the doublespeak of the Nixon administration.

Persuasion by Ann Christine Heintz, B.V.M. Chicago: Loyola
University Press, 1970.

A combination textbook-workbook which sets out to help students
discover techniques of persuasion and to build their own persuasive skills. Teacher's Guide.

Persuasion and Propaganda in War and Peace by Gladys and Mar-
cella Thum. Evanston, Illinois: McDougal, Littell & Company,
1974.

All illustrated reader covering military, political, economic (advertising), religious, and racial propaganda from the time of the
American revolution to the present. Also covers foreign propaganda and offers some thoughts about the propaganda of the
future.

Persuasion: Reception and Responsibility by Charles U. Larson.
Belmont, California: Wadsworth Publishing Co., 1973.

College text written to prepare students as receivers of persuasive
messages.

*Persuasion: The Theory and Practice of Manipulative Communica-
tion* by George N. Gordon; New York: Hastings House, 1971.
$16.50.

Approaches a study of persuasion from three perspectives: logical,
psychological, and humanistic. Includes a section on groups, such
as blacks, youth, women.

The Politics of Communication by Claus Mueller. Oxford University Press, 1973, $7.95.

Deals with distorted communication as a tool used by political organizations to justify their policies and keep the public ignorant of their activities. It defines distorted communication as that use of language which filters and obscures understanding so that a governmental institution can continue to maintain its authority based on law and order.

The Politics of Lying by David Wise, New York: Vintage, 1973.

According to this author, lying is institutionalized because of official secrecy, classification of information, and government control of information channels.

Pop Culture by Arthur Asa Berger. Dayton: Pflaum/Standard, 1973.

A series of essays dealing with subjects such as amusements and entertainments, advertising, styles, symbols and social phenomena. The author's idea is that by learning about our popular culture we learn something about ourselves. Instructor's program guide.

Popular Writings in America by Donald McQuade and Robert Atwan. New York: Oxford University Press, 1974. (and teaching guide)

A collection of writings suited to particular audiences in 19th and 20th century America. Includes writing from advertising, newspapers, magazines, best sellers, classics. Supplementary text.

Power to Persuade: Mass Media and the News by Robert Cirino. New York: Bantam Books, 1974, $1.25.

Deals with objectivity, censorship, the public interest, etc. Geared to the secondary school classroom, it contains over 150 case studies as well as questions for discussions and class activities.

The Press and Its Problems by Curtis D. MacDougall. Dubuque; Wm. E. Brown, 1964.

A college textbook concerned with the role and responsibility of the press and its relationship with the law and the individual.

The Process of Social Influence: Readings in Persuasion edited by Thomas Beisecker and Donn Parson. Englewood Cliffs, N.J.: Prentice-Hall, Inc., 1972.

Attempts to synthesize primarily experimental studies of the process of social influence. Covers the psychological context; the source: properties of speaker credibility; characteristics of the message; and the effects of persuasion.

Propaganda and Public Opinion: Strategies of Persuasion by Bernard Rubin. Xerox Corp., 1973.

Pamphlet includes sections on manipulating opinion, war propaganda, public opinion and public diplomacy.

210

Propaganda, Polls, and Public Opinion by Malcolm G. Mitchell. Englewood Cliffs, New Jersey: Prentice-Hall, Inc., 1970.

One book of a series of sixteen dealing with important contemporary social and political issues. Each book presents an in-depth study of a particular problem.

Propaganda: The Formation of Men's Attitudes by Jacques Ellul. New York: Vintage, 1973.

Discussion of characteristics, effects and effectiveness of propaganda. The author holds the view that propaganda is a greater danger to mankind than any of the other threats hanging over the human race.

Psycholinguistics by Dan I. Slobin. Glenview: Scott, Foresman Basic Psychological Concept Series, 1971.

An introductory college text emphasizing the role of language in human behavior.

Responsibility in Mass Communication (rev. ed.) by William L. Rivers and Wilbur Schramm. New York: Harper and Row, 1969.

A book on the relationship between the mass media and the public. Among issues the authors discuss are freedom and governmental control, the public's "right to know," and censorship.

The Survival of English: Essays in Criticism of Language by Ian Robinson. Cambridge University Press, 1973, $11.50.

On the misuse of language in Great Britain. Covers politics, advertising, and the media.

Teaching as a Subversive Activity by Neil Postman and Charles Weingartner. New York: Dell Publishing Co., 1969, $2.25.

Describes ways in which to make what goes on inside the classroom have some bearing on students' lives outside of school. (One indication of its value: It was one of the books stolen from the committee display.)

Techniques of Persuasion by J.A.C. Brown. Middlesex, England: Penguin Books, 1963.

A scholarly book on persuasion theory written by a psychiatrist.

Test Pattern for Living by Nicholas Johnson. New York: Bantam, 1972.

Examines the difficulties of developing a rational life-style in a "corporate state"; first part emphasizes the influence of television on values.

To Kill a Messenger by William Small. New York: Hastings House, 1970.

A study by a former executive with CBS News. The making of

TV news coverage from war, riots, political conventions to routine newscasts.

True, False, or In Between by Donald Hiatt. Lexington, Mass.: Ginn and Company, 1975, $2.00.

A 140 page paperback text for high school students which studies the ways in which language is used to persuade improperly, to evade, and to confuse.

T.V. Action Book by Jeffrey Schrank. Evanston: McDougall, Littell & Co., 1974.

A textbook which discusses the use of the television channels—programming, ownership of stations, the Fairness Doctrine, advertising. A substantial part of the book is a logbook to help students analyze local television.

The Use and Misuse of Language edited by S.I. Hayakawa. Greenwich, Conn.: Fawcett, 1962.

A collection of 18 essays selected from the files of the quarterly journal *ETC., A Review of General Semantics,* arranged under four headings: The Art of Communication, Semantics Around Us, The Arts: Low, Middle and High, Human Insight.

The War of Ideas: America's International Identity Crisis by George N. Gordon and Irving A. Falk. New York: Hastings House, 1973.

Written for "every socially and politically alert American," the book deals with the issues of international communication.

The Waste Makers by Vance Packard. New York: Pocket Books, 1960.

A discussion of the strategies marketing experts use to insure a constant demand for products, and some suggested courses the citizen and consumer might follow to maintain human values and guard against gross materialism.

What Do You Think? by Alvin Schwartz. New York: E.P. Dutton & Co., 1966.

An introduction to public opinion: how it forms, how it functions, and how it affects our lives.

Magazines and Journals

(A few of the many which might be of interest)

Advertising Age (Crain Communications, Inc., 740 North Rush, Chicago, Illinois). The weekly newspaper of the advertising industry.

The Consumer Educator (1201 16th Street, N.W., Washington, D.C.) a monthly fact sheet co-sponsored by the National Association of Secondary School Principals and the Better Business Bureau.

Consumer Reports (Consumers Union, P.O. Box 1000, Orangeburg,

NY 10962—$11 year) Often contains analyses of the wording of manufacturers' claims and advertisements.

Columbia Journalism Review (700 Journalism Building, Columbia University, New York, NY 10027) a respected press watchdog.

English Journal and *College English* (NCTE, 1111 Kenyon Rd., Urbana, IL 61801) Both contain Committee columns and other articles dealing with doublespeak.

ETC. A Review of General Semantics (International Society for General Semantics, San Francisco, CA) Contains frequent references to the use of general semantics for the study of language misuse.

Better Broadcasts News (11 King Street, Madison, WI 53703—$2.00 year, five issues) publication of the American Council for Better Broadcasts which coordinates efforts to "improve by educational means the quality of radio and television."

Multi-Media

The Propaganda Game. WFF'N PROOF Publishers, Box 71, New Haven, CT 06501—$6.00 plus postage and handling.

Teaches players how to recognize such techniques as quotation out of context, technical jargon, and faulty analogy.

The Persuasion Box, Jeffrey Schrank. Palatine, IL: The Learning Seed, Co., 1974.

Contains The Propaganda Game, Carl Wrighter's *I Can Sell You Anything*, a 16mm film of a commercial, The Claim Game, a filmstrip, and a teacher's guide. Suitable for use with a secondary class or an individual student.

Doublespeak: What Is Deceptive Advertising. An 87 minute tape cassette of speeches by Alvin Achenbaum of J. Walter Thompson Advertising Company and Wendell Reid of the Federal Trade Commission, 1973. (Available from NCTE for $6.00, Stock No. 71354)

Achenbaum argues that advertising doesn't manipulate people. The audience argues that it does.

Curriculum Materials

What follows is a list of a few curriculum guides and course syllabi which contain material appropriate for the study of doublespeak. Many of these items can be located through the ERIC system; others are available from the individual authors.

Language and Communication: A Resource Book K–12. Department of Instruction, Department of Education, State of Minnesota, St. Paul, 1975. (Available for $6.50 from: Documents Section, Rm. 140 Central Bldg., St. Paul, MN 55155)

Employs a general semantics approach to improve communication and reduce conflict. Includes a catalogue of materials available from the International Society for General Semantics and a record containing three songs dealing with the ways that language affects human relationships. (A television series—six 30-minute programs—is being used to introduce the guide in Minnesota. Committee member Gerald Kincaid played a key role in developing the guide and the TV programs.)

Advanced Persuasive Speaking, English, Speech: 5114.112. By the Dade County (Florida) Public Schools, 25 pp. (ED 084 618).

A quinmester unit of teaching strategies for a course which analyzes speeches from *Vital Speeches of the Day,* political speeches, television commercials, etc.

The Language of Persuasion, English, Vocabulary: 5114.68. By Irving Groff. Dade County Public Schools, 23 pp. (ED 084 563).

A quinmester unit of teaching strategies for a course studying the speaker or writer as persuader, the identification of the logical and psychological tools of persuasion, and examination of the levels of abstraction, the techniques of propaganda, and effective forces in advertising.

"Syllabus for Counter-Propaganda—Module #3940V" by Hugh Rank, Governors State University, 1974, 2 pp.

Contains performance objectives, a list of required and recommended books, and a day-by-day breakdown of activities for the eight-week course geared to secondary and junior college teachers of English.

"Syllabus for Freedom & Responsibility in Communication" by Richard L. Johannesen. Northern Illinois University. 9pp.

Lists textbooks, requirements, selected sources for case studies in Freedom and Responsibility in Communication, selected sources on ethics in communication, selected sources on freedom of speech, and additional sources.

Language Arts: The Language of Persuasion by Irvin Groff. Miami, Fla.: Dade County Public Schools, 1972, 20 p.

One of the Dade County Quinmester products, this guide describes a minicourse on persuasion and propaganda. Though it's brief, it contains a number of good classroom exercises and a short bibliography and filmography. It will soon be indexed in the ERIC system.

Words and What They Do to You by Catherine Minteer. Lakeville, CT: Institute of General Semantics, 1965, 128 pp.

Sixteen lessons for 7th and 8th graders. Employs a general semantics approach to study the relationship between language and thought, the scientific use of language, and the misuse of language.

Language Arts: A Curriculum Guide, Levels K–12. Las Vegas: Clark County School District, 1971, 420 pp. (available for $6.00 from: Dept. of Instructional Services, 2832 E. Flamingo Rd., Las Vegas, NV 89109).

Contains materials for teaching about mass media, advertising, propaganda, critical thinking, and critical listening.

English 7–8: Modern Media of Communication by Madelon McGowan. California: San Diego City Schools, 1971, 10 pp. (ED 075 884).

A one-year course designed to enhance students' preparation for functioning in a media environment. Includes film production and media analysis.

The English Language Arts and Basic Skills Program of the Bellevue Public Schools. Elementary Level. Bellevue (Washington) Public Schools. 1972, 418pp. (ED 074 487).

Contains some materials on euphemisms, advertising, etc., though it is but a small portion of a very large guide.

Vocational Consumer Education: Homemaking, Grades 6–8 by Doris West et al. Fort Worth Public Schools, 1972, 98 pp. (ED 080 747).

One of the six sections deals with consumer education and contains suggestions on how to evaluate advertising and labels, how to recognize consumer fraud, and how to make intelligent purchasing decisions.

Mass Media and Propaganda by Bruce Reeves, Acalanes High School, May 1972, (9 pp.)

Lists the philosophy, goals, objectives, and activities which Bruce uses in his high school course.

Social Dimensions of Language: The Age of Doublethink by Donald Lazere, University of California, Spring 1971. Berkeley, (1 p.)

A one page syllabus listing required texts, recommended texts and a tentative schedule for Don's college course.

[Composition] by Donald Lazere, University of California, Berkeley, Fall 1973.

A two page syllabus for an introductory composition course which includes the study of propaganda.

The Mass Media and Society by Joseph Lyford, University of California, Berkeley, Fall 1973.

A 4½ page syllabus for a journalism course studying "the roles, responsibilities, and performance of the mass media in modern U.S. society."

Public Opinion by Mr. Bellquist, University of California, Berkeley, Fall 1973.

A two-page syllabus for a political science course on public opinion. The course deals with public relations and political power.

Articles and Dissertations

The following list is offered as an addendum to the forty articles and dissertations which have been listed in past issues of the *Public Doublespeak Newsletter*.

"Critically Reading for Propaganda Techniques in Grade Six" by Bonnie Smith. M.A. Thesis submitted at Rutgers University, October 1974. (Soon to be in the ERIC system.)

"The experiment seems to indicate that sixth grade students are able to differentiate among the seven types of propaganda."

"Eat, Drink and Be Wary" by Jeffrey Schrank. *Media and Methods,* September 1974, pp. 36–38, & 65.

Describes a unit on food education for secondary school students which deals with advertising claims and honesty in labeling.

"The Electric Carrot: The Rhetoric of Advertisement" by D.G. Kehl. *College Composition and Communication,* May 1975, pp. 134–140.

Suggests a few of the possibilities for language analysis in advertisement.

"Public Doublespeak: Cable TV, Media Systems, and Doublespeak" by Sidney J. Hormell. *English Journal,* May 1975, pp. 18–19.

"Many characteristics of doublespeak get into the message due to the very nature of the mass communication process." Cable TV, a non-mass medium, avoids constraints inherent in mass communication systems.

"Public Doublespeak: Doublespeak in Advertising" by Walker Gibson. *College English,* February 1975, pp. 14–15.

Describes the "ingenious achievement of the adwriters in manipulating current social concerns of their own advantage," concentrating on the purpose and effect of the ideological ad.

"Public Doublespeak: On Expletives Deleted and Characterizations Omitted" by Terence P. Moran. *College English,* February 1975, pp. 689–693.

Examines the transcripts of the White House tapes and provides a fill-in-the-blanks test of readers' understanding of the language of the White House Oval Office during the Nixon tenure.

"Public Doublespeak: On Mistakes and Misjudgments" by Terence P. Moran. *College English,* March 1975, pp. 837–842.

The third of a three-part series on the language of Watergate.

"The Process of Defining Reality and Television Use" by Dennis

Davis, Ph.D. Dissertation at the University of Minnesota, 1973 (See *Dissertation Abstracts International,* January 1974, p. 4304A).

Examines the use of television content to distract or divert attention from problems of everyday life (escape); as a source of definitions for imaginary worlds (fantasy); and as a source of definitions for violent or aggressive action (violence).

"Some Thoughts on Studying Media" by Robert H. Weston. *Media & Methods,* April 1974, pp. 22–25.

Briefly explores the power of television over our lives.

Papers

The following are a few of the papers on doublespeak which have been brought to the attention of the committee. To obtain copies, write to the authors of the papers or, if the author's address is not listed, write to the Committee on Public Doublespeak.

"In-Class Checks on Doublespeak?" by Gloria Glissmeyer.

Suggests classroom exercises to use in teaching about doublespeak. Contains two questionnaires for use in analyzing sexism in language and discusses what preventive, offensive, and redirective procedures are possible in dealing with doublespeak.

"Language in the Marketplace: On Teaching about Doublespeak" by Daniel Dieterich. Paper presented at the annual Conference of the Canadian Council of Teachers of English, Saskatoon, Saskatchewan, August 22, 1974, 19pp.

Outlines reasons why education to prepare students to cope with doublespeak should be included in the English curriculum at all levels, elementary school through college. Describes several techniques for teaching about doublespeak.

"Nominalized Passive" by Julia Stanley. 1972.

"The nominalized passive permits us the illusion of having stated a fact when it is really only an opinion." Concentrates on the language of B.F. Skinner for examples.

"On Doublespeak" by Daniel Dieterich. Paper given at Niles College of Loyola University, Chicago, Illinois, on December 9, 1974, 17pp.

Written for a group of seminarians, the paper describes ways in which public language is misused and suggests precautions which they might take to avoid misusing language when they write sermons.

"Passive Motivation" by Julia Stanley. 1971.

Concludes that "the immediate result of the passive form is to draw our attention away from the agent carrying out the action of the verb, especially when that agent has been deleted, and to focus our attention elsewhere."

"Speaking of Watergate: Language and Moral Accountability" by Brenda Danet, 1975, 29pp.

Contains sections on "Accounting for Watergate," "Accountability and Indirection in Speech," and "The Eight Deadly Sins of Watergate Talk."

"Perceptions of Television Advertising Directed at Children: An Investigation of the Views of an Entire Community" by Frank N. Pierce, et al. Paper presented at the Annual Meeting of the Advertising Division of the Association for Education in Journalism, San Diego, 1974.

A survey of 900 residents of Gainesville, Florida. Those polled felt most children's television commercials did not present a true picture of the product advertised; that advertising does not help develop a child's ability to make good consumer decisions, that most advertisers do not make a sincere effort to present their product truthfully; etc.

"The Questionable Rationale for Advertising Puffery as Revealed in Early English and American Legal Precedents" by Ivan Preston. Paper presented at the annual convention of the Association for Education in Journalism, 1974 (soon to be in the ERIC system).

A study of puffery, a type of subjective opinion claim defended by the law on the ground that it does not deceive the public even though false. Concludes that "puffery is no more justified today than would be any of the now-rejected aspects of caveat emptor which once prevailed."

"The Stylistics of Appropriateness: A Redefinition" by Julia Stanley. Paper delivered to the Conference on College Composition and Communication, 1973.

Calls attention to the two most prevalent methods of lying in our society, syntactic overkill and semantic pollution, stressing the point that when language is used to deceive, oppress, or coerce, it is "inappropriate" because it is dishonest.

"The Stylistics of Belief" by Julia Stanley. Paper delivered to the Conference on College Composition and Communication, Anaheim, California, 1974 (Soon to be indexed in the ERIC system).

Urges the study of "the stylistics of belief," the study of the ways in which language is used by speakers to express their beliefs, to convince other people that they are right, or to avoid committing themselves to particular beliefs." Concentrates particularly on the deception of the reader through "syntactic exploitation" and through word-choice.

"Summary of Thoughts on Doublespeak" by Gloria Glissmeyer. Pa-

218

per presented at the Berkeley Committee Meeting, April 1974, 4 pages.

One and a half pages of text and a two page questionnaire on the "sexist discrimination inherent in or evidenced by certain language use."

"Syntactic Exploitation: Passive Adjectives in English" by Julia Stanley. 1972.

Concludes that passivized prenominal adjectives create a "discourse loop" from which the hearer/reader cannot extricate himself. Concludes from a study of such adjectives in the writing of B.F. Skinner that such constructions force us into a yes/no deadend in discourse.

"The Watergate Mentality and the Ethics of Public Communication" by Richard L. Johannesen. Paper delivered at the Central States Speech Association Convention, April 6, 1974. 9pp.

Describes the language of Watergate and its implications for the teacher of communication. "As teachers of communication we must sensitize our students to the ethical issues in communication."